ENCYCLOPAEDIA OF TEACHING OF INTERNET

Encyclopaedia of Teaching of Internet

(Volume – Two)

Editor-in-Chief

A. Kumar

INSTITUTE FOR SUSTAINABLE DEVELOPMENT
LUCKNOW
&
ANMOL PUBLICATIONS PVT. LTD.
NEW DELHI - 110 002 (INDIA)

ANMOL PUBLICATIONS PVT. LTD.
4374/4B, Ansari Road, Daryaganj
New Delhi - 110 002
Ph.: 23261597, 23278000
Visit us: www.anmolpublications.com

Encyclopaedia of Teaching of Internet

First Edition, 2004

ISBN 81-261-2031-2 (Set)

PRINTED IN INDIA

Published by J.L. Kumar for Anmol Publications Pvt. Ltd., New Delhi and Printed at Mehra Offset Press, Delhi.

Contents

Preface

Internet, computer-based worldwide information network. The Internet is composed of a large number of smaller interconnected networks called internets. The Internet contains the WWW and also includes all the hardware (computers, supercomputers, and connections) and non-WWW software and protocols in which the WWW runs. The difference between the Internet and the WWW is similar to the distinction between a computer and a multimedia program that runs on the computer. Individuals, companies, and institutions use the Internet in many ways. Businesses use the Internet to provide access to complex databases, such as financial databases. Individuals use the Internet for communication, entertainment, finding information, and to buy and sell goods and services.

The Internet is based on the concept of a client-server relationship between computers, also called a client/ server architecture. In a client/server architecture, some computers act as servers, or information providers, while other computers act as clients, or information receivers. Personal computer and workstations, however, are now capable of acting as Internet servers due to advances in computing technology. A client computer is any computer that receives information from a server and is often a personal computer.

To access information on the Internet, a user must first log on, or connect, to the client computer's host network. A host network is a network that the client computer is part of, and is usually a local area network (LAN). If the information requested by the user resides on one of the computers on the host network, that information is quickly retrieved and sent to the user's terminal. Once the client computer makes a connection with the server containing the requested information, the server sends the information to the client in the form of a file. A special computer program called a browser enables the user to view the file. Examples of Internet browsers are Mosaic, Netscape, and Internet Explorer. Most Internet files are multimedia documents-that is, text, graphics, photographs, audio, and video may be combined in a single document. Multimedia files on the Internet are called hypermedia documents.

Access to the Internet falls into two broad categories: dedicated access and dial-up access. With dedicated access, the computer is directly connected to the Internet via a router, or the computer is part of a network linked to the Internet. A great many companies, called Internet Service Providers (ISPs), provide dial-up access to the Internet for a modest fee. This system, called packet-switching, uses a series of protocols, or rules, known as TCP IIP (Transmission Control Protocol/Internet Protocol). To be part of the Internet a computer must have a unique Internet Protocol (IP) network address so that messages can be directly routed to and from the machine over the Internet. Internet addresses are called URLs (Uniform Resource Locators). The most widely used tool on the Internet is electronic mail, or e-mail. Before the introduction of the World Wide Web, various standards and types of software existed for transmitting data over the Internet. Telnet allows an Internet user to connect to a distant computer and use that computer as if he or she were using it directly: This original network, the very first computer network, was called ARPANET (ARPANETwork). To meet the needs of data transmission standards, computer scientists developed the Transmission Control Protocol (TCP) and the Internet Protocol (IP). In 1989 English computer scientist limothy Berners-Lee introduced the World Wide Web. As Internet applications become more sophisticated, and as more people around the world use the Internet, the amount of information transmitted across the Internet will demand very high bandwidth connections.

In order to accommodate the increasing number of users, the non-profit organization University Corporation for Advanced Internet Development (UCAill) is working on the construction of Internet 2. Internet 2 will add more bandwidth, or available communication lines, to the current information superhighway in order to accommodate larger packets of data.

The issue of business being conducted over the Internet raises important security issues. Similarly, government facilities, universities, and institutions must ensure that access to their computers over the Internet is strictly regulated.

Individuals, companies, and institutions use the Internet in many ways. Businesses use the Internet to provide access to complex databases, such as financial databases. Individuals use the Internet for communication, entertainment, finding information, and to buy and sell goods and services.

Computer-based network of information resources that a user can move through by using links from one document to another. The information on the World Wide Web is spread over computers allover the world. The World Wide Web is often referred to simply as "the Web." The Web has become a very popular resource since it first became possible to views images and other multimedia on the Internet, a worldwide network of computers, in 1993. Anyone with access to a computer connected to the Web can view most of that information. A small percentage of information on the Web is only accessible to subscribers or other authorized users. The Web also carries information in a wide spectrum of formats.

Like all computer networks, the Web connects two types of computers-clients and servers-using a standard set of rules for communication between the computers. The server computers store the information resources that make up the Web, and Web users use client computers to access the resources. A computer-based network may be a public network-such as the worldwide Internet-or a private network, such as a company's internet. The Web is part of the Internet. The Internet also encompasses other methods of linking computers, such as Telnet, File Transfer Protocol, and Gopher, but the Web has quickly become the most widely used part of the Internet. Enabling client computers to display Web pages with pictures and other media was made possible by the introduction of a type of software called a browser. Almost every Web page or Web document includes links, called hyperlinks, to other Web sites. Client computers connect to the Web in one of two ways. Client computers with dedicated access to the Web connect directly to the Web through a router (a piece of computer hardware that determines the best way to connect client and server computers) or by being part of a larger network with a direct connection to the Web. Client computers with dial-up access to the Web connect to the Web through a modem, a hardware device that translates information from the computer into signals that can travel over telephone lines. The client computer and the Web server use a set of rules for passing information back and forth. Web servers hold Web documents and the media associated with them. Client computers access information from Web servers, and any computer that a person uses to access the Web is a client, so a client could be any type of computer. The Web, and all Internet formats, uses the 'protocol called TCP /IP (Transmission Control Protocol/Internet Protocol). However, each part of the Internet-such as a the Web, gopher systems, and File Transfer Protocol (FTP) systems-uses a slightly different system to transfer files between clients and servers.

The address of a Web document helps the client computer find and connect to the server that holds the page. The next part of the URL, *encarta.msn.com*, gives the name, or unique Internet address, of the server on which the Web site is stored. Client-server communication, URLs, and HTML allow Web sites to incorporate hyperlinks, which users can use to navigate through the Web. Hyperlinks are often phrases in the text of the Web document that link to another web document by providing the document's URL when the user clicks their mouse on the phrase. The web also contains directories of e-mail and postal mail addresses and phone numbers.

Web users can shop at Web sites of major bookstores, clothing sellers, and other retailers. Some businesses, especially publishers, provide limited information to ordinary Web users, but offer much more to users who buy a subscription. Operating systems are the basic software that control computers. The Web's methods of storing information associatively, retrieving documents with hypertext links, and naming Web sites with URLs make it a smooth extension of the rest of the Internet. This allows easy access to information between different parts of the Internet.

Some computers even use ordinary television sets, instead of special computer monitors, to display content from the Web. This work contains latest and useful information on Internet and information technology. Due to highly scientific and technical nature of Internet and IT, the material gathered herein is drawn from various authoritative sources. We are thankful to all those computer wizards/ experts whose opinions and erudition is borrowed.

A number of colleagues and friends have provided valuable advice and assistance, hence we will be failing in our duty if we do not express our gratitude to them. We also express our gratitude to Mr. J.L. Kumar, Managing Director, Mr. Kripal Joshi, Editor, Anmol Publications Pvt. Ltd., New Delhi for publishing this manuscript in a very limited time.

—A. Kumar

12

System Maintenance

Preventive maintenance is the key to obtaining years of trouble-free service from your computer system. A properly administered preventive maintenance programme pays for itself by reducing problem behavior, data loss, component failure, and by ensuring a long life for your system. In several cases, I have "repaired" an ailing system with nothing more than a preventive maintenance session. Preventive maintenance also increases your system's resale value because it will look and run better. This chapter describes preventive maintenance procedures and how often you should perform them.

You will also learn the importance of creating backup files of data and the various backup procedures available. A sad reality in the computer repair and servicing world is that hardware can always be repaired or replaced, but data cannot. Most hard disk troubleshooting and service procedures, for example, require that a low-level format be done. This low-level format overwrites any data on the disk.

Because data recovery depends a great deal on the type and severity of damage and the expertise of the recovery specialist, data-recovery services are very expensive. Most recovery services charge a premium and offer no guarantees that the data will be completely recovered. Backing up your system as discussed in this chapter is the only guarantee you have of seeing your data again.

Most of the discussion of backing up systems in this chapter is limited to professional solutions that require special hardware and software. Backup, solutions that employ floppy disk drives, such as the DOS backup software, are insufficient and too costly in most cases for hard disk backups. It would take 1,456 1.44M floppy disks, for example, to backup the 2G hard disk in my portable system! That would cost more than $1,000 in disks, not to mention the rime involved. A tape system can put 4G to 8G on a single $15 tape.

Finally, the last section in this chapter discusses the standard warranties and optional service contracts available for many systems. Although most of this book is written for people who want to perform their own maintenance and repair service, taking advantage of a good factory warranty that provides service for free definitely is prudent. Some larger computer companies, such as IBM, offer attractive service contracts that, in some cases, are cost-justified over self service. These types of options are examined in the final section.

DEVELOPING A PREVENTIVE MAINTENANCE PROGRAMME

Developing a preventive maintenance programme is important to everyone who uses or manages personal computer systems. Two types of preventive maintenance procedures exist: active and passive.

Active preventive maintenance includes steps you apply to a system that promote a longer, trouble-free life. This type of preventive maintenance primarily involves periodic cleaning of the system and its components. This section describes several active preventive maintenance procedures, including cleaning and lubricating all major components, reseating chips and connectors, and reformatting hard disks.

Passive preventive maintenance includes steps you can take to protect a system from the environment, such as using power-protection devices; ensuring a clean, temperature-controlled environment; and preventing excessive vibration. In other words, passive preventive maintenance means treating your system well. This section also describes passive preventive maintenance procedures.

Active Preventive Maintenance Procedures

How often you should implement active preventive maintenance procedures depends on the system's environment and the quality of the system's components. If your system is in a dirty environment, such as a machine shop floor or a gas station service area, you might need to clean your system every three months or less. For normal office environments, cleaning a system every one to two years is usually fine. However, if you open your system after one year and find dust bunnies inside, you should shorten the cleaning interval.

Another active preventive maintenance technique discussed in this section is reformatting hard disks. Low-level reformatting restores the track and sector marks to their proper locations and forces you to back up and restore all data on the drive. Not all drives require this procedure, but if you are using drives with a stepper motor head actuator, periodic reformatting is highly recommended. Most drives with voice-coil head actuators run indefinitely without reformatting due to their track following servo mechanisms which prevent temperature induced mistracking.

Other hard disk preventive maintenance procedures include making periodic backups of critical areas such as Boot Sectors, File Allocation Tables, and Directory structures on the disk.

Cleaning a System. One of the most important operations in a good preventive maintenance programme is regular and thorough cleaning of the system. Dust buildup on the internal components can lead to several problems. One is that dust acts as a thermal insulator which prevents proper system cooling. Excessive heat shortens the life of system components and adds to the thermal stress problem caused by wider than normal temperature changes between power-on and power-off states. Additionally, dust may contain conductive elements that can cause partial short circuits in a system. Other elements in dust and dirt can accelerate corrosion of electrical contacts and cause improper connections. In all, the removal of any layer of dust and debris from within a computer system benefits that system in the long run.

All IBM and IBM-compatible systems use a forced-air cooling system that allows for even cooling inside the system. A fan is mounted in, on, or near the power supply and pushes air outside. This setup depressurizes the Interior of the system relative to the outside air. The lower pressure inside the system causes outside air to be drawn into openings in the system chassis and cover. This draw-through, or depressurisation, is the most efficient cooling system that can be designed without an air filter. Air filters typically are not used with depressurisation systems because there is no easy way to limit air Intake to a single port that can be covered by a filter.

Some industrial computers from IBM and other companies use a forced-air system that uses the fan to pressurize, rather than to depressurize, the case. This system forces air to exhaust from any holes in the chassis and case or cover. The key to the pressurisation system is that all air intake for the system is at a single location—the fan. The air flowing into the system therefore can be filtered by simply integrating a filter assembly into the fan housing. The filter must be cleaned or changed periodically. Because the interior of the case is pressurised relative to the outside air, airborne contaminants are not drawn into the system even though it may not be sealed. Any air entering the system must pass through the fan and filter housing, which removes the contaminants. Pressurisation cooling systems are used primarily in industrial computer models designed for extremely harsh environments.

Most systems you have contact with are depressurisation systems. Mounting any sort of air filter on these types of systems is impossible because air enters the system from too many sources. With any cooling system in which incoming air is not filtered, dust and other chemical matter in the environment is drawn in and builds up inside the computer. This buildup can cause severe problems if left unchecked.

One problem that can develop is overheating. The buildup of dust acts as a heat insulator, which prevents the system from cooling properly. Some of the components in a modern PC can generate an enormous amount of heat which must be dissipated for the component to function. The dust also might contain chemicals that conduct electricity. These chemicals can cause minor current shorts and create electrical signal paths where none should exist. The chemicals also cause rapid corrosion of cable connectors, socket-installed components, and areas where boards plug into slots. All can cause intermittent system problems and erratic operation.

Tip

Cigarette smoke contains chemicals that can conduct electricity and cause corrosion of computer parts. The smoke residue can infiltrate the entire system, causing corrosion and contamination of electrical contacts and sensitive components such as floppy drive read/write heads and optical drive lens assemblies. You should avoid smoking near computer equipment and encourage your company to develop and enforce a similar policy.

Floppy disk drives are particularly vulnerable to the effects of dirt and dust. Floppy drives are a large "hole" within the system through which air continuously flows. Therefore, they accumulate a large amount of dust and chemical buildup within a short time. Hard disk drives do not present quite the same problem. Because the head disk assembly (HDA) in a hard disk is a sealed unit with a single barometric vent, no dust or dirt can enter without passing through the barometric vent filter. This filter ensures that contaminating dust or particles cannot enter the interior of the HDA. Thus, cleaning a hard disk requires simply blowing the dust and dirt off from outside the drive. No internal cleaning is required.

Disassembly and Cleaning Tools. To properly clean the system and all the boards inside requires certain supplies and tools. In addition to the tools required to disassemble the unit you should have these items:

- Contact cleaning solution
- Canned air
- A small brush
- Lint-free foam cleaning swabs
- Antistatic wrist-grounding strap

You might also want to acquire these optional items:

- Foam tape
- Low-volatile room-temperature vulcanising (RTV) sealer

- Silicone type lubricant
- Computer vacuum cleaner

These simple cleaning tools and chemical solutions will allow you to perform most common preventive maintenance tasks.

Chemicals. You can use several different types of cleaning solutions with computers and electronic assemblies. Most fall into the following categories:

- Standard Cleaners
- Contact Cleaner/Lubricants
- Dusters

Tip

The makeup of many of the chemicals used for cleaning electronic components has been changing because many of the chemicals originally used are now considered environmentally unsafe. They have been attributed to damaging the Earth's ozone layer, a nature protective barrier in the stratosphere which prevents harmful ultraviolet (UV-B) radiation from reaching Earth. Chlorine atoms from chlorofluorocarbons (CFCs) and chlorinated solvents attach themselves to ozone molecules and destroy them. Many of these chemicals are now strictly regulated by federal and international agencies in an effort to preserve the ozone layer. Most of the companies that produce chemicals used for system cleaning and maintenance have had to introduce environmentally safe replacements. The only drawbacks is that many of these safer chemicals cost more and usually do not work as well as those they replace.

Many specific chemicals are used in cleaning and dusting solutions, but five types are of particular interest. The EPA has classified ozone-damaging chemicals into two classes: Class I and Class II. Chemicals that fall into these two classes have their usage regulated. Other chemicals are nonregulated. Class I chemicals include:

- Chlorofluorocarbons (CFCs)
- Chlorinated solvents

Class I chemicals can only be sold for use in professional service and not to consumers. A new law that went into effect on May 15, 1993, requires that the containers, for Class I chemicals be labeled with a warning that the product "Contains substances which harm public health and the environment by destroying ozone in the atmosphere." Additionally, electronics manufacturers and other industries must also apply a similar warning label to any products that use Class I chemicals in the production process. This means that any circuit board or computer that is manufactured with CFCs will have this label!

The most popular Class I chemicals are the various forms of Freon, which are CFCs. A very popular cleaning solution called 1,1,1 Trichloroethane is a chlorinated solvent and is also strictly regulated. Up until the last year or so, virtually all computer or electronic cleaning solutions contained one or both of these chemicals. While you can still purchase them, regulations and limited production have made them more expensive and more difficult to find.

Class II chemicals include hydrochlorofluorocarbons (HCFCs). These are not as strictly regulated as Class I chemicals because they have a lower ozone depletion potential. Many cleaning solutions have switched to HCFCs, because they do not require the restrictive labeling required by Class I chemicals and are not as harmful. Most HCFCs have only one tenth the ozone damaging potential of CFCs.

Other nonregulated chemicals include Volatile Organic Compounds (VOCs) and Hydrofluorocarbons (HFCs). These chemicals do not damage the ozone layer but actually contribute to ozone production, which, unfortunately, appears in the form of smog or ground level pollution. Pure isopropyl alcohol is an example of a VOC that is commonly used in electronic part and contact cleaning. HFCs are used as a replacement for CFCs because the HFCs do not damage the ozone layer.

The EPA has developed a method to measure the ozone damaging capability of a chemical. The Ozone Depletion Potential (ODP) of a chemical solution is the sum of the depletion potentials of each of the chemicals used in the solution by weight. The ODP of Freon R12 (Automotive Air Conditioning Freon), is 1.0 on this scale. Most modern CFC replacement chemicals have an ODP rating of 0.0 to 0.1, as opposed to those using CFCs and chlorinated solvents that usually have ODP ratings of 0.75 or higher.

Standard Cleaners. Standard cleaning solutions are available in a variety of types and configurations. You can use pure isopropyl alcohol, acetone, Freon, trichloroethane, or a variety of other chemicals. Most are now leaning to the alcohol, acetone, or others that do not cause ozone depletion and that comply with government regulations and environmental safety. You should be sure that your cleaning solution is designed to clean computers or electronic assemblies. In most cases this means that the solution should be chemically pure and free from contaminants or other unwanted substances. You should not, for example, use drugstore rubbing alcohol for cleaning electronic parts or contacts because it is not pure and could contain water or perfumes. The material must be moisture-free and residue-free. The solutions should be in liquid form, not a spray. Sprays can be wasteful and you almost never spray the solution directly on components. Instead, wet a foam or chamois swab used for wiping the component. These electronic-component cleaning solutions are available at any good electronics parts stores.

Contact Cleaner/Lubricants. These are very similar to the standard cleaners but include a lubricating component. The lubricant eases the force required when plugging and unplugging cables and connectors, which reduces strain on the devices. The lubricant coating also acts as a conductive protectant that insulates the contacts from corrosion. These chemicals can greatly prolong the life of a system by preventing intermittent contacts in the future.

Contact cleaner/lubricants are especially effective on I/O slot connectors, adapter card edge and pin connectors, disk drive connectors, power supply connectors, and virtually all connectors in the PC.

An excellent contact enhancer and lubricant is Stabilant 22. It is more effective than conventional contact cleaners or lubricants. This chemical is available in several forms. Stabilant 22 is the full strength concentrated version, while Stabilant 22a is a version diluted with isopropyl alcohol in a 4 to 1 ratio. An even more diluted 8 to 1 ratio version is sold in many high end stereo and audio shops under the name "Tweet" Just 15ml of Stabilant 22a sells for about $40, while a liter of the concentrate costs about $4,000. While Stabilant 22 is expensive, very little is required and an application can provide protection for a long time. Stabilant is manufactured by D. W. Electrochemicals, which is listed in Appendix B, the "Vendor List."

Dusters. Compressed gas often is used as an aid in system cleaning. The compressed gas is used as a blower to remove dust and debris from a system or component. Originally, these dusters used CFCs such as Freon, while modern dusters now use HFCs or carbon dioxide, neither of which is damaging to the ozone layer. Be careful when you use these devices because some of them can generate a static charge when the compressed gas leaves the nozzle of the can. Be sure that you are using the kind approved for cleaning or dusting off computer equipment, and consider wearing a static grounding strap as a precaution. The type of compressed-air cans used for cleaning camera equipment can sometimes differ from the type used for cleaning static-sensitive computer components.

Most older computer-grade canned gas dusters consisted of dichlorodifluoromethane (Freon R12), the same chemical used in many automotive air-conditioning systems built until 1995, when a ban of the manufacture and use of R12 takes place. In 1992 many automobile manufacturers began switching to an ozone safe chemical called R134a. Manufacturing of R12 will cease by 1995, and the regulations placed on its use have forced companies to use other products such as carbon dioxide for compressed gas dusters. In addition to the environmental concerns about depleting the ozone layer, Freon can be dangerous if exposed to an open flame.

Caution

If you use any chemical with the propellant Freon R12 (dichlorodifluoromethane), *do not expose the gas to an open flame or other heat source.* If you burn this substance, a highly toxic gas called *phosgene* is generated. Phosgene, used as a nerve gas in World War II, can be deadly.

Related to compressed-air products are chemical-freeze sprays. These sprays are used to quickly cool down a suspected failing component, which often temporarily restores it to operation. These substances are not used to repair a device, but to confirm that you have found a failed device. Often, a component's failure is heat-related and cooling it temporarily restores it to function. If the circuit begins operating normally, the device you are cooling is the suspect device.

Vacuum Cleaners. Some people prefer to use a vacuum cleaner instead of canned gas dusters for cleaning a system. Canned gas is usually better for cleaning in small areas. A vacuum cleaner is more useful when you are cleaning a system loaded with dust and dirt. You can use the vacuum cleaner to suck out dust and debris instead of blowing them on other components, which sometimes happens with canned air. For outbound servicing (when you are going to the location of the equipment instead of the equipment coming to you), canned air is easier to carry in a toolkit than a small vacuum cleaner.

Brushes and Swabs. A small brush (makeup, photographic, or paint) can be used to carefully loosen accumulated dirt and dust before spraying with canned air or using the vacuum cleaner. Be careful about generating static electricity. In most cases the brushes should not be used directly on circuit boards but should be used instead on the case interior and other parts such as fan blades, air vents, and keyboards. Wear a grounded wrist strap if you are brushing on or near any circuit boards, and brush slowly and lightly to prevent static discharges from occurring.

Use cleaning swabs to wipe off electrical contacts and connectors, disk drive heads, and other sensitive areas. The swabs should be made of foam or synthetic chamois material that does not leave lint or dust residue. Unfortunately, proper foam or chamois cleaning swabs are more expensive than the typical cotton swabs. Do not use cotton swabs be cause they leave cotton fibers on everything they touch. Cotton fibers are conductive in some situations and can remain on drive heads, which can scratch disks. Foam or chamois swabs can be purchased at most electronics-supply stores.

One item to avoid is an eraser for cleaning contacts. Many people (including myself) nave recommended using a soft pencil type eraser for cleaning circuit board contacts. Testing has proven this to be bad advice for several reasons. One is that any such abrasive wiping on electrical contacts generates friction and an electrostatic discharge (ESD). This ESD can be damaging to boards and components, especially with newer low voltage devices made using CMOS (Complimentary Metal Oxide Semiconductor) technology. These devices are especially static sensitive, and cleaning the contacts without a proper liquid solution is not recommended. Also the eraser will wear off the gold coating on many contacts, exposing the tin contact underneath, which will rapidly corrode when exposed to air. Some companies sell premoistened contact cleaning pads that are soaked in a proper contact cleaner and lubricant. These pads are safe to wipe on conductor and contacts with no likelihood of ESD damage or abrasion of the gold plating.

Foam Tape or RTV Sealer. Hard disks usually use a small copper, strap to ground the spindle of the disk assembly to the logic board, thus bleeding off any static charge carried by the spinning disk platters. Unfortunately, this strap often can begin to harmonize, or vibrate, and result in an annoying squealing or whining noise. (Sometimes the noise is similar to fingernails dragged across a chalkboard.)

To climinate the source of irritation, you can stop the strap from vibrating by weighting it. One method is to use a piece of foam tape cut to match the size of the strap and stuck to the strap's back side. Another way to dampen the vibration is to apply a low-volatile RTV sealer. You apply this silicone-type rubber to the back of the grounding strap. After it hardens to a rubber-like material, the sealer stops the vibrations that produce the annoying squeal. You can buy the RTV sealer from an automotive-supply house.

I prefer using the foam tape rather than the RTV because it is easier and neater to apply. If you use the RTV, be sure that it is the low-volatile type, which does not generate acid when it cures. This acid produces the vinegar smell common to the standard RTV sealer, and can be highly corrosive to the strap and anything else it contacts. The low-volatile RTV also eliminates the bad vinegar smell. You can purchase the foam tape at most electronics-supply houses, where it often is sold for attaching alarm switches to doors or windows. The low-volatile RTV is available from most auto-supply stores. To be sure that you buy low-volatile RTV, look for the packaging to state specifically that the product is either a low-volatile type or is compatible with automobile oxygen sensors.

Silicone Lubricants. Silicone lubricants are used to lubricate the door mechanisms on floppy disk drives and any other part of the system that may require clean, non-oily lubrication. Other items you can lubricate are the disk drive head slider rails or even printer-head slider rails, which allow for smooth operation.

Using silicone instead of conventional oils is important because silicone does not gum up and collect dust and other debris. Always use the silicone sparingly. Do not spray it anywhere near the equipment as it tends to migrate and will end up where it doesn't belong (such as on drive heads). Instead, apply a small amount to a toothpick or foam swab and dab the silicone on the components where needed. You can use a lint-free cleaning stick soaked in silicone lubricant to lubricate the metal print-head rails in a printer.

Remember that some of the cleaning operations described in this section might generate a static charge. You may want to use a static grounding strap in cases in which static levels are high to ensure that you do not damage any boards as you work with them.

Obtaining Required Tools and Accessories. Most cleaning chemicals and tools can be obtained from a number of electronics-supply houses, or even the local Radio Shack. A company called Chemtronics specializes in chemicals for the computer and electronics industry. These and other companies which supply tools, chemicals, and other computer and electronic cleaning supplies are listed in Appendix B, the "Vendor List." With all these items on hand, you should be equipped for most preventive maintenance operations.

Disassembling and Cleaning Procedures. To properly clean your system, it must at least be partially disassembled. Some people go as far as to remove the motherboard. Removing the motherboard results in the best possible access to other areas of the system but in the interest of saving time, you probably need to disassemble the system only to where the motherboard is completely visible.

All plug-in adapter cards must be removed, along with the disk drives. Although you can dean the heads of a floppy drive with a cleaning disk without opening the system unit's cover, you probably will want to do more thorough cleaning. In addition to the heads, you also should clean and lubricate the door mechanism and dean any logic boards and connectors on the drive. This procedure usually requires removing the drive.

Next, do the same procedure with a hard disk: clean the logic boards and connectors, as well as lubricate the grounding strap. To do so, you must remove the hard disk assembly. As a precaution, be sure it is backed up before removal.

Reseating Socketed Chips. A primary preventive maintenance function is to undo the effects of chip creep. As your system heats and cools, it expands and contracts, and the physical expansion and contraction causes components plugged into sockets to gradually work their way out of those sockets. This process is called *chip creep*. To correct its effects, you must find all socketed components in the system and make sure that they are properly reseated.

In most systems, all the memory chips are socketed or are installed in socketed SIMMs (Single Inline Memory Modules). SIMM devices are retained securely in their sockets by a positive latching mechanism and cannot creep out. Memory SIPP (Single Inline Pin Package) devices (SIMMs with pins rather than contacts) are not retained by a latching mechanism and therefore can creep out of their sockets. Standard socketed memory chips are prime candidates for chip creep. Most other logic components are soldered in. You can also expect to find the ROM chips, the main processor or CPU, and the math coprocessor in sockets. In most systems, these items are the only components that are socketed; all others are soldered in.

Exceptions, however, might exist. A socketed component in one system might not be socketed in another—even if both are from the same manufacturer. Sometimes this difference results from a parts-availability problem when the boards are manufactured. Rather than halt the assembly line when a part is not available, the manufacturer adds a socket instead of the component. When the component becomes available, it is plugged in and the board is finished. Many newer systems place the CPU in a Zero Insertion Force (ZIF) socket, which has a lever that can release the grip of the socket on the chip. In most cases there is very little creep with a ZIF socket.

To make sure that all components are fully seated in their sockets, place your hand on the underside of the board and then apply downward pressure with your thumb (from the top) on the chip to be seated. For larger chips, seat the chip carefully in two movements, and press separately on each end of the chip with your thumb to be sure that the chip is fully seated. (The processor and math coprocessor chips can usually be seated in this manner). In most cases, you hear a crunching sound as the chip makes its way back into the socket. Because of the great force sometimes required to reseat the chips, this operation is difficult if you do not remove the board.

For motherboards, forcibly seating chips can be dangerous if you do not directly support the board from the underside with your hand. Too much pressure on the board can cause it to bow or bend in the chassis, and the pressure can crack it before seating takes place. The plastic standoffs that separate and hold the board up from the metal chassis are spaced too far apart to properly support the board under this kind of stress. Try this operation only if you can remove and support the board adequately from underneath.

You may be surprised to know that, even if you fully seat each chip, they might need reseating again within a year. The creep usually is noticeable within a year or less.

Cleaning Boards. After reseating any socketed devices that may have crept out of their sockets, the next step is to clean the boards and all connectors in the system. For this step, the cleaning solutions and the lint-free swabs described earlier are needed.

First, clean the dust and debris off the board and then dean any connectors on the board. To clean the boards, it is usually best to use a vacuum cleaner designed for electronic assemblies and circuit boards or a duster can of compressed gas. The dusters are especially effective at blasting any dust and dirt off the boards.

Also blow any dust out of the power supply, especially around the fan intake and exhaust areas. You do not need to disassemble the power supply to do this, just use a duster can and blast the compressed air into the supply through the fan exhaust port. This will blow the dust out of the supply and clean off the fan blades and grille which will help with system airflow.

Caution

Be careful with electrostatic discharge (ESD), which can damage components, when cleaning electronic components. Take extra precautions in the dead of winter in an extremely dry, highstatic environment. You can apply antistatic sprays and treatments to the work area to reduce the livelihood of ESD damage.

An antistatic wrist-grounding strap is recommended. This should be connected to a ground on the card or board you are wiping. This strap ensures that no electrical discharge occurs between you and the board. An alternative method is to keep a finger or thumb on the ground of the motherboard or card as you wipe it off. It is easier to ensure proper grounding while the motherboard is still installed in the chassis, so it is good idea not to remove it.

Cleaning Connectors and Contacts. Cleaning the connectors and contacts in a system promotes reliable connections between devices. On a motherboard, you will want to clean the slot connectors, power-supply connectors, keyboard connector, and speaker connector. For most plug-in cards, you will want to clean the edge connectors that plug into slots on the motherboard as well as any other connectors, such as external ones mounted on the card bracket.

Submerge the lint-free swabs in the liquid cleaning solution. If you are using the spray, hold the swab away from the system and spray a small amount on the foam end until the solution starts to drip. Then, use the soaked foam swab to wipe the connectors on the boards. Pre-soaked wipes are the easiest to use. Simply wipe them along the contacts to remove any accumulated dirt and leave a protective coating behind.

On the motherboard, pay special attention to the slot connectors. Be liberal with the liquid; resoak the foam swab repeatedly, and vigorously clean the connectors. Don't worry if some of the liquid drips on the surface of the motherboard. These solutions are entirely safe for the whole board and will not damage the components.

Use the solution to wash the dirt off the gold contacts in the slot connectors, and then douse any other connectors on the board. Clean the keyboard connector, the grounding positions where screws ground the board to the system chassis, power-supply connectors, speaker connectors, battery connectors, and so on.

If you are cleaning a plug-in board, pay special attention to the edge connector that mates with the slot connector on the motherboard. When people handle plug-in cards, they often touch the gold contacts on these connectors. Touching the gold contacts coats them with oils and debris, which prevents proper contact with the slot connector when the board is installed. Make sure that these gold contacts are free of all finger oils and residue. It is a good idea to use one of the contact cleaners that has a conductive lubricant, which both allows connections to be made with less force, and also protects the contacts from corrosion.

Caution

Many people use a common pink eraser to rub the edge connectors clean. I do not recommend this procedure for two reasons. One, the eraser eventually removes some of the gold and leaves the tin solder or copper underneath exposed. Without the gold, the contact corrodes rapidly and requires cleaning. The second reason to avoid cleaning with the eraser is that the rubbing action can generate a static charge. This charge can harm any component on the board. Rather than use an eraser, use the liquid solution and swab method described earlier.

You also will want to use the swab and solution to clean the ends of ribbon cables or other types of cables or connectors in a system. Clean the floppy drive cables and connectors, the hard disk cables and connectors, and any others you find. Don't forget to clean off the edge connectors that are on the disk drive logic boards as well as the power connectors to the drives.

Cleaning Floppy Drives. "Floppy Disk Drives and Controllers, explains the procedure for cleaning floppy drives, the information is not repeated here. The basic idea is to use a canned gas duster to dust off the interior of the drive, use the silicone lubricant on whatever items need lubrication, and follow with a head cleaning, either manually with a foam swab or most likely with a chemical-soaked cleaning disk.

For hard disks, take this opportunity to dampen or lubricate the grounding strap if you have a noise problem as described earlier. Dampening is the recommended solution because if you lubricate this point, the lubricant eventually dries up and the squeal can come back. Because the dampening is usually a more permanent fix for this sort of problem, I recommend it whenever possible. Most newer hard disks have this dampening material applied at the factory and are not likely to generate noise like older drives.

Cleaning the Keyboard and Mouse. Keyboards and mice are notorious for picking up dirt and garbage. If you ever open an older keyboard, you often will be amased at the junk you will find.

To prevent problems, it is a good idea to periodically clean out the keyboard with a vacuum cleaner. An alternative method is to turn the keyboard upside down and shoot it with a can of compressed gas. This will blow out the dirt and debris that has accumulated inside the keyboard and possibly prevent future problems with sticking keys or dirty keyswitches.

If a particular key is stuck or making intermittent contact, you can soak or spray that switch with contact cleaner. The best way to do this is to first remove the keycap and then spray the cleaner into the switch. This usually does not require complete disassembly of the keyboard. Periodic vacuuming or compressed gas cleaning will prevent more serious problems with sticking keys and keyswitches.

Most mice are easily cleaned. In most cases there is a twist off locking retainer that keeps the mouse ball retained in the body of the mouse. By removing the retainer, the ball will drop out. After removing the ball, you should clean it with one of the electronic cleaners. I would recommend a pure cleaner instead of a contact cleaner with lubricant because you do not want any lubricant on the mouse ball. Then you should clean off the rollers in the body of the mouse with the cleaner and some swabs.

Periodic cleaning of a mouse in this manner will eliminate or prevent skipping or erratic movement that can be frustrating. I also recommend a mouse pad for most ball type mice because the pad will prevent the mouse ball from picking up debris from your desk.

Mice often need frequent cleaning before they start sticking and jumping, which can be frustrating. If you never want to clean a mouse again, I suggest you look into the Honeywell mouse. These mice have a revolutionary new design that uses two external wheels rather than the conventional ball and roller system. The wheels work directly on the desk surface and are unaffected by dirt and dust. Because the body of the mouse is sealed, dirt and dust cannot enter it and gum up the positional sensors. I find this mouse excellent to use with my portable system because it works well on any surface. This mouse is virtually immune to the sticking and jumping that plague ball and roller designs and never needs to be cleaned, so it is less frustrating than conventional mice.

Hard Disk Maintenance

Certain preventive maintenance procedures protect your data and ensure that your hard disk works efficiently. Some of these procedures actually minimize wear and tear on your drive, which will prolong its life. Additionally, a high level of data protection can be implemented by performing some simple commands periodically. These commands provide methods for backing up (and possibly later restoring) critical areas of the hard disk that, if damaged, would disable access to all your flies.

Defragmenting Files. Over time, as you delete and save flies to a hard disk, the files become fragmented. This means that they are split into many noncontiguous areas on the disk. One of the best ways to protect both your hard disk and the data on it is to periodically defragment the flies on the disk. This serves two purposes. One is that by ensuring that all of the files are stored in contiguous sectors on the disk, head movement and drive wear and tear will be minimised. This has the added benefit of improving the speed at which files will be retrieved from the drive by reducing the head thrashing that occurs every time a fragmented file is accessed.

The second major benefit, and in my estimation the more important of the two, is that in the case of a disaster where the File Allocation Tables (FATs) and Root Directory are severely damaged, the data on the drive can usually be recovered very easily if the files are contiguous. On the other hand, if the files are split up in many pieces across the drive, it is virtually impossible to figure out which pieces belong to which files without an intact File Allocation Table (FAT) and directory system. For the purposes of data integrity and protection. I recommend defragmenting your hard disk drives on a weekly basis, or immediately after you perform any major backup.

- Three main functions are found in most defragmenting programmes:
- File Defragmentation
- File Packing (Free Space Consolidation)
- File Sorting

Defragmentation is the basic function but most other programmes also add file packing. Packing the flies is optional on some programmes because it usually takes additional time to perform. This function packs the files at the beginning of the disk so that all free space is consolidated at the end of the disk. This feature minimizes future file fragmentation by eliminating any empty holes on the disk. Because all free space is consolidated into one large area, any new files written to the disk will be able to be written in a contiguous manner with no fragmentation necessary.

The last function, file sorting, is not usually necessary and is performed as an option by many defragmenting programmes. This function adds a tremendous amount of time to the operation, and has little or no effect on the speed at which information is accessed. It can be somewhat beneficial for disaster recovery purposes because you will have an idea of which files came before or after other files if a disaster occurs. These benefits are minimal compared to having the files be contiguous no matter what their order. Not all defragmenting programmes offer file sorting, and the extra time it takes is probably not worth any benefits you will receive. Other programmes can sort the order that files are listed in directories, which is a quick and easy operation compared to sorting the file ordering the disk.

Several programmes are available that can defragment the files on a hard disk but the one available to most people is the DEFRAG programme built into DOS 6.x. This reduced function version of the SPEEDISK programme is a part of the Symantec Norton Utilities. If you have the Norton Utilities, by all means use SPEEDISK instead of DEFRAG. The DOS DEFRAG programme offers all three functions including defragmenting, packing, and sorting. The SPEEDISK programme performs these operations faster and with more efficient use of memory. Many of these programmes will have problems on very large disks, and SPEEDISK will work on drives as large as 2G (the maximum DOS volume size), while DEFRAG is limited to disks of about 5 12M or less due to memory constraints.

Several afterrnarket defragmenting programmes are more powerful or faster than the DOS DEFRAG programme. They include:

- SPEEDISK by Symantec (Norton Utilities)
- Power Disk by PC-KWIK

- Optune by Gazelle
- VOPT by Golden Bow

All of these are highly recommended and usually perform much better than the DEFRAG programmeme in DOS. The Power Disk, Optune, and VOPT programmes are also much faster than DEFRAG. The VOPT programme is the simplest and quickest of these. It is a command line programme not a menu driven programme like the others and does not offer a sort capability while all the others do. What it does offer is the ultimate in speed and efficiency in defragmenting and packing flies. Currently, most of these programmes will work on drives up to 1G while some will handle drives of up to 2G. These programmes are updated constantly; contact the manufacturer for more detailed specifications if you are interested. Each of these manufacturers is listed in Appendix B, the "Vendor List."

No matter which programme you end up using, defragmenting and packing your disk helps to reduce drive wear and tear by minimising the amount of work required to load flies. It also greatly increases the chances for data recovery in the case of serious corruption in the File Allocation Tables (FATs) and directories on the disk.

Backing Up the FAT and Directory System. The operating system uses several areas on a formatted disk to manage the files stored on the disk. These areas are extremely critical. If they are damaged, all access to the drive volume may be compromised or completely disabled. In some cases, these critical areas can be rebuilt using known data recovery procedures and tools, but the easiest and best way to recover from damage to these areas is to simply have a backup of them to restore.

The critical areas of a hard disk file system are the following:

- Master (Partition) Boot Record (MBR)
- Extended (Partition) Boot Record (EBR)
- DOS Boot Record (DBR)
- File Allocation Tables (FATs)
- Root Directory

These areas are stored on the disk in the order listed, except that each volume starts with an MBR or EBR but not both. Unlike complete file backups of the entire hard disk, a backup of these system areas is relatively quick and easy. This is because these areas are very small in comparison to the remainder of the drive and normally occupy a fixed amount of space on the disk. For example, the MBR, EBRs and DBRs are only one sector long each, while the two FATs used on each volume cannot exceed 512 sectors (256K), and the Root Directory is limited to 32 sectors (15K). This means that even for the largest hard disk drive, these areas do not consume more than about 300K of space.

The boot record (sector) areas do not change during day to day usage of the disk. These areas will change only if you reformat, repartition, or change operating system versions. Because they are relatively constant, it makes good sense to back up these areas to a file on a floppy disk for later, to restore if necessary.

Each normal disk volume will have two File Allocation Tables and a single Root Directory: These areas change constantly as files are written and deleted from the disk. A backup of these areas is only good for temporary purposes and can be useful when trying to undelete files. Because of this, these backups are often written on the hard disk in a special hidden file near the end of the disk. Other recovery or restoration programmes can then look for this special file and use the information within it to rebuild the FATs or directory system. Often this type of backup is very useful in a situation where files need to be undeleted.

DOS 5.0 provided the MIRROR command for backups of all of these areas. MIRROR has two functions: it can back up the boot sector areas on the hard disk to a file on a floppy disk as well as back up the FAT and directory areas to the end of the hard disk as a special hidden file that recovery programmes can find. To use MIRROR to back up the boot sectors to a floppy disk, execute the command as follows:

MIRROR /PARTN

This will create a special file called PARTNSAV.FIL on a floppy disk you designate. This file contains an image of all of the boot sectors across all of the DOS accessible partitions oh your hard disk. This information can later be restored by the UNFORMAT command as follows:

UNFORMAT/PARTN

The UNFORMAT programme will ask for the disk containing the PARTNSAV.FIL file and restore the boot sector information to the hard disk.

MIRROR can also b e used to backup the FATs and Directory structure to a special hidden file on the disk by simply executing the command with no parameters at all:

MIRROR

By executing the command in this manner, a special file called MIRROR.FIL, as well as a hidden file called MIRRORSAV.FIL, will be created in the root directory, and a copy of the FAT and Directory structures will be copied into some free space at the end of the drive. The actual FAT and Directory data is not stored in a normal file with a filename but is instead written to empty sectors at the end of the drive. These sectors will eventually be overwritten, which is why it is a good idea to run the MIRROR command frequently. The second time you run it, it will actually create a second backup and retain the first. Every subsequent run will retain the previous one as a secondary backup. It is a good idea to put the MIRROR command in your AUTOEXEC.BAT file so that these critical areas of the disk are backed up every time your system boots. Usually, MIRROR only takes a few seconds to perform its backup functions so there will be little delay in booting.

To restore the FAT and Directory area backups, you would use the UNFORMAT programme, also with no parameters. This programme will then search the disk for the MIRROR backups and prompt you for a possible restore. Be careful in restoring these areas as they may be out of sync somewhat with the actual files on your disk. You should always run MIRROR after defragmenting your drive because the defragmenting process moves many files on the disk, making the MIRROR backup obsolete.

There is one unfortunate problem with the MIRROR programme; both Microsoft and IBM removed it from DOS 6. Fortunately, you can retain your copy of MIRROR from DOS 5, or you can download the DOS 6 supplemental disk from the MSDOS forum on CompuServe. This package will provide you with a number of utilities left out of DOS 6 but the MIRROR command is the most useful. You can also order this disk directly from Microsoft for $5 using an order form in the back of the DOS 6 manual from Microsoft.

Many other data recovery programmes offer the ability to back up these areas on the disk. The Norton Utilities by Symantec is one of the best and most well known data recovery packages on the market. It offers this capability and does a much better job than DOS alone. Norton uses an IMAGE command instead of MIRROR, and also has a special programme called RESCUE that creates a rescue disk with not only the boot sector areas on it, but copies of your AUTOEXEC.BAT and CONFIG.SYS files, the DOS system flies, and the CMOS RAM data from your system. Also included on the rescue disk are copies of the appropriate Norton Utilities programmes that can be used to restore these areas.

Checking for Virus Programmes. Both Microsoft and IBM now provide standard anti-virus software in DOS 6.x. The Microsoft Anti-Virus programme is actually a reduced function version of the Central Point Anti-Virus software. IBM has written a package called the IBM Anti-Virus programme. Many aftermarket utility packages are available that will scan for and remove virus programmes. One of the best known is the McAfee Associates SCANV programme, which is also one of the easiest to run because it is a command line utility. The McAfee programme is also distributed through BBS systems and is often site-licensed to large companies.

No matter which of these programmes you use, it is a good idea to perform a scan for virus programmes periodically, especially before making hard disk backups. This will help to ensure that you catch any potential virus problem before it spreads and becomes a major hassle.

Reformatting a Hard Disk. Periodically reformatting a hard disk is an operation often overlooked as part of a preventive maintenance plan. Reformatting serves two purposes. On non-servo controlled drives (stepper motor head actuators) the low level format rewrites the sector header information in alignment with current head positions, which can drift in stepper motor head actuator drives because of temperature- and stress-induced dimensional changes between the platters and heads. If these alignment variations continue unchecked, they eventually will cause read and write errors. Note that this reformatting operation applies to stepper motor head actuator drives only and not to voice-coil drives, which maintain their positional accuracy due to the closed loop servo control mechanism that guides the heads.

The second function of a Low Level Format is to locate and mark or spare out any new defective sectors. This can be accomplished during the Low Level Format and also by a subsequent surface analysis.

Reformatting a hard disk lays down new track and sector ID marks and boundaries, remarks the manufacturer's defects, and performs a surface scan for new defects that might have developed since the last format. With Zone Recorded drives, only the defect mapping and surface analysis are performed. The sector headers are usually not completely rewritten. Temperature variations, case flexing, and physical positioning can add up to eventual read and write errors in a stepper motor head actuated hard disk. This type of failure sometimes appears as a gradually increasing number of disk retries and other read and write problems. You also might notice difficulties when you boot the disk for the first time each day or if the system has been turned off for some time. The cause of these problems is a mistracking between where the data has actually written on the drive and where the track and sector ID marks are located. If the drive is used in a variety of temperatures and environmental conditions, dimensional changes between the heads and planers can cause the data to be written at various improper offsets from the desired track locations.

The reformatting procedure for hard disks is the equivalent of aligning a floppy drive. For hard disks, however, the concern is not for the actual location of each track, but that the drive heads are positioned accurately to the same track location each time. Because of the inherent problems in tracking with stepper motor drives and the lack of a track-following system, mistracking errors accumulate and eventually cause a failure to read or write a particular location. To correct this problem, you must lay down a new set of track and sector ID marks that correspond as closely as possible to the position from which the heads actually read and write data. To do this (with stepper motor drives), you must perform a low-level format.

To make the new format effective, you must do it at the drive's full operating temperature and with the drive in its final mounted position. If the drive runs on its side when it is installed, the format must be done in that position.

For inexpensive drives that lack a proper shock-mounting system (such as the Seagate ST-225, -238, -251, or any ST-2XX drive), make sure that the drive is completely installed before beginning low-level formatting. When you attach the mounting screws to these drives, you are placing screws almost directly into the Head Disk Assembly (HDA), which can cause the HDA to bend or warp slightly depending on how much you tighten the screws. Turn the screws just until they are snug. Do not over tighten them, or your drive might fail if the screws ever loosen and the HDA stress is relaxed. Screws that are too tight can cause continuous read and write problems from stress in the HDA. Having this type of drive completely installed when you are formatting places the HDA under the same physical stress and distortion that it will be under when data is read and written, which makes the format much more accurate.

The frequency with which you should reformat a hard disk depends primarily on the types of drives you have. If the drives are inexpensive stepper motor types (the Seagate ST-2XX series, for example) you probably should reformat the drives once a year. People who must support large numbers of these cheaper drives become known as "hard disk reformatting specialists." A joke in the industry is that some of these drives require winter and summer formats because of temperature sensitivity. This joke, unfortunately, can be somewhat truthful in some cases.

High-quality voice-coil drives usually are formatted only once, either at the factory, as in the case of most IDE or SCSI drives, or by the installer, as is the case with most other types of hard disks. With these drives, a reformat is only performed when the drive begins to exhibit problems reading or writing any sectors on the disk. This might appear in the form of DOS "Abort, Retry, Fail, Ignore error messages, or other read or write errors. Upon encountering difficulty with any sectors on the disk, it should be fully backed up and then a reformat should be performed. In this case, the reformat and subsequent surface analysis will locate and mark off or spare out the marginal sectors, thus restoring the drive to proper operation.

As mentioned earlier, voice-coil drives do not require reformatting the hard disk as do stepper motor drives. Voice-coil drives do not usually develop difficulties with *hysteresis*, a measurement of how accurately a drive can repeatedly locate to a specified position. Hysteresis is measured by commanding a drive to position itself at a particular cylinder and later (at a different temperature), commanding the drive to position itself at the same cylinder. The voice-coil drive always positions itself at the same position relative to the disk platter because of the track-following servo guide head. The stepper motor drive, however, is fooled by temperature and other environmental or physical stress changes because it is essentially a *blind* positioning system.

"Hard Disk Drives and Controllers," which describes hard disk formatting procedures, for more information about the proper tools and procedures for reformatting the different types of hard disk drives.

Passive Preventive Maintenance Procedures

Passive preventive maintenance involves taking care of the system in an external manner: basically, providing the best possible environment—both physical as well as electrical—for the system to operate in. Physical concerns are conditions such as ambient temperature, thermal stress from power cycling, dust and smoke contamination, and disturbances such as shock and vibration. Electrical concerns are items such as electrostatic discharge (ESD), power line noise, and radio-frequency interference. Each of these environmental concerns is discussed in this section.

Examining the Operating Environment. Oddly enough, one of the most overlooked aspects of microcomputer preventive maintenance is protecting the hardware—and the sizable financial investment it represents—from environmental abuse. Computers are relatively forgiving, and they generally are safe in an environment that is comfortable for people. Computers, however, often are treated with no more respect than desktop calculators. The result of this type of abuse is a system failure.

Before you acquire a system, prepare a proper location for your new system, free of airborne contaminants such as smoke or other pollution. Do not place your system in front of a window: the system should not be exposed to direct sunlight or temperature variations. The environmental temperature should be as constant as possible. Power should be provided through properly grounded outlets, and should be stable and free from electrical noise and interference. Keep your system away from radio transmitters or other sources of radio frequency energy. This section examines these issues in more detail.

Heating and Cooling. Thermal expansion and contraction from temperature changes place stress on a computer system. Therefore, keeping the temperature in your office or room relatively constant is important to the successful operation of your computer system.

Temperature variations can lead to serious problems. You might encounter excessive chip creep, for example. If extreme variations occur over a short period, signal traces on circuit boards can crack and separate, solder joints can break, and contacts in the system can undergo accelerated corrosion. Solid-state components such as chips can be damaged also, and a host of other problems can develop.

Temperature variations can play havoc with hard disk drives also. Writing to a disk at different ambient temperatures can, on some drives, cause data to be written at different locations relative to the track centers. Read and write problems then might accelerate later.

To ensure that your system operates in the correct ambient temperature, you first must determine your system's specified functional range. Most manufacturers provide data about the correct operating temperature range for their systems. Two temperature specifications might be available, one indicating allowable temperatures during operation and another indicating allowable temperatures under non-operating conditions. IBM, for example, indicates the following temperature ranges as acceptable for most of its systems:

System on: 60 to 90 degrees Fahrenheit
System off: 50 to 110 degrees Fahrenheit

For the safety of the disk and the data it contains, avoid rapid changes in ambient temperatures. If rapid temperature changes occur—for example, when a new drive is shipped to a location during the winter and then brought indoors—let the drive acclimate to room temperature before turning it on. In extreme cases, condensation forms on the platters inside the drive head disk assembly—disastrous for the drive if you him it on before the condensation can evaporate. Most drive manufacturers specify a timetable to use as a guide in acclimating a drive to room temperature before operating it. You usually must wait several hours to a day before a drive is ready to use after it has been shipped or stored in a cold environment.

Most office environments provide a stable temperature in which to operate a computer system, but some do not. Be sure to give some consideration to the placement of your equipment.

Power Cycling (On/Off). As you have just learned, the temperature variations a system encounters greatly stress the system's physical components. The largest temperature variations a system encounters, however, are those that occur during system warm-up when you initially turn it on. Turning on (also called powering on) a cold system subjects it to the greatest possible internal temperature variations. For these reasons, limiting the number of power-on cycles a system is exposed to greatly improves its life and reliability.

If you want a system to have the longest, most trouble-free life possible, you should limit the temperature variations in its environment. You can limit the extreme temperature cycling in two simple ways during a cold start-up: leave the system off all the time or leave it on all the time. Of these two possibilities, of course, you want to choose the latter option. Leaving the power on is the best way I know to promote system reliability. If your only concern is system longevity, the simple recommendation would be to keep the system unit powered on (or off!) continuously. In the real world, however there are more variables to consider, such as the cost of electricity, the potential fire hazard of unattended running equipment, and other concerns as well.

If you think about the way light bulbs typically fail, you can begin to understand that thermal cycling can be dangerous. Light bulbs burn out most often when you first turn them on, because the filament must endure incredible thermal stress as it changes temperature—in less than one second—from ambient to several thousands of degrees. A bulb that remains on continuously lasts longer than one that is turned on and off repeatedly.

Some people argue that the reason you should leave a computer system on continuously is to prevent the electrical "shock" from the inrush of power when you start up a system. The cause of failure in a low-voltage solid-state circuit repeatedly powered on and off, however, is not in-rushing electrons, but rather physical stresses caused by thermal expansion and contraction of the components. Component engineers agree, and tests prove, that a device left on continuously outlasts one that is powered on and off repeatedly.

Where problems can occur immediately at power-on is in the power supply. The start-up current draw for the system and for any motor during the first few seconds of operation is very high compared to the normal operating-current draw. Because the current must come from the power supply, the supply has an extremely demanding load to carry for the first few seconds of operation, especially if several disk drives will be started. Motors have an extremely high power-on current draw. This demand often overloads a marginal circuit or component in the supply and causes it to bum or break with a "snap." I have seen several power supplies the the instant a system was powered up. To enable your equipment to have the longest possible life, try to keep the temperature of solid-state components relatively constant, and limit the number of start-ups oń the power supply. The only way I know to do so is to leave the system on.

Although it sounds as though I am recommending that you leave all of your computer equipment on 24 hours a day, seven days a week, I no longer recommend this type of operation. A couple of concerns have tempered my urge to leave everything running continuously. One is that an unattended system that is powered on, represents a fire hazard. I have seen monitors start themselves on fire after internally shorting, and systems whose cooling fans have frozen, enabling the power supply and entire system to overheat. I do not leave any system running in an unattended building. Another problem is wasted electrical power. Many companies have adopted austerity programmes that involve turning lights and other items off when not in use. The powei consumption of some of today's nigh-powered systems and accessories is not trivial. Also, an unattended operating system is more of a security risk than one that is powered off and locked.

Realities—such as the fire hazard of unattended systems running during night or weekend hours, security problems, and power-consumption issues—might prevent you from leaving your system on all the time. Therefore, you must compromise. Power on the system only one time daily. Don't power the system on and off several times every day. This good advice is often ignored, especially when several users share systems. Each user powers on the system to perform work on the PC and then powers off the system. These systems tend to have many more problems with component failures.

If you are concerned about running your hard disk continuously, let me dispel your fears. Running your hard disk continuously might be the best thing you can do for your drive. Leaving the drive powered on is the best method for reducing read and write failures caused by temperature changes. If you arc using extremely inexpensive drives with stepper motor actuators, leaving the drive on greatly improves reliability and increases the time between low-level formats caused by mistracking. A drive's bearings and motors also function longer if you reduce the power-on temperature cycling. You might have had a disk that didn't boot after you turned the drive off for a prolonged period (over the weekend, for example) and you fixed the problem with a subsequent low-level format, but you most likely wouldn't have had the problem if you had left your drive on.

If you are in a building with a programmable thermostat, you have another reason to be concerned about temperatures and disk drives. Some buildings have thermostats programmed to turn off the heat overnight or over the weekend. These thermostats are programmed also to quickly raise the temperature just before business hours every day. In Chicago, for example, outside temperatures in the winter can dip to 20 degrees below 0 (not including a wind-chill factor). An office building's interior temperature can drop as low as 50 degrees during the weekend. When you arrive Monday morning, the heat has been on for only an hour or so, but the hard disk platters might have not yet reached even 60 degrees when you turn on the system unit. During the first 20 minutes of operation, the disk platters rapidly rise in temperature to 120 degrees or more. If you have an inexpensive stepper motor hard disk and begin writing to the disk at these low temperatures, you are setting yourself up for trouble. Again, many systems with these "cheap" drives don't even boot properly under these circumstances and must be warmed up before they even boot DOS.

Tip

If you do not leave a system on continuously, at least give it 15 minutes or more to warm up before writing to the hard disk. Power up the system and go get a cup of coffee, read the paper, or do some other task. This practice does wonders for the reliability of the data on your disk, especially cheaper units.

If you do leave your system on for long periods of time, make sure that the screen is blank or displays a random image if the system is not in use. The phosphor on the picture tube can burn if a stationary image is left on-screen continuously. Higher-persistence phosphor monochrome screens are most susceptible, and the color displays with low-persistence phosphors are the least susceptible. If you ever have seen a monochrome display with the image of some programme permanently burned in—even with the display off—you know what I mean. Look at the monitors that display flight information at the airport—they usually show the effects of phosphor burn.

Screen savers or blankers will either blank the screen completely or display some sort of moving random image to prevent burn in. This can be accomplished by either a manual or automatic procedure as follows:

- *Manual.* Turn the brightness and contrast levels all the way down, or even power the display off completely. This technique is effective but it is a manual method; you must remember to do it.

- *Automatic. Many* types of programmes can cause the screen to blank or display random images automatically at a predetermined interval. Screen savers are built into most Graphical User Interfaces (GUIs) such as Windows and OS/2. These can easily be enabled, and you can also specify the time delay before they activate. If you run under plain DOS, you can use a number of public domain as well as commercial screen saver programmes. These programmes usually run as terminate-and-stay-resident (TSR) programmes. The programme watches the clock as well as the keyboard and mouse ports. If several minutes pass with nothing typed at the keyboard or no mouse movement, the programme activates and either shuts off all signals to the display or creates an image that moves around oh the screen to prevent burn in.

Static Electricity. Static electricity can cause numerous problems within a system. The problems usually appear during the winter months when humidity is low or in extremely dry climates where the humidity is low year-round. In these cases, you might need to take special precautions to ensure that the system functions properly.

Static discharges outside a system-unit chassis are rarely a source of permanent problems within the system. The usual effect of a static discharge to the case, keyboard, or even in dose proximity to a system, is a parity check (memory) error or a locked-up şystem. In some cases, I have been able to cause parity checks or system lockups by simply walking past a system. Most static-sensitivity problems such as this one are caused by improper grounding of the system power. Be sure that you always use a three-prong, grounded power cord plugged into a properly grounded outlet. If you are unsure about the outlet, you can buy an outlet tester at most electronics-supply or hardware stores for only a few dollars.

Whenever you open a system unit or handle circuits removed from the system, you must be much more careful with static. You can damage permanently a component with a static discharge if the charge is not routed to a ground. I usually recommend handling boards and adapters first by a grounding point such as the bracket to minimize the potential for static damage.

An easy way to prevent static problems is with good power-line grounding, which is extremely important for computer equipment. A poorly designed power-line grounding system is one of the primary causes of poor computer design. The best way to prevent static damage is to prevent the static charge from getting into the computer in the first place. The chassis ground in a properly designed system serves as a static guard for the computer, which redirects the static charge safely to ground.

For this ground to be complete, therefore, the system must be plugged into a properly grounded three-wire outlet.

If the static problem is extreme, you can resort to other measures. One is to use a grounded static mat underneath the computer. Touch the mat first before you touch the computer, to ensure that any static charges are routed to ground and away from the system unit's internal parts. If problems still persist you might want to check out the electrical building ground. I have seen installations in which three-wire outlets exist but are not grounded properly. You can use an outlet tester to be sure that the outlet is wired properly.

Power Line Noise. To run properly, a computer system requires a steady supply of clean, noise-free power. In some installations, however, the power line serving the computer serves heavy equipment also, and the voltage variations resulting from the on-off cycling of this equipment can cause problems for the computer. Certain types of equipment on the same power line also can cause voltage *spikes*—short transient signals of sometimes 1,000 volts or more—that can physically damage a computer. Although these spikes are rare, they can be crippling. Even a dedicated electrical circuit used only by a single computer can experience spikes and transients, depending on the quality of the power supplied to the building or circuit.

During the site-preparation phase of a system installation, you should be aware of these factors to ensure a steady supply of clean power.

- If possible, the computer system should be on its own circuit with its own circuit breaker. This setup does not guarantee freedom from interference, but it helps.
- The circuit should be checked for a good, low-resistance ground, proper line voltage, freedom from interference, and freedom from brownouts (voltage dips).
- A three-wire circuit is a must but some people substitute grounding-plug adapters to adapt a grounded plug to a two-wire socket. This setup is not recommended; the ground is there for a reason.
- Power line noise problems increase with the resistance of the circuit, which is a function of wire size and length. To decrease resistance, therefore, avoid extension cords unless absolutely necessary, and then use only heavy-duty extension cords.
- Inevitably, you will want to plug in other equipment later. Plan ahead to avoid temptations to use too many items on a single outlet. If possible, provide a separate power circuit for noncomputer-related accessories.

Air conditioners, coffee makers, copy machines, laser printers, space heaters, vacuum cleaners, and power took are some of the worst corrupters of a PC system's power. Any of these items can draw an excessive amount of current and play havoc with a PC system on the same electrical circuit. I've seen offices in which all the computers begin to crash at about 9.05 a.m. daily, which is when all the coffee makers are turned on!

Also, try to ensure that copy machines and laser printers do not share a circuit with other computer equipment. These devices draw a large amount of power.

Another major problem in some companies is partitioned offices. Many of these partitions are prewired with their own electrical outlets and are plugged into one another in a sort of power line daisy chain, similar to chaining power strips together. I pity the person in the cubicle at the end of the electrical daisy chain, who will have very flaky power!

As a real-world example of too many devices sharing a single circuit, I can describe several instances in which a personal computer had a repeating parity check problem! All efforts to repair the system had been unsuccessful. The reported error locations from the parity check message also were inconsistent, which normally indicates a problem with power. The problem could have been the power supply in the system unit or the external power supplied from the wall outlet. This problem was solved one day as I stood watching the system. The parity check message was displayed at the same instant someone two cubicles away turned on a copy machine. Placing the computers on a separate line solved the problem.

By following the guidelines in this section, you can create the proper power environment for your systems and help to ensure trouble-free operation.

Radio-Frequency Interference. Radio-frequency interference (RFI) is easily overlooked as a problem factor. The interference is caused by any source of radio transmissions near a computer system. Living next door to a 50,000-watt commercial radio station is one sure way to get RFI problems, but less powerful transmitters cause problems too. I know of many instances in which portable radio-telephones have caused sporadic random keystrokes to appear, as though an invisible entity were typing on the keyboard. I also have seen RFI cause a system to lock up. Solutions to RFI problems are more difficult to state because every case must be handled differently. Sometimes, reorienting a system unit eliminates the problem because radio signals can be directional in nature. At other times, you must invest in specially shielded cables for cables outside the system unit, such as the keyboard, cable.

One type of solution to an RFI noise problem with cables is to pass the cable through a *toroidal iron con*, a doughnut-shaped piece of iron placed around a cable to suppress both the reception and transmission of electromagnetic interference (EMI). If you can isolate an RFI noise problem in a particular cable, you often can solve the problem by passing the cable through a toroidal core. Because the cable must pass through the center hole of the core, it often is difficult, if not impossible, to add a toroid to a cable that already has end connectors installed.

Radio Shack sells a special snap-together toroid designed specifically to be added to cables already in use. This toroid looks like a thick-walled tube that has been sliced in half. You just lay the cable in the center of one of the halves, and snap the other half over the first. This type of construction makes it easy to add the noise-suppression features of a toroid to virtually any existing cable.

IBM also makes a special 6-foot long PS/2 keyboard cable with a built-in toroid core (part number 27F4984) that can greatly reduce interference problems. This cable has the smaller 6-pin DIN (PS/2 style) connector at the system end and the standard SDL (Shielded Data Link) connector at the keyboard end; it costs about $40.

The best, if not the easiest, way to eliminate the problem probably is to correct it at the source. You likely won't convince the commercial radio station near your office to shut down but if you are dealing with a small radio transmitter that is generating RFI, sometimes you can add to the transmitter a filter that suppresses spurious emissions. Unfortunately, problems sometimes persist until the transmitter is either switched off or moved some distance away from the affected computer.

Note that your own computer systems can be a source of RFI. Computer equipment must meet one of these two classifications to be certified and salable, according to the FCC (Federal Communications Commission): Class A or Class B. The Class A specification applies to computing devices sold for use in commercial, business, and industrial environments. Class B indicates that the equipment has passed more stringent tests and can *be* used in residential environments, in addition to any environments allowed under Class A.

The FCC does not really police users or purchasers of computer equipment so much as it polices the equipment manufacturers or vendors. Therefore, if you are using a Class A-rated system in your home, you don't need to worry about radio police showing up at your door. You must obtain a Class B certification for systems that meet one of the following conditions:

- Marketed through retail or direct-mail outlets
- Sold to the general public rather than commercial users only

- Operates on battery or 120-volt AC electrical power

Notice that a system has to fit each of these three categories to be considered a personal computer and be subject to the stricter Class B rules. Notice also that the FCC considers all portable computer systems as meeting Class B standards because their portability makes them likely to be used in a residential setting.

The FCC standards for Class A and Class B certification govern two kinds of emissions: conductive emissions, radiated from the computer system into the power cord, and radio-frequency emissions, radiated from the computer system into space. Table 1 shows the conductive and radio-frequency emissions limitations to be eligible for both Class A and Class B ratings.

TABLE 1

FCC Class A and Class B Emission Limitations

Conductive Emissions: Maximum Signal Level (mv)

Frequency	*Class A*	*Class B*
0.45 to 1.705 MHz	1000	250
1.705 to 30.0 MHz	3000	250

Conductive Emissions: Maximum Field Strength (uv/M)

Frequency	*Class A (10M)*	*Class B(3M)*
30 to 88 MHz	90	100
88 to 216 MHz	150	150
217 to 960 MHz	210	200
960 MHz and up	300	500

MHz = Megahertz
10M Measured at 10 meters
3M = Measured at 3 meters
mv = Millivolt
uv/M = Microvolts per meter

Notice that although some of the specific numbers listed for Class A seem lower than those required for Class B, you must consider that field strength measurements normally decline under the inverse square law: the strength of the signal decreases as the square of the distance from the source. A rating of 100 microvolts per meter at 3 meters, therefore, would be approximately equal to a rating of about 9 microvolts per meter at 10 meters. This calculation just means that the limits to pass Class B certification are much tougher than they look, and certainly are much tougher than

Class A limits. Additionally, Class A certification is tested and verified entirely by the manufacturer; Class B certification requires a sample of the equipment to be sent to the FCC for testing.

IBM and most other responsible manufacturers ensure that all systems they sell meet the stricter Class B designations. One of the primary reasons for the Micro Channel Architecture design was to meet, and also greatly exceed these FCC classifications. IBM knew that as computing clock speeds go up, so do the radio emissions. As clock rates of 66, 75, and 100 MHz and higher become more common (and they will soon), IBM will have a distinct advantage over manufacturers still using the AT or EISA bus designs because vendors using ISA or EISA bus designs will have to invest in more expensive chassis and case shielding to combat the emission problem. IBM and other Micro Channel clones will gain a distinct manufacturing cost advantage.

Dust and Pollutants. Dirt, smoke, dust, and other pollutants are bad for your system. The power-supply fan carries airborne particles through your system, and they collect inside. If your system is used in an extremely harsh environment, you might want to investigate some of the industrial systems on the market designed for harsh conditions.

IBM used to sell industrial model XT and AT systems but discontinued them after introducing the PS/2. IBM has licensed several third-party companies to produce industrial versions of PS/2 systems.

Compatible vendors also have industrial systems; many companies make special *hardened* versions of their systems for harsh environments. Industrial systems usually use a different cooling system from the one used in a regular PC. A large cooling fan is used to pressurize the case rather than depressurize it, as most systems do. The air pumped into the case passes through a filter unit that must be cleaned and changed periodically. The system is pressurised so that no contaminated air can flow into it; air flows only outward. The only way air can enter is through the fan and filter system.

These systems also might have special keyboards impervious to liquids and dirt. Some flat-membrane keyboards are difficult to type on, but are extremely rugged; others resemble the standard types of keyboards, but have a thin, plastic membrane that covers all the keys. You can add this membrane to normal types of keyboards to seal them from the environment.

A new breed of humidifier can cause problems with computer equipment This type of humidifier uses ultrasonics to generate a mist of water sprayed into the air.

The extra humidity helps cure problems with static electricity resulting from a dry climate, but the airborne water contaminants can cause many problems. If you use one of these systems, you might notice a white ash-like deposit forming on components. The deposit is the result of abrasive and corrosive minerals suspended in the vaporised water. If these deposits collect on the disk drive heads, they will ruin the heads and scratch disks. The only safe way to run one of these ultrasonic humidifiers is with pure distilled water. If you use a humidifier, be sure it does not generate these deposits.

If you do your best to keep the environment for your computer equipment clean, your system will run better and last longer. Also, you will not have to open your unit as often for complete preventive maintenance cleaning.

USING POWER-PROTECTION SYSTEMS

Power-protection systems do just what the name implies: they protect your equipment from the effects of power surges and power failures. In particular, power surges and spikes can damage computer equipment, and a loss of power can result in lost data. In this section, you learn about the four primary types of power-protection devices available and under what circumstances you should use them.

Before considering any further levels of power protection, you should know that the power supply in your system (if your system is well-made) already affords you a substantial amount of protection. The power supplies in IBM equipment are designed to provide protection from higher-than-normal voltages and currents, and provide a limited amount of power line noise filtering. Some of the inexpensive aftermarket power supplies probably do not have this sort of protection; be careful if you have an inexpensive clone system. In those cases, further protecting your system might be wise.

IBM's PS/2 power supplies will stay within operating specifications and continue to run a system if any of these power line disturbances occur:

- Voltage drop to 80 volts for up to 2 seconds
- Voltage drop to 70 volts for up to .5 seconds
- Voltage surge of up to 143 volts for up to 1 second

IBM also states that neither their power supplies nor systems will be damaged by the following occurrences:

- Full power outage
- Any voltage drop (brownout)
- A spike of up to 2,500 volts

Because of the high quality power supply design that IBM uses, they state in their documentation that external surge suppressors are not needed for PS/2 systems. Most other high quality name brand manufacturers also use high quality power supply designs. Companies like Astec, PC Power and Cooling, and others make very high quality units.

To verify the levels of protection built into the existing power supply in a computer system, an independent laboratory subjected several unprotected PC systems to various spikes and surges up to *6,000 volts*—considered the maximum level of surge that can be transmitted to a system by an electrical outlet. Any higher voltage would cause the power to arc to ground within the outlet itself. Note that none of the systems sustained permanent damage in these tests; the worst thing that happened was that some of the systems rebooted or shut down if the surge was more than 2,000 volts. Each system restarted when the power switch was toggled after a shutdown.

I do not use any real form of power protection on my systems, and they have survived near-direct lightning strikes and powerful surges. The most recent incident, only 50 feet from my office, was a direct lightning strike to a brick chimney that *blew the top of the chimney apart.* None of my systems (which were running at the time) were damaged in any way from this incident; they just shut themselves down. I was able to restart each system by toggling the power switches. An alarm system located in the same office, however, was destroyed by this strike. I am not saying that lightning strikes or even much milder spikes and surges cannot damage computer systems—another nearby lightning strike did destroy a modem and serial adapter installed in one of my systems. I was just lucky that the destruction did not include the motherboard.

This discussion points out an important oversight in some power-protection strategies: you may elect to protect your systems from electrical power disturbances, but do not forget to provide similar protection also from spikes and surges on the phone line.

The automatic shutdown of a computer during power disturbances is a built-in function of most high-quality power supplies. You can reset the power supply by flipping the power switch from on to off and back on again. Some power supplies, such as those in most of the PS/2 systems, have an *auto-restart function.* This type of power supply acts the same as others in a massive surge or spike situation: it shuts down the system. The difference is that after normal power resumes, the power supply waits for a specified delay of three to six seconds and then resets itself and powers the system back up. Because no manual switch resetting is required, this feature is desirable in systems functioning as a network file server or in a system in a remote location.

The first time I witnessed a large surge cause an immediate shutdown of all my systems, I was extremely surprised. All the systems were silent, but the monitor and modem lights were still on. My first thought was that everything was blown, but a simple toggle of each system-unit power switch caused the power supplies to reset, and the units powered up with no problem. Since that first time, this type of shutdown has happened to me several times, always without further problems.

The following types of power-protection devices are explained in the sections that follow:

- Surge suppressors
- Line conditioners
- Standby power supplies (SPS)
- Uninterruptible power supplies (UPS)

Surge Suppressors (Protectors)

The simplest form of power protection is any of the commercially available surge protectors; that is, devices inserted between the system and the power line. These devices, which cost between $20 and $200, can absorb the high-voltage transients produced by nearby lightning strikes and power equipment. Some surge protectors can be effective for certain types of power problems, but they offer only very limited protection.

Surge protectors use several devices, usually metal-oxide varistors (MOVs), that can clamp and shunt away all voltages above a certain level. MOVs are designed to accept voltages as high as 6,000 volts and divert any power above 200 volts to ground. MOVs can handle normal surges, but powerful surges such as a direct lightning strike can blow right through them. MOVs are not designed to handle a very high level of power, and self-destruct while shunting a large surge. These devices, therefore, cease to function after a single large surge or a series of smaller ones. The real problem is that you cannot easily tell when they no longer are functional; the only way to test them is to subject the MOVs to a surge, which destroys them. Therefore, you never really know if your so-called surge protector is protecting your system.

Some surge protectors have status lights that let you know when a surge large enough to blow the MOVs has occurred. A surge suppressor without this status indicator light is useless because you never know when it has stopped protecting.

Underwriters Laboratories has produced an excellent standard that governs surge suppressors, called UL 1449. Any surge suppressor that meets this standard is a very good one, and definitely, offers an additional line of protection beyond what the power supply in your PC already does. The only types of surge suppressors worth buying, therefore, should have two features: conformance to the UL 1449 standard and a status light indicating when the MOVs are blown. Units that meet the UL 1449 specification say so on the packaging or directly on the unit. If this standard is not mentioned, it does not conform, and you should avoid it.

Another good feature to have in a surge suppressor is a built-in circuit breaker that can be reset rather than a fuse. The breaker protects your system if the system or a peripheral develops a short. These better surge suppressors usually cost about $40.

Phone Line Surge Protectors

In addition to protecting the power lines, it is critical to provide protection to your systems from any phone lines that are connected. If you are using a modem or fax board which is plugged into the phone system, any surges or spikes that travel the phone line can potentially damage your system. In many areas, the phone lines are especially susceptible to lightning strikes, which is the largest cause of fried modems and computer equipment attached to them.

Several companies manufacture or sell simple surge protectors that plug between your modem and the phone line. These inexpensive devices can be purchased from most electronics supply houses. Most of the cable and communication product vendors listed in Appendix B sell these phone line surge protectors.

Line Conditioners

In addition to high-voltage and current conditions, other problems can occur with incoming power. The voltage might dip below the level needed to run the system and result in a brownout. Other forms of electrical noise other than simple voltage surges or spikes might be on the power line, such as radio-frequency interference or electrical noise caused by motors or other inductive loads.

Remember two things when you wire together digital devices (such as computers and their peripherals). A wire is an antenna and has a voltage induced in it by nearby electromagnetic fields, which can come from other wires, telephones, CRTs, motors, fluorescent fixtures, static discharge, and, of course, radio transmitters. Digital circuitry also responds with surprising efficiency to noise of even a volt or two, making those induced voltages particularly troublesome. The wiring in your building can act as an antenna and pick up all kinds of noise and disturbances. A line conditioner can handle many of these types of problems.

A line conditioner is designed to remedy a variety of problems. It filters the power, bridges brownouts, suppresses high-voltage and current conditions, and generally acts as a buffer between the power line and the system. A line conditioner does the job of a surge suppressor, and much more. It is more of an active device functioning continuously rather than a passive device that activates only when a surge is present. A line conditioner provides true-power conditioning and can handle myriad problems. It contains transformers, capacitors, and other circuitry that temporarily can bridge a brownout or low-voltage situation. These units usually cost several hundreds of dollars, depending on the power-handling capacity of the unit.

Backup Power

The next level of power protection includes backup power-protection devices. These units can provide power in case of a complete blackout, which provides the time needed for an orderly system shutdown. Two types are available: the standby power supply (SPS) and the uninterruptible power supply (UPS). The UPS is a special device because it does much more than just provide backup power: it is also the best kind of line conditioner you can buy.

Standby Power Supplies (SPS). A standby power supply is known as an *off-line device:* it functions only when normal power is disrupted. An SPS system uses a special circuit that can sense the AC line current. If the sensor detects a loss of power on the line, the system quickly switches over to a standby battery and power inverter. The power inverter converts the battery power to 110-volt AC power, which then is supplied to the system.

SPS systems do work, but sometimes a problem occurs with the switch to battery power. If the switch is not fast enough, the computer system unit shuts down or reboots anyway, which defeats the purpose of having the backup power supply. A truly outstanding SPS adds to the circuit a *ferroresonant transformer,* a large transformer with the capability to store a small amount of power and deliver it during the switch time. Having this device is similar to having on the power line a buffer that you add to an SPS to give it almost truly uninterruptible capability.

SPS units also may or may not have internal line conditioning of their own; most cheaper units place your system directly on the regular power line under normal circumstances and offer no conditioning. The addition of a ferroresonant transformer to an SPS gives it additional regulation and protection capabilities due to the buffer effect of the transformer. SPS devices without the ferroresonant transformer still require the use of a line conditioner for full protection. SPS systems usually cost from $200 to several thousands of dollars, depending on the quality and power-output capacity.

Uninterruptible Power Supplies (UPS). Perhaps the best overall solution to any power problem is to provide a power source that is both conditioned and that also cannot be interrupted—which describes an uninterruptible power supply. UPSs are known as online systems because they continuously function and supply power to your computer systems. Because some companies advertise ferroresonant SPS devices as though they were UPS devices, many now use the term *true UPS* to describe a truly on-line system. A true UPS system is constructed much the same as an SPS system; however, because you always are operating from the battery, there is no switching circuit.

In a true UPS, your system always operates from the battery, with a voltage inverter to convert from 12 volts DC to 110 volts AC. You essentially have your own private power system that generates power independently of the AC line. A battery charger connected to the line or wall current keeps the battery charged at a rate equal to or greater than the rate at which power is consumed.

When power is disconnected, the true UPS continues functioning undisturbed because the battery-charging function is all that is lost. Because you already were running off the battery, no switch takes place and no power disruption is possible. The battery then begins discharging at a rate dictated by the amount of load your system places on the unit, which (based on the size of the battery) gives you plenty of time to execute an orderly system shutdown. Based on an appropriately scaled storage battery, the UPS functions continuously, generating power and preventing unpleasant surprises. When the line power returns, the battery charger begins recharging the battery, again with no interruption.

UPS cost is a direct function of both the length of time it can continue to provide power after a line current failure, and how much power it can provide; therefore, purchasing a UPS that gives you enough power to run your system and peripherals as well as enough time to dose files and provide an orderly shutdown would be sufficient. In most PC applications, this solution is the most cost-effective because the batteries and charger portion of the system must be much larger than the SPS type of device, and will be more costly.

Many SPS systems are advertised as though they were true UPS systems. The giveaway is the unit's "switch time." If a specification for switch time exists, the unit cannot be a true UPS because UPS units never switch. Understand, however, that a good SPS with a ferroresonant transformer can virtually equal the performance of a true UPS at a lower cost.

Because of a UPS's almost total isolation from the line current, it is unmatched as a line conditioner and surge suppressor. The best UPS systems add a ferroresonant transformer for even greater power conditioning and protection capability. This type of UPS is the best form of power protection available. The price, however, can be very high. A true UPS costs from $1 to $2 per watt of power supplied. To find out just how much power your system requires, look at the UL sticker on the back of the unit. This sticker lists the maximum power draw in watts, or sometimes in just volts and amperes. If only voltage and amperage are listed; multiply the two figures to calculate a wattage figure.

As an example, the back of an IBM PC AT Model 339 indicates that the system can require as much as 110 volts at a maximum current draw of 5 amps. The maximum power this AT can draw is about 550 watts. This wattage is for a system with every slot full, two hard disks and one floppy—in other words, the maximum possible level of expansion. The system should never draw any more power than that; if it does, a 5-ampere fuse in the power supply blows. This type of system normally draws an average 300 watts; to be safe when you make calculations for UPS capacity, however, be conservative and use the 550-watt figure. Adding a monitor that draws 100 watts brings the total to 650 watts or more. To run two fully loaded AT systems, you need an 1,100-watt UPS. Don't forget two monitors, each drawing 100 watts; the total, therefore, is 1300 watts. Using the $1 to $2 per watt figure, a UPS of at least that capacity or greater will cost from $1,300 to $2,600 dollars—expensive, but unfortunately what the best level of protection costs. Most companies can justify this type of expense for only a critical-use PC, such as a network file server.

In addition to the total available output power (wattage), several other factors can differentiate one UPS from another. The addition of a ferroresonant transformer improves a unit's power conditioning and buffering capabilities. Good units have also an inverter that produces a true sine wave output; the cheaper ones may generate a square wave. A square wave is an approximation of a sine wave with abrupt up-and-down voltage transitions. The abrupt transitions of a square wave signal are not compatible with some-computer equipment power supplies. Be sure that the UPS you purchase produces a signal compatible with your computer equipment. Every unit has a specification for how long it can sustain output at the rated level. If your systems draw less than the rated level, you have some additional time. Be careful, though: most UPS systems are not designed for you to sit and compute for hours through an electrical blackout. They are designed to provide power to whatever is needed, to remain operating long enough to allow for an orderly shutdown. You pay a large amount for units that provide power for more than 15 minutes or so.

There are many sources of power protection equipment, but two of the best are Best Power and Tripp Lite. These companies sell a variety of UPS, SPS, line, and surge protectors. They are listed in Appendix B.

USING DATA-BACKUP SYSTEMS

Making a backup of important data on a computer system is one thing that many users fail to do. A backup is similar to insurance: you need it only when you are in big trouble! Because of the cost in not only dollars, but also in time and effort, many users do not have adequate backup—which is not a problem until the day you have a catastrophe and suddenly find yourself without your important data or files. This section discusses several forms of backup hardware and software that can make the job both easier and faster, and—hopefully—cause more users to do it.

Backup is something a service technician should be aware of. After I repair a system that has suffered some kind of disk crash, I can guarantee that the disk subsystem will be completely functional. I cannot guarantee, however, that the original files are on the disks; in fact, the drive may have to be replaced. Without a backup, the system can be physically repaired, but the original data may be lost forever.

Nothing destroys someone's faith in computer technology faster than telling them that the last year or more of work (in the form of disk files) no longer exists. When I visit a customer site to do some troubleshooting or repair, I always tell my clients to back up the system before I arrive. They may be reluctant to do so at first, but it is better than paying a technician by the hour to do it. A backup must be done before I operate on a system, because I do not want to be liable if something goes wrong and data is damaged or lost. If the system is so dysfunctional that a backup cannot be performed, I make sure that the client knows that the service technician is not responsible for the data.

A good general rule is never to let a backup interval be longer than what you are willing to lose some day. You always can reload or even repurchase copies of software programmes that might have been lost, but you cannot buy back your own data. Because of the extremely high value of data compared to the system itself, I have recommended for some time that service technicians become familiar with data-recovery principles and procedures. Being able to perform this valuable service gives you a fantastic edge over technicians who can only fix or replace the hardware.

Backup Policies

All users and managers of computer systems should develop a plan for regular disk backups. I recommend that one person in an office have the responsibility for performing these backups so that the job is not left undone.

A backup interval should be selected based on the amount of activity on the system. Some users find that daily backups are required, and others find that a weekly arrangement is more suitable. Backups rarely must be scheduled at more than weekly intervals. Some users settle on a mixed plan: perform weekly disk backups and daily backups of only the changed files.

The procedures for backing up and for dealing with copy protection are explained in the following sections.

Backup Procedures

You should back up to removable media such as cartridge or tape, which you remove from a system and store in a safe place. Backups performed on nonremovable media, such as another hard disk, are much more vulnerable to damage, theft, or fire; also, having multiple backups is much more expensive.

Because of the relatively low cost of hard disks, some users unfortunately install two hard disks and back up one to the other. Worse, some users split a single disk into two partitions and back up one partition to the other. These backups are false backups. If the system were subjected to a massive electrical surge or failure, the contents of both drives could be lost. If the system were stolen, again, both backups would be lost. Finally, if the system were physically damaged, such as in a fire or other mishap, both the data and the backup would be lost. These are good reasons that it is important to back up to removable media.

Perform your backups on a rotating schedule. I recommend using a tape-backup system with at least three tapes per drive, in which you back up data to the first tape the first week. The second week, you use a second tape. That way, if the second tape has been damaged, you can use the preceding week's backup tape to restore data.

The third week, you should use still another, third, tape and place the first tape in a different physical location as protection against damage from fire, flood, theft, or another disaster.

The fourth week, you begin to rotate each tape so that the first (off-site) tape is used again for backup, and the second tape is moved off-site. This system always has two progressively older backups on-site, with the third backup off-site to provide for disaster insurance. Only removable media can provide this type of flexibility, and tape is one of the best forms of removable media for backup.

Dealing with Copy Protection. One thing standing in the way of proper backups of some of your software is copy protection, a system in which the original disk the software is on is modified so that it cannot be copied exactly by your system. When the programmes on the disk are run, they look for this unique feature to determine whether the original disk is in the system. Some software makers force you to use master copies of their programmes by using this technique to require that the original disks be placed in the floppy drive for validation even though the system might have the software loaded on the hard disk.

Some forms of copy protection load the software on a hard disk only from an original disk, and modify the hard disk loaded version so that it runs only if it remains on the system in a specified set of sectors. If the programme ever is moved on the disk, it fails to operate. Because these requirements make the software highly prone to failure, copy protection has no place on software used in a business environment.

My personal response to copy protection is to refuse to use, buy, or recommend any software from a company engaged in this practice. With rare exceptions, I simply do not buy copy-protected software. Unprotected alternatives always are available for whatever type of programme you want. You might even discover that the unprotected alternative is a better programme. If you don't make the software-purchasing decisions in your organisation, however, you may have little choice in this matter.

Experienced computer users know that you never should use original disks when you install or configure software. After I purchase a new programme, I first make a copy and store the original disks. In fact, I use the original disks solely for making additional backup copies. Following this procedure protects me if I make a mistake in installing or using the software. Because of the need for backup and the fact that copy protection essentially prevents proper backup, a solution has been devised.

When you must use a piece of protected software, you can purchase special programmes that enable you to back up and even to remove the protection from most copy-protected programmes on the market. Two such programmes are CopyWrite, by Quaid Software Ltd., and Copy II PC, by Central Point Software. These programmes cost about $50 and are absolutely necessary when you are forced to deal with copy-protected software.

Note that no matter what a software license agreement says, you have a legal right to back up your software; this right is guaranteed under US copyright law. Do not let a software license agreement bamboozle you into believing otherwise.

The best way to fight copy protection is with your wallet. Most companies respond to this economic pressure; many respond by removing the protection from their programmes. Fortunately, because of this economic pressure by influential users, the scourge of copy protection has been almost eliminated from the business-software marketplace. Only a few remaining programmes have this unfortunate defect; I hope that the protection will be eradicated from them as well.

Backup Software

In considering how to back up your system, you should be aware of both the hardware and software options available. This section first explores the software-only options; that is, using either what you get with DOS, or some more powerful aftermarket software to back up using a floppy drive. You will learn that the aftermarket software usually offers many features and capabilities that the standard DOS BACKUP programme does not have. After discussing software alternatives, this section looks at complete, dedicated hardware and software backup systems. Using specialised hardware is the best way to have an easy, effective, and safe way of backing up your system.

The DOS BACKUP Command

The most basic backup software you can use are the DOS commands BACKUP and RESTORE. Since their introduction in Version 2.0 of DOS, and up to Version 3.3, these commands have frustrated users with their bugs and other problems. The versions supplied with DOS V4.0 and higher have been greatly improved, but they still do not offer what many aftermarket products offer. Because of the way BACKUP and RESTORE use the floppy drive as the hardware device, you can use this software only for backing up systems with low-capacity hard drives.

New Backup Software with DOS 6.x

Both Microsoft and IBM have included new backup software with their respective versions of DOS 6.x. These programmes far outstrip the capabilities of the original BACKUP command and are much easier and safer to use.

In MS-DOS, Microsoft supplies a limited version of the Norton Backup software called MSBACKUP. This programme is a full-featured menu-driven programme that is designed to back up to floppy drives only. It is very easy to use, and represents a great leap from the older BACKUP and RESTORE commands. Because it is really a restricted version of the Norton Backup programme by Symantec, you can easily upgrade to the more full-featured Norton Backup programme and still retain compatibility with ail of your existing backups.

IBM went a different route in PC DOS and supplies an only slightly limited version of the Central Point Backup programme called CPBACKUP. This offers a great deal more functionality than the MSBACKUP programme supplied by Microsoft. CPBACKUP can back up to a variety of different devices, including tape drives. It is also an easy to use menu-driven programme, but can also be completely automated with an extensive number of command line options. Again, a more full-featured version can be obtained directly from Central Point which would be compatible with your existing backups.

Aftermarket Software for Floppy Backups

Most aftermarket software offers convenience and performance features not found in the DOS BACKUP and RESTORE commands. If you are relegated to using the floppy disk drive as your backup hardware, you should do yourself a favor and investigate some of the aftermarket software designed for backup. I recommend FASTBACK, by fifth Generation Systems, as well as the Norton (Symantec) and Central Point backup programmes. The latter two are included in utility packages from these companies, including Norton Desktop for Windows and PC Tools.

Even with these programmes, however, backing up a hard disk larger than 20 to 40 megabytes is not recommended because it requires using a large number of floppy disks. To explain, consider the system I use. My main portable system has a 1-gigabyte disk drive, which requires *728* 1.44M floppy disks for backup. Some backup programmes perform data compression that can reduce that number by a third to a half; optimistically, therefore, you still would need nearly 400 high-density disks. Because I always perform backups to a rotating set of media, with three backups in the rotation, I need somewhere from *1,200* to 2,184 *HD disks for my backup.* That number handles only one of my systems; I have an aggregate of more than 1 gigabyte of disk space on several other systems as well. When you imagine trying to manage more than a thousand HD floppy disks, not to mention feeding 400 or more of them into a system for a day or so to perform each backup, you can see the problem associated with backing up large drives to floppy disks.

One solution is to back up the drive using either an 8mm videotape drive or a 4mm digital audio tape (DAT) drive. Either type of tape system easily backs up more than one gigabyte to a single tape and can perform a complete backup of a full drive in just over three hours. Partial backups take only seconds or minutes.

Another feature of a tape drive is that, because it is an external unit, I can carry it around and use it to back up all my systems. Also, the media costs for tape are much less than for floppy disks: the 4mm 1.3 gigabyte tapes cost only $20 or less. Therefore, I can have three backups that cost less than $60—using floppy media would cost from $1,000 to $2,000 or more. You may not have a gigabyte of on-line storage to back up, but any amount over 40 megabytes starts to become unwieldy when you are using a floppy drive.

For a total of about $1,500 for some of the less-expensive DAT or 8mm units, I have a reliable, complete, high-speed, and simple backup of every system I own. If you have more than 40M to back up—or more than one system—a tape-backup device is the best way. Various tape-backup products are discussed in the following section.

Dedicated Backup Hardware

As explained earlier, you can choose from software and hardware options when you consider backup equipment. In this section, you learn about dedicated backup hardware, usually a tape or cartridge device designed for high-speed, high-capacity backup purposes.

Backup Systems

A good, reliable backup is important when you're using a large hard disk. With a disk of 40M or more, you should consider some form of hardware backup device other than only the floppy drive. Tape backup is available in configurations easily supporting hundreds of megabytes and more. Tape backup is fast and accurate.

Because your data is probably worth much more to you than the physical hardware on which it is stored, it is important to develop a backup system you will use. A tape system makes the backup convenient and, therefore, helps to ensure that you will complete it. If backing up your system is a difficult, time-consuming operation, you or the person responsible for doing it probably will not do it regularly (if ever). Tape units also can be set to perform unattended automatic backups during times when you are not using your computer, such as during the middle of the night.

Basic parameters of different tape-backup devices include the following:

- Type of media used
- Hardware interface
- Backup software

These parameters are explained in the following sections.

QIC Standards

The Quarter-Inch Committee (QIC) issues standards for such things as tape-drive controller adapters, the tape cartridges, and commands that tape drives understand. You will find them listed in Appendix B, the "Vendor List."

The QIC organisation was formed to develop standard formats for DC-600 and DC-2000 data cartridge tape drives. Because quarter-inch tapes typically have been the market leaders, even suppliers of other systems generally follow QIC standards, such as the SCSI command set in QIC-104, and QIC-122 or QIC-123, which define data-compression methods. Data compression allows you to store more data on a certain length of tape. Vendors can change their backup software so that the codes are inserted at the beginning of the tape. Then, if the tape is read back by other tape drives, the read back drive can determine the method used.

Tape Media

I like to use systems that employ industry-standard media. *Media* refers to the type of tape format used. The type of media you select dictates the capacity of the tape-unit storage. Many different types of systems use many different types of media, but I am concerned with only a handful of standard media types. Four primary standards are the 3M Data Cartridge 600 (or DC-600), the DC-2000, the 4mm digital audio tape (DAT), and the 8mm (video) cartridge media. I recommend any of these types, depending on your requirements for capacity and performance. This list shows the different media types:

- *DC-600 cartridges.* Invented by 3M, the DC-600 cartridge is a relatively large tape, 4 x 6 x 0.665 in L x W x D, and has a heavy metal base plate. This long-running standard was introduced in 1971. Many variations of the DC-600 tapes exist; longer lengths have capacities anywhere from 60M, at the low end, to 525M or more at the high end.
- *DC-2000 cartridges.* Also invented by 3M, this cartridge is one of the most popular media for backup purposes. This tape is 2.415 x 3.188 x 0.570 inches in L x W x D, with a heavy metal base plate. Although

early versions held only 20M, the most common ones now hold 80M or more. A variety of capacities result from the different tape formats available.

- 4mm *DAT (digital audio tape) cartridges.* At first glance, this cartridge looks like a regular audiocassette but is slightly smaller. These cartridges come in several recording formats. The most widely used is digital data storage, or DDS for short. Another format, DataDAT, is also available. The recording technology is similar to digital audio tape decks and is done in a Helical-Scan format; it is licensed by Sony (the original DAT developer). DAT tapes can hold as much as 1.3 gigabytes (1 gigabyte = 1,024M).
- *8mm cartridges.* These cartridges, which use the 8mm videotape developed by Sony for camcorders, comprise one of the highest-capacity backup systems available. Most units store 2.3G but larger-capacity units are available. The recording is done physically as a Helical-Scan, the same method used in a video recorder.

The DC-600 drives now store from 60M to 525M or more, depending on the format and quality of tape use the DC-2000 media stores only 40M to 80M or more per tape and might be suitable for low-end (such as home) use. Because the larger-capacity 4mm and 8mm units store more than 1 or 2 gigabytes on a tape, they are ideal for network server applications. These large-capacity units can cost from $1,500 to $6,000 or more, depending on the features included and — of course — where you buy it.

Make sure that the system is capable of handling your largest drive either directly or through the use of multiple tapes. With this unit, you can change tapes in the middle of a backup session to accommodate greater capacities; because this method is inconvenient and requires an operator, however, you eliminate unattended, overnight backups. For network applications or large storage requirements, or anything else for which you need top performance and the most reliable backup, you should select DC-600 or the 4mm or 8mm rather than the DC-2000 media.

I recommend only tape systems that use these media because they offer the greatest value per dollar, are the most reliable, and hold a large amount of data. Stay away from devices that use the 3M DC-1000 tapes, Phillips audio tapes, or VHS VCR tape systems. These systems often are slow, error prone, and inconvenient to use; some do not handle larger capacities, and they are not standard.

Interfaces for Tape Backup Systems

Of the three primary hardware-interface standards., virtually all professional backup systems use the QIC-02 (few Quarter-Inch Committee 02) or SCSI (for *Small Computer Systems Interface)*, and more recently, the parallel port interface. Some low-end systems use the Shugart Associates 400 (SA-400) interface, which is the standard floppy controller. The interface you select controls the backup speed, whether an adapter card and slot are required, and the reliability and capacity of the units.

In the PC and XT systems with their 4-drive floppy controllers, you can use the extra connector on the back of the existing floppy controller for some tape-backup units. This connector saves the use of a slot in these systems. Unfortunately, the AT systems require some sort of multiplexer card to enable sharing one of the internal floppy ports or another complete floppy controller so that these systems can work.

I don't recommend these floppy interface systems in general because they are slow, and the floppy controller lacks any form of error-detection and correction capability, which can make the backups unreliable. A system using the SA-400 interface has a maximum data rate of 2M per minute, less than half the QIC-02 or SCSI interfaces. These floppy interface systems are suitable for home computer users on a tight budget but should not be used in business or professional environments. Another problem is that the interface limits the capacity to 40M, and you might have to format the tapes before using them.

The QIC-02 interface, designed specifically for tape-backup products, represents an industry standard. Many companies offer products that use this interface. The QIC-02 can back up at a rate of 5M per minute. The interface usually is a short adapter card that requires a free slot in the system. You can buy these adapters separately and enable many systems to use the same externally mounted drive. A free slot is required, however, and might not be available with a regular PC.

Perhaps the best hardware interface is the Small Computer Systems Interface (SCSI), which enables your PC to back up at high data rates. The data throughput of the SCSI interface is either 5MB or 10MB per minute for standard and fast 8-bit SCSI respectively. There are currently no tape drives or hard disks that can sustain this rate of transfer, so the performance is dictated by the drives rather than the SCSI interface. Because of the high speed of the SCSI interface relative to the tape and hard disk drives, when faster media and drives are available, SCSI can easily take advantage of the greater speed.

The SCSI interface is supplied as a SCSI host adapter card that plugs into the system unit and can connect to the tape drive. The SCSI host adapter requires an expansion slot, but it can connect to other devices such as hard disk drives or tape drives with embedded SCSI interfaces. The use of a single host adapter for as many as six hard disk drives and one tape unit is a strong case in favor of SCSI as a general disk and tape interface. The only real problem with SCSI is that you will need drivers which support both your particular tape drive as well as your particular host adapter. Most tape drivers support host adapters that have ASPI (Advanced SCSI Programmeming Interface) or CAM (Common Access Method) drivers. In other words, you will need the ASPI or CAM driver for your host adapter, and a tape driver that connects to ASPI or CAM for your tape drive. Although there can sometimes be problems getting the correct drivers for a particular system, SCSI is still the highest performance and most flexible interface for tape backup systems.

Another interface gaining wide acceptance is the parallel port. It is used for more than just printers, as several companies have introduced versions of their backup hardware and software systems that use the parallel port to connect to your system. The parallel port offers a high speed data transfer interface with easy configuration and cabling. Unlike serial ports, there is usually no confusion as to how the cables are wired for parallel port connections.

Several companies, like MicroSolutions and Colorado, offer complete external backup systems including all hardware, software, and cables needed to connect to the parallel port of any system. These types of backup systems offer independence from a particular type of system, which is especially useful in a mixed machine or mixed bus environment.

Other companies, like Trantor, offer parallel port SCSI adapters, to which you can connect any SCSI device including hard disk, CD-ROM, tape backup, scanners, and so on. If you are out of slots or desire to set up an external backup system that will attach to and back up several systems, I recommend using one of these parallel port SCSI adapters like the Trantor MiniSCSI Plus. Using a parallel port SCSI adapter and one of the higher performance DAT tape drives, you can set up a highly capable external backup system that can function on virtually any machine.

Tape Backup Driven and Software

Now you need to consider the software that will run the tape system. Some manufacturers have written their own software, which is proprietary and used only by that manufacturer. In other words, even though you might be using a tape unit with the same media and interface, if the software is different you cannot interchange data between the units. One type of software does not recognize the data formats of another proprietary software system. Other tape software packages are designed to run on a variety of tape hardware rather than a single manufacturer's system. Several hardware independent backup software packages support a variety of tape drives such as SyTOS (Sytron Tape Operating System) by Sytron, Novaback by Novastor, and Central Point Backup by Central Point. All of these products work with a number of different tape drives. SyTOS is somewhat of an industry standard because it is endorsed (and sold) by IBM and many other vendors, as well as having versions that work on all major PC operating systems.

SyTOS has been selected by IBM as the standard software for its units. Because of market pressures to be compatible with IBM, Compaq and other system and tape-drive vendors are offering SyTOS with their tape systems. Because two systems that use the same media, interface, and software can read and write each other's tapes, you can have data interchangeability among different tape-unit manufacturers. You should consider using a system that runs SyTOS software for those reasons. Of course, the proprietary software is generally just as good, if not better. You can exchange data tapes only with other users of the same systems.

All software should be capable of certain basic operations. Make sure that your software does what you want, and consider buying only software that has these features:

- Can back up an entire DOS partition (full volume backup)
- Can back up any or all flies individually (file-by-file backup)
- Allows a selective file-by-file restore from a volume backup as well as a file-by-file backup
- Can combine several backups on a single tape
- Can run the software as commands from DOS BATCH flies
- Works under a network
- Can span a large drive on multiple tapes
- Can be completely verified

If the software you are considering does not have any of these essential features, look for another system.

Physical Location: Internal or External

Physical location of the tape-backup units is a simple factor often not considered in detail. I almost never recommend any tape-backup unit mounted internally in a system unit. I recommend that you buy a tape unit externally mounted in its own chassis and one that connects to the system unit through a cable and connectors.

Tape units are relatively expensive, and I never want to tie up a backup unit for only one system. The amount of time that just one system spends using the unit makes this proposition wasteful. With an external unit, many systems can share the backup unit. I just equip every system unit with the required interface, if they aren't already equipped. Extra QIC-02 cards are available for about $100 each, and SCSI host adapters are about $200. Note that many systems now include a SCSI host adapter as part of the motherboard, or as a card already installed. I already share my system among more than five computers and will continue adding systems to the backup pool. In some companies, the backup unit is mounted on a wheeled cart so that workers easily can move it from computer to computer.

If you have only one system or if all your data is stored in a single file-server system, you might have a legitimate argument for using an internal tape drive. You might wish that you had an external system, however, on the day a new system arrives, or when the server is down and you have to get a new one up and running.

Recommended Backup System

Although a variety of backup systems are available, I recommend units from any manufacturer that meets these requirements:

Type of media: DC-2000, DC-600, 4mm DAT, or 8mm
Hardware interface: QIC-02, Parallel Port or SCSI

My preferences lean towards the 4mm DAT drives because of their high capacity (4G plus with built-in data compression) and relatively high performance. Also, the media cost is very low, around $15 per cartridge. DAT devices almost always use a SCSI interface, which means you would need a SCSI host adapter installed in the system. This could be either a standard type of SCSI host adapter in a slot (or integrated into the motherboard of some systems), or for a lower cost portable solution, you could run the SCSI DAT drive from a parallel port with one of the parallel to SCSI adapters like those from Trantor. The parallel port adapters make it easy to use a single external DAT drive to back up a variety of systems.

PURCHASING WARRANTY AND SERVICE CONTRACTS

Extended warranties are a recent trend in the computer industry. With the current fierce competition among hardware vendors, a good warranty is one way for a specific manufacturer to stand out from the crowd. Although most companies offer a one year warranty on their systems, others offer longer warranty periods, such as two years or more.

In addition to extended-length warranties, some manufacturers offer free or nearly free on-site service during the warranty period. Many highly competitive mail-order outfits offer service such as this for little or no extra cost. Even IBM has succumbed to market pressure to lower service costs, and has an option for converting the standard one year warranty into a full-blown, on-site service contract for only $40. This same option can be extended to cover monitors and printers for only a small additional cost.

Tip

IBM and other companies are beginning to offer extended-length warranties and free or low-cost on-site service. IBM has a somewhat unknown option to upgrade the standard one year warranties on its PS/2 systems into a full-blown, on-site service contact. Under this option, you can upgrade the standard Customer Carry-in Repair warranty to an IBM On-site Repair warranty for only $40 for the first year.

If you have only the carry-in warranty, as its name implies you must carry in your computer to a depot for service; with the on-site warranty, the service technician comes to you. One car trip to a service center costs me more than $40 in wasted gasoline and time. I gladly pay the fee to have the service technician come to see me. Be sure to ask for this option when you buy your system. If your dealer is unfamiliar with it, ask that your order include IBM feature code #9805.

In most normal cases, service contracts are not worth the price. In the retail computer environment, a service contract is often a way for a dealer or vendor to add income to a sale. Most annual service contracts add 10 to 15 per cent of the cost of the system. A service contract for a $5,000 system, for example, *costs $500 to 1750 per year.* Salespeople in most organisations are trained to vigorously sell service contracts. Much like in the automobile sales business, these contracts are largely unnecessary except in special situations.

The high prices of service contracts also might affect the quality of service you receive. Technicians could try to make their work seem more complex than it actually is to make you believe that the contract's price is justified. For example, a service technician might replace your hard disk or entire motherboard with a spare when all you need is low-level formatting for the hard disk or a simple fix for the motherboard such as a single memory chip. A "defective" drive, for example, probably is just returned to the shop for low-level formatting. Eventually, it ends up in somebody else's system. Replacing a part is faster and leaves the impression that your expensive service contract is worth the price because you get a "new" part. You might be much less impressed with your expensive service contract if the service people visit, do a simple troubleshooting procedure, and then replace a single $2 memory chip or spend 15 minutes reformatting the hard disk.

With some basic troubleshooting skills, some simple tools, and a few spare parts, you can eliminate the need for most of these expensive service contracts. Unfortunately, some companies practice deceptive servicing procedures to justify the expensive service contracts they offer. Users are made to believe that these types of component failures are the norm, and they have a mistaken impression about the overall reliability of today's systems.

> **Tip**
>
> If you have many systems, you can justify carrying a spare-parts inventory, which can also eliminate the need for a service contract. For less than what a service contract costs for five to ten systems, you often can buy a complete spare system each year. Protecting yourself with extra equipment rather than service contracts is practical if you have more than ten computers of the same make or model. For extremely time-sensitive applications, you might be wise to buy a second system along with the primary unit—such as in a network file-server application. Only you can make the appropriate cost-justification analysis to decide whether you need a service contract or a spare system.

In some instances, buying a service contract can be justified and beneficial. If you have a system that must function at all times and is so expensive that you cannot buy a complete spate system, or for a system in a remote location far away from a centralised service operation, you might be wise to invest in a good service contract that provides timely repairs. Before contracting for service, you should consider your options carefully. These sources either supply or authorize service contracts:

- Manufacturers
- Dealers or vendors
- Third parties

Although most users take the manufacturer or dealer service, sometimes a third-party tries harder to close the deal; for example, it sometimes includes all the equipment installed, even aftermarket items the dealers or manufacturers don't offer. In other cases, a manufacturer might not have its own service organisation; instead, it makes a deal with a major third-party nationwide service company to provide authorised service.

After you select an organisation, several levels of service often are available. Starting with the most expensive, these levels of service typically include:

- Four-hour on-site response
- Next-day on-site response
- Courier service (a service company picks up and returns a unit)
- Carry-in, or "depot", service

The actual menu varies from manufacturer to manufacturer. For example, IBM offers only a full 24-hours-a-day, 7-days-a-week, on-site service contract. IBM claims that a technician is dispatched usually within four hours of your call. For older systems, but not the PS/2, IBM also offers a courier or carry-in service contract. Warranty work, normally a customer carry-in depot arrangement, can be upgraded to a full on-site contract for only $40. After the first-year $40 contract upgrade expires, you can continue the full on-site service contract for standard rates. Table 2 lists the rates for IBM service contracts after expired.

If you have bought a service contract in the past, these prices might surprise you. With the PS/2 systems, IBM has rewritten the rules for PC servicing. The same type of on-site annual contract for an earlier 20M AT system, for example, costs nearly $600 annually, compared with $220 for the PS/2 Model 50. Smaller third-party service companies are having difficulty competing with these newer prices. IBM claims that the PS/2 systems are five times more reliable than the earlier systems, and the service-contract pricing is about one-third what the earlier systems cost. If the claims of additional reliability are true, IBM is doing well even with lower pricing. If the claims are not true (which is unlikely), then IBM would be losing money on its service contracts.

Tip

In summary, for most standard system, a service contract beyond what is included with the original warranty is probably a waste of money. For other systems that have not yet achieved commodity status or for systems that must be up and running at all time service contract option, even though you might be fully qualified and capable of servicing the system.

The PS/2 systems are a somewhat special case; they have low-priced, on-site warranty upgrades and fairly inexpensive service contracts compared to the costs of the systems. Remember, however that you can buy most, if not all, parts for these systems from non-IBM sources; also, third-party companies that specialize in difficult items such as motherboards and power supplies can repair these items. Only after carefully weighing every option and cost involved can you decide how your systems should be serviced.

TABLE 2
PS/2 Service Contract Fees after Warranty for Annual IBM On Site Repair (IOR) Service

PS/2 Model	*Contract.*	*PS/2 Model*	*Contract*
8525-x01/x02	$95	8570-0x1/1x1	$450
8525-x04/x05	$110	8570-Axx	595
8525-x06/x36	$210	8570-Bx1	645
8530-001	$190	8573-031/061	385
8530-002	$140	8573-121	385.
8530-021	$190	8573-161	750
8530-E01/E21	$190	8573-401	850
8530-E31/E41	$190	8580-041	360
8535-all	$260	8580-071	425
8540-all	$400	8580-081	550
8543-044	$430	8580-111/121	500
8550-021	$220	8580-161	600
8550-031/061	$220	8580-311	575
8555-0x1	$260	8580-321	605
8555-LT0/LE0	$260	8580-A21	675
8557-045/049	$400	8580-A16/A31	785
8560-041	$310	8590-0G5/0G9	800
8560-071	$345	8590-0J5/0J9	850
8565-061	$425	8590-0KD	950
8565-121	$475	8595-0G9/0GF	1,400
8565-321	$550	8595-0Jx	1,450
8570-E61	$415	8595-0Kx	1,550

Summary

This chapter has presented the steps you can take tc ensure proper operation of your system. It has examined active and passive preventive maintenance—the key to a system that gives many years of trouble-free service. You have learned about the procedures involved in preventive maintenance and the frequency with which these procedures should be performed.

Backup was discussed as a way to be prepared when things go wrong. The only guarantee for being able to retrieve data is to back it up. In this chapter, you also have learned about backup options.

Finally, you have learned about the commonly available warranty and service contracts provided by computer manufacturers. Sometimes the contracts can save you from worrying about tough-to-service systems or systems whose parts are largely unavailable on short notice.

13

Hypertext: From Modern Utopia to Postmodern Dystopia?

When Vannevar Bush, in his 1945 article *As We May think*, presented his vision of the *Memex,* the proposed information retrieval system that later served as an inspiration for Ted Nelson's *Hypertext* concept, this vision was clearly and necessarily rooted in *modernity* as it appeared, unchallenged, at the end of World Warn.

Bush held the view that science, having been in the service of destructive forces for the duration of the war, now was able to return to its main objective — to secure progress of mankind. It was to this end that he proposed the *Memex* system:

> Presumably man's spirit should be elevated if he can better review his shady past and analyse more completely and objectively his present problems. He has built a civilisation so complex that he needs to mechanise his records more fully if he is to push his experiment to its logical conclusion and not merely become bogged down part way there by overtaxing his limited memory (Bush 1945:108).

This Utopian modem optimism elicited by Bush, was considerably tempered by the time Ted Nelson's *Computer Lib* appeared in 1974 , a book that clearly places Nelson within the social critical tradition of the American intellectual left in the 1960s. His critical stance was augmented by the ecological awareness of the 1970s expressed through journals like *Co-Evolution Quarterly* and *The Whole Earth Catalogue,* and it is no coincidence that the editor of these two publications, Stewart Brand, wrote the introduction to the 1987 edition of *Computer Lib.* Nevertheless, Nelson's plea in 1974 for the necessity of "understanding computers" is closely linked to the Enlightenment paradigm, as the possible answer to the environmental threats to human society:

> Humanity may end with a bang (thermonuclear exchanges or just desultory firings until we're all poisoned or sterile), or a whimper (universal starvation), or, I would anticipate, some spastic combination of the two, and all within the (possible) lifetime of the average reader.

> ...as the problems increase and move toward our heartland, it'll be blamed on environmentalists and on the news media, till bang.
>
> Or maybe not. Just maybe.
>
> But we've all got to ... look for holes or strategies. If computer modelling systems doing this kind of work are made widely enough available, perhaps some precocious gradeschooler or owlish hobbyist will find some way out that the others haven't hit on.
>
> *(Nelson* 1987a: 177)

This dramatic conclusion to the 1974 text belies the prevalent enthusiasm of *Computer Lib,* and may be viewed as a "politically correct" afterthought. The rest of Nelson's book presents a firmly consistent belief in modern man's capability to control and influence his destiny with the help of computers ("You can and must understand computers NOW"), and the 1974/87 "companion" book, *Dream Machines,* prophesies a pivotal role for hyper-textual computer design in this respect.

1984 has come and gone and a good many of Nelson's predictions in *Computer Lib* and *Dream Machines* have come true, especially those pertaining to technological development Another striking aspect of this book today is a consistent argumentation that clearly places Nelson on one side of an ongoing debate between modernism and postmodernism.

Critical modernism has during the last decade been challenged by various versions *of postmodern* theory, from writers, artists, and theoreticians who all express either doubts about or outright rejection of the central pillars of modernity. In this critical discourse the distinction between modernism and modernity has become increasingly important in order to avoid confusion with the old modemist/ antimodernist debates, *modernity* being identified with the general direction of philosophical and social thought of the Enlightenment.

MTV, a media phenomenon universally proclaimed as "postmodernist," announces a daily series of new music videos under the heading *Postmodern,* lending further credibility to the view that "postmodern" in today's everyday language has taken over many of the meanings "modern" contained in the everyday usage yesterday, with the music video as a major metaphor. The word now connotes the transitory, the ephemeral, the fragmented, the multifaceted, as well as leaning strongly to a hedonist philosophy.

As for the word "postmodernism" itself, it is, as Fredric Jameson has pointed out, with its multitude of meanings and uses symptomatic for postmodern thought — "the sheer enumeration of changes and modifications." (Jameson, 1991). Jameson comments on his 1984 article on postmodernism, *The Cultural Logic of Late Capitalism*, by pointing out that the main change in the general view on postmodernism as a phenomenon in 1984 and 1989 was that in the latter year it was nearly impossible, on principle grounds, to *avoid* using the word "postmodern."

Postmodern Traits of Hypertext Example: Hyperland

In 1990 The BBC produced a television program that presented and demonstrated the potentiality of hypertext as a harbinger of *nonlinear television*. In the program, Douglas Adams (author of *The Hitchhiker's Guide to the Galaxy)* is transported into the near future where he is confronted with a "fully customizable," on-line, humanoid guide through the world of non-linearity.

Adams is presented with a control panel of *micons*, or icons containing small loops of digitised video. These micons represent hypertext nodes, and pointing at a micon, or a part of it, will take him to that hypertext node. Thus the following sequence is initiated:

> By pointing at a micon representing Vannevar Bush, a video sequence consisting of archive film and explanatory soundtrack appears, giving information on Bush and the article presenting the *Memex-idea*.. This micon is titled *Atlantic Monthly*. At the touch of the word *Atlantic*, several new micons pop up on a background of a rolling ocean with titles like *Oceanography*, *Live Feed*, *Literature*, and *Shipping*.

The *Live Feed* micon then takes the user to a concurrent video image from the weather satellite MarSat West in orbit over the Southern Atlantic. Over this image then two more micons representing submersible observation stations in the Atlantic, and a touch on one of these takes the astounded Adams to a live video of dolphins curiously looking at the camera.

From here, a touch on the "Return" icon on the screen, again brings up the five micons of the *Atlantic* menu. The *Literature* micon brings up the images and names of Melville, Coleridge, Conrad, C.S. Forrester, and Hemingway, the appearance of each micon accompanied by selected lines from the works of these authors read aloud on the soundtrack. By touching *Coleridge*, a micon representing *The Rime of the Ancient Mariner* appears over a portrait of Coleridge, accompanied by further micons related to this author. Another touch, this time on *More works*, brings up a new series of choices, among those *Kubla Khan*. After choosing this poem, it is read while the text scrolls in "Star Wars" fashion over the screen. Pointing at any word in the text will stop the text and lead to an explanation of some sorts. Moving our fingers over the phrase "widening chasm," we are informed that this may be viewed as a "metaphor for the female sexual organ," a touch on the word "dulcimer" opens up for a discourse on mediaeval music, as well as a treatise on rhombic shapes, and in the middle of all this, up pops the micon with Ted Nelson's continually shaking head. Why? Because the on-line hypertext system for organising literature that Nelson has been working on for almost two decades is called — "had to be called," as Nelson puts it — *XANADU.*

I will use this example to illustrate how the hypertext idea is marked by a series of contradictions typical of the modern/postmodern controversy. Although it may be contended that the chosen example is a hypothetical one, and an example of dubious hypertextual design at that, there is no doubt that it represents a very real simulation, based on the current state of the art in the field of hypermedia. Furthermore, the obvious design "faults" in the program are very helpful in illustrating inherent problems in the hyper-textual presentation.

Hypertext in the Modern/Postmodern Controversy: The "Checklist" of Ihab Hassan

In his article *Concepts of Postmodernism,* Ihab Hassan (Hassan, 1987) has compiled a "postmodern checklist" consisting of a dual listing of "modem" phenomena presented with their postmodern counterparts. In this list we find four pairs of contrasting concepts with a definite relevance to the situation experienced by the watcher of *Hyperland:*

Modernism	*Postmodernism*
Purpose	Play
Design	Chance
Centering	Dispersal
Hierarchy	Anarchy

This set of contradictions can easily be found to be contained within the practice of hypertextual structures.

Although the idea behind hypertext is based on a very strong sense of *purpose,* the *Hyperland* film ends up with a strong emphasis on the *playfulness* of the medium, with a tour-de-force presentation of virtual reality "goggles." In the sequence referred to, the user clearly falls prey to playful curiosity as the beckoning micons pop up, one after another.

Play and games are central components of the computer culture as such, as a visit to any computer store and a look at any BBS files list should bear witness to. The counterpart to the purpose-oriented "computer programmer" is the play-oriented "hacker."

This contradiction, between purpose and play, spills over into the next pair of concepts. In authoring languages and systems for interactive multimedia, an area of application where hypertext holds a central position, purposeful *design* is what textbooks and courses propagate. Although the interface with the user should appear as "friendly" as possible, presenting the user with what seems to be a wide choice of options, the program in the background is specifically designed in order to fulfil a stated purpose behind the program, usually didactically defined.

At every hypertext node this design is challenged by *chance* in the form of possible "wrong" choices of links or paths. A critical part of multimedia design is therefore to minimise chances of "wrong" decisions, at the same time keeping up the appearance of presenting "real" choices.

A first glance at a design chart for a hypertext program can thus easily give the false impression of an information flow that lead in all directions, seemingly at random. This impression of information *dispersal* is in turn contrasted with the previously mentioned *centering* represented by the many pointers imbedded in the program design aimed at leading the user through a presumed meaningful discourse. The implied *hierarchy* of instructional design is made as a defense against the playful *anarchy* that is the didactic lure of computer-assisted learning programs.

These four major contradictions within the concept of hypertext-based learning programs all point to the contested ground of *space* in the ongoing debate on modernity and post-modernity, and lead to a detour to the field of architecture and urban geography.

Getting Lost in Postmodern Hyperspace

The case for the modern conception of orientation in space is perhaps best made by Kevin Lynch in his classic study from 1960, *The Image of the City*. This book is especially interesting in our context because some of Lynch's key concepts for city geography bear close resemblance to important principles of hypertext Lynch defines five types of elements pertaining to the physical form of the city: *paths, nodes, landmarks, districts, and edges.*

These elements are crucial in our perception of the city, as they help us define the *legibility* of the urban environment *Paths* are the routes of frequent travel, and are invariably related to the concept of *nodes* defined as strategic junction points and, according to Lynch, a dominant feature in the individual's image of the city. *Landmarks* are reference points, usually in some form of physical shape, like monuments of buildings that facilitates navigation in the city landscape. *Districts* are areas with a common identity, and *edges* are linear structures representing the boundaries between areas (Lynch, 1960: 46-49).

All of these five elements can and have been transferred to hypertext, where concepts like nodes and paths (links) are part of any definition of the concept, like the one made by McKnight, Dillon, and Richardson in their book *Hypertext in Context:* "Simply stated, hypertext consists of *nodes* (or "chunks") of information and *links* between them" (McKnight, Dillon, Richardson, 1991: 2).

Further on in that book, the authors make extensive use of the geography analogy in order to cast light over the problem of *navigation* in hypertext. Referring to several empirical studies of learning efficiency in hypertext programs as compared to line text presentation of the same subject matter, the authors conclude that hypertextual presentation is no guarantee of better performance, and emphasise the problem of navigation:

> Interestingly, these studies seem to suggest that the hypertext structure places an extra burden on the reader in terms of navigation and consequently leads to poorer performance. And: With the advent of hypertext it has become widely accepted that the departure from the so-called "linear" structure of paper increases the likelihood of readers or users of getting lost.

Lynch frequently points to the *horror* of getting lost in his book:

> To become completely lost is perhaps a rather rare experience for most people in the modern city. We are supported by the presence of others and by special way-finding devices: maps, street numbers, route signs, bus placards. But let the mishap of disorientation once occur, and the sense of anxiety and even terror that accompanies it reveals to us how closely it is linked to our sense of balance and well-being. The very word "lost" in our language means much more than geographical uncertainty; it carries overtones of utter disaster.
>
> (*Lynch*, 1960: 4).

This danger of getting lost is underscored by the authors of *Hypertext in Context*, who devote an entire chapter to the problem of navigation in hypertextual space, based on the (surprisingly scant, according to the authors) research done in the psychology of navigation with an emphasis on the development of *cognitive mapping*.

Cognitive Mapping: A Counter Strategy to Hyperspace

The question of cognitive mapping is also prominent in the work of Fredric Jameson on postmodernism. In his 1991 book on the subject, he elaborates on the points of view set forth in his 1984 article, where he places the postmodern phenomenon in a wider social and cultural context. Unlike other theoreticians with a Marxist background who have rejected the postmodern argumentation (for example, Callinicos, 1989), Jameson has set out to "historise" a concept that appears to be ahistorical.

Postmodernism, Jameson contends, is the cultural logic of late capitalism, representative for an epoch where capital expands truly *multinationally*, not only imperialistically. It is the period when the last pre-capitalist enclaves in modem time — nature and the unconscious — are invaded by omnipresent multinational capital. Instead of viewing postmodernism as something that transcends the ideology of capitalism, Jameson sees postmodernism as the cultural logic of "late capitalism" as defined by the Marxist economist Ernest Mandel.

Jameson turns to architecture to illustrate his point and uses John Portman's Westin Bonaventure Hotel in Los Angeles as an analysis example. This building, prominent among its large number of siblings all over the industrialised world, sticks out in the city landscape with its rejective glass facade (Jameson uses the word "repulsive"), signaling itself as a self-contained world. Which it in a way is, with its combination of habitation (hotel) and consumption (restaurants and shopping arcades).

The visitor, when entering the building through one of its inconspicuous entrances, is sucked into a shopping, eating, and living machine where orientation becomes almost impossible with its multitude of levels and panorama elevators, and criss-crossing escalators combine to elicit what Jameson calls *postmodern hyperspace*. And he sees in this spatial disorientation a metaphor for postmodernism as such:

> So I come finally to ray principal point here, that this latest mutation in space — postmodern hyperspace — has finally succeeded in transcending the capacities of the individual to locate itself, to organise its immediate surroundings perceptually, and cognitively to map its position in a mappable external world. It may now be suggested that this alarming disjunction point between body and its built environment... can itself stand as the symbol and analogon of that even sharper dilemma which is the incapacity of our minds... to map the great global multinational and decentered communi-cational network in which we find ourselves caught as individual subjects.
>
> (*Jameson*, 1991: 44).

It is interesting to note that Jameson uses the word "alarming" in this context, thus echoing the horror of getting lost expressed by Kevin Lynch, and he has followed this up in his 1988 article *Cognitive Mapping* (Jameson, 1988) by suggesting a counter strategy of cognitive mapping based on acceptance of the idea of a *social totality*. This is where Jameson departs from other theoreticians of the postmodern (like Lyotard and Baudrillard) for whom the rejection of any social totality is one of the very hallmarks of the postmodern condition.

A similar strategy, underscoring the historical importance of mapping, is proposed by David Harvey in his book. *The Condition of Postmodernity*. Harvey points out how the accessibility, appropriation, domination, and production of space has been crucial in the development of modem society from the first, primitive stages of capitalism and up to today's "flexible accumulation," which is his more precise definition of Jameson's "late capitalism."

Linking the growth of capitalism with the concept of spatial control, Harvey shows that, historically, the fragmentation and pulverisation of space was a major factor in achieving this, and that the development of accurate maps was one of the tools facilitating this. ("Space can be conquered only through the production of space.")

During the last hundred years, this development has, quite literally, been "speeded up," mainly as a result of the development in communication, represented by the now so-trite metaphor about "the shrinking world" or, as Harvey put it, the annihilation of space through time. This time-space compression has resulted in the "great global multinational and decentered communicational network" that Jameson points to, which has given rise to a cultural homogenisation that Harvey describes this way: "Extraordinary decentralisation and proliferation of industrial production ends up putting Bennetton or Laura Ashley in almost every serially produced shopping mall in the advanced capitalist world" (Harvey, 1989: 296).

Loss of Place-identity

One obvious effect of this is what Harvey terms as a "loss of place-identity" — the inability of the individual to identify his or her world geographically — and there seem to be two distinct reactions to this in contemporary thinking. One reaction, emanating from what could be termed "postmodern ideology," is to view this as a positive phenomenon, where the individual ought to take advantage of this new cultural pluralism, freed from the shackles of the old hierarchic, moralistic, place-bound, and static culture.

An early manifestation of this view is to be found in one of the seminal texts of postmodern theory, *Learning from Las Vegas*, by Robert Venturi, Denise Scott Brown, and Steven Izenour. This book on architecture was published in 1972 and proposed an architecture of the "ugly and ordinary" by using popular and commercial building styles as examples for an architecture in opposition to the dominating modern and functionalist architecture.

The authors suggested that by drawing lessons from the way urban architecture in America had developed on its own, outside the world of systemised and institutionalised modern architecture, an alternative position to modernist architecture could be developed. The geographical expression of this is *the urban sprawl*, as it has grown organically in the automobile oriented culture of the United States. The counterpart and identified enemy to this expression of popular, "low culture" and commercial city non-planning in *Learning from Las Vegas,* is the planned, elitist, "high culture," modern city planning tradition identified as *megastructure.*

Using a contrasting table very much like Hassan's modern/postmodern "checklist," the authors go through a list of how urban sprawl and megastructure differ fundamentally: ugly and ordinary vs. heroic and original, mixed media vs. pure architecture, popular life-style, vs. "correct" life-style, vital mess vs. "Total Design," building for men (markets) vs. building for Man, to name a few of the 30 pairs in question. (Venturi, Brown, and Izenour. 1972: 84). The aim is clearly to "rehabilitate" the "vital mess" of urban sprawl, pointing to Los Angeles and Las Vegas as the Rome and Florence for future generations of architects. For the postmodern architects, loss of place-identity is no great loss.

For the other view, we can return to Kevin Lynch and his description of the urban sprawl of Jersey City as it appeared through interviews with inhabitants: "In studying the individual sketches and interviews, it became apparent that none of the respondents had anything like a comprehensive view of the city they had lived in for many years. The maps were often fragmented, with large, blank areas" (Lynch, 1960:29).

Jersey City is made into a negative example by Lynch by the very lack of place-identity that it elicits, and Lynch is absolutely clear on the alternative to this in his conclusion: "By appearing as a remarkable and well-knit *place.* the city could provide a ground for the clustering and organisation of ... meanings and associations. Such a sense of place in itself enhances every human activity that occurs there."

Harvey points out that the apparently liberating function of antiauthoritar-ian, anti-structural "organic" growth has some sinister overtones. The accelerating speed of time-space compression is not matched by a similar speedily reorientation of our mental maps and this loss of place-awareness may have serious political implications. One such implication that Harvey suggests, the retreat into geopolitical fragmentation, has been strongly emphasised by recent developments (winter of 1992) in the former Soviet Union and Yugoslavia.

Another negative aspect to this loss of space pertains to the experience of *space as a reality.* During the Gulf War of 1991, the television audience of the world was bombarded by high-tech images from the war, to an extent that it was referred to as *the Nintendo effect.* This metaphor very revealingly points to a loss of reality in perception — reality extended to the level where the borders between play and physical reality becomes obscure, the realm of postmodern *hyperreality.*

Going Off on an Ice-lolly: The Digression as Master

In *Hyperland* an exasperated Douglas Adams finally asks his "guide": "Where were we before we went off on this — what do you call it?" Guide: "You can call it anything you like." "What if I call it an ice-lolly?" "Very good!" "So what happened when we went off on this ice-lolly?"

And since the field of hypertext is an uncharted one, with numerous ' nameless concepts yet to be mapped and named, let us appropriate Douglas Adams' new word into the hyperspeak vocabulary and look closer at the ice-lolly" as a hypertext phenomenon.

In ordinary conversation the ice-lolly is known as a *digression,* the situation where two partners engage in a conversation on one topic and end up on a completely different topic.

The digression in turn, has relevance to the *coherence* of the text. Coherence, recent work in text linguistics suggests (for example, Agar and Hobbs, 1982), comes in three versions that act together. *Thematic coherence* refers to our ability to relate a proposition to an,explicit theme. It is the quality that enables us to recognise what a certain text "is about" Closely connected to this, is *local coherence* where one sentence is obviously linked to the next, virtually "pointing" at it, without necessarily referring to the thematic coherence. The footnote is a typical example of local coherence Thematic coherence and local coherence are participating in building a third kind of encompassing coherence that enables us to perceive series of isolated propositions as a whole — a *global coherence.*

What happens in the *Hyperland* example is that local coherence becomes dominant at the cost of thematic and global coherence and we feel the need to retrace the path to find our bearings. Local coherence is the stuff that di-gressions are made of.

The rapidly expanding field of hypertext theory take diverging views on the dangers of digression, and these views fall roughly along the separating lines of the followers and adversaries of postmodern ideology referred to above. One clear contradiction seems to follow the purpose/play dichotomy set forth by Hassan, with George P. Landow as a stern defender of purpose and global coherence.

In the article *The Rhetoric of Hypermedia: Some Rules for Authors,* Landow also invokes the navigation metaphor, noting that any user of a hypertext will assume that links represent useful and interesting relationships, hence Landow's first and third rules (of altogether nineteen) for hypertext authors:

Rule 1. The very existence of links in hypermedia conditions the reader to expect useful, important relationships between linked materials.

Rule 3. Since Hypermedia systems predispose users to expect such significant relationships among documents, those documents that disappoint these expectations appear particularly incoherent and nonsignificant

Landow treats hypertext as the modern learning-efficient tool that Bush and Nelson expected it to be, and his set of rules contributes to this. His 19 rules construct a useful set of concepts for those wanting to map and structure the seemingly chaotic field of hypertext In fact, what Landow does is provide the hypertext authors with rules that help them create maps for the users to navigate by in the "urban sprawl" of multi-linear hypertext.

In his Rule 6, Landow echoes Lynch's ideas of an imaginable city:

Rule 6. Devices of orientation permit readers (a) to determine their present location, (b) to have some idea of that location's relation to other materials, (c) to return to their starting, and (d) to explore material not directly linked to those in which they presently find themselves.

Another and different stance on the question of digression and lack of coherence in hypertext is taken by Terence Harpold, who puts the phenomenon of digression into a psychoanalytic context (Harpold, 1991). Turning to the French psychoanalytic tradition from Lacan, Harpold delivers a "defense" for the digression in hypertext that is strongly reminiscent of psychoanalytically oriented film theory.

The common concept here is what Jacques-Alain Millar named *suture* literally the "sewing together" of the "cut" or "gap" in the signifying chain, representing the death of the subject. In Lacanian and Althusserian inspired film theory, *suture* is used to explain how the "seamless" narrative techniques of the Hollywood film is able to elicit pleasure in the viewer by representing a "whole" subject, a world where all the uncomfortable gaps have been "sewn together."

For Harpold, *suture* similarly represents "knots" that tie together the unwanted gaps in hypertext links, the gaps that open to innumerable other narrations. When these knots are loosened it has the effect of erasing subjectivity:

> These loopings and the knots that bind them are the traces of collective structures enclosing and obscuring the gap of subjectivity. What distinguishes hypertexts as collaborative forms of textuality-as-detour is that they concretise in a social form the significance of the structures of gap and erasure in narrative digression.
>
> (*Harpold*, 1991: 178).

Thus digression becomes a revealing agent in the process of de-centering the subject, and hypertext appears to be an ideal medium for making this more visible. Instead of being an anarchic detour into meaninglessness and nothingness, the digression actually allows for greater insight.

Stewart Moulthorpe takes this view even further, when he suggests hypertext as an answer to Jameson's scepticism about the possibility of a politically relevant postmodern art (Aarseth, 1991: 81).

Knowing Where You are, or Getting Lost and Enjoying it

In this chapter I have pointed out how some of the crucial aspects of hypertext and hypermedia de in with the continuing controversy around postmodern thought Popularly it can be stated as a controversy between upholding the modernist vision of "knowing where you are" or succumbing to the temptation of the postmodern position of "getting lost and enjoying it."

From the debate in architecture between modern and postmodern, represented by the views of Lynch and Venturi et al., this contradiction can be said to crystallise between the "imaginable city" of Lynch and the "urban sprawl" of Venturi, with the first emphasising the need for *knowledge and control* and the latter pointing to the *enjoyment* aspect of popular culture.

These two stances can be viewed as representing the same dialectics conveyed by the selected pairs from Hassan's postmodern "checklist" — purpose/play, design/chance, centering/dispersal, and hierarchy/anarchy, where special consideration should be given to the first pair, that of purpose *versus* play.

When we look to hypertextual practices in the present and in the near future, it is quite obvious that this debate does not easily resolve into an either/or. In the established field of interactive hypermedia (mainly interactive video learning programs), the question of "correct" navigation and securely structured pathways is and will definitely be the main concern, clearly signalling a bias toward "purpose." "Interactive design" has for several years existed as an academic discipline at American universities, adjusting and im-proving the purpose-related hypertext tools of interactive authoring systems.

On the other hand, development in hypertextual literary systems seems to have developed a duality. In addition to normative work on the rhetoric of hypertext, such as Landow's, there is also a marked emphasis on the "playful," in theory as well as in practice, as the examples cited from Harpold and Moulthorpe suggest

In certain areas of hypertextual practices, the "play" side seems to be totally dominating. In a recent master's thesis, Espen Aarseth focuses on the practices of *MUDs* — multi-user dungeons — which has developed into a sub-culture within the on-line community. Admittedly, the practices of online role-playing in a constantly changing cybernetic environment stretches the hypertext concept to its outer limit, but Aarseth maintains that "if we can study the games within a text, then why not study the texts within a game?" (Aarseth, 1991: 84-85).

This raises the question where to place the latest technological innovation related with hypertext — *virtual reality* where the postmodern simulacrae described by Baudrillard and others is taken to the extreme. With the help of a pair of "goggles" connected to a powerful three-dimensional graphic computer, the "reader" can enter the text pseudo-physically, seemingly without having to resort to representing devices like film. TV, or a book. At the bottom of this experience (or really pseudo-experience) Des a hypertext design with links and nodes that only differ from "ordinary" hypertext in its computational complexity.

According to recent rumors, commercial versions of virtual reality programs are expected to be available as the next generation of video games in the near future. We will then have an extraordinary example illustrating the paradox of "the postmodern condition" in the fact that large, centralised entertainment corporations, with the help of tightly, hierarchically designed virtual reality programs, will provide the public with pseudo-realities invoking playful multiplicity and chance.

This result does definitely not confirm with the utopian views of Bush and Nelson, and it hardly conforms with the implicit promise of "subversive hypertext" set forth by the theoreticians of postmodern hypertext. However, it points to an interdependent duality between modern and postmodern expressions in hypertextual practice that seems to belie the seemingly unbridgeable gap that theory has constructed.

Could it be that we are looking at two sides of the same coin?

REFERENCES

Aarseth, E. (1991). *Texts of Change. Towards a Poetics of Nonlinearity.* Unpublished M.A. thesis. Bergen: Department of Comparative Literature, University of Bergen, Norway.

Agar, M., Hobbs, J. (1982). Interpreting discourse. In *Discourse Processes,* 5 pp. 1-32.

Bush, V. (1945). As We May Think. *Atlantic Monthly* 176, July 1945, pp.101-108.

Callinicos, A. (1989). *Against Postmodernism.* Cambridge: Polity Press.

Delany, P., Landow, G. (1991). *Hypermedia and Literary Studies.* Cambridge, Mass.: The MIT Press.

Evensen, L. (1988). Lokal og global koherens i elevers skriving. In *TRANS — Trondheim Papers in Applied Linguistics,* IV.

Harpold, T. (1991). Threnody: Psychoanalytic Digressions on the Subject of Hypertext In *Hypermedia and Literary Studies,* eds. Delaney, Landow, pp.171-181. Cambridge, Mass.: The MIT Press.

Harvey, D. (1989). *The Condition of Postmodernity.* Oxford: Basil Blackwell.

Hassan, I. (1987). *The postmodern turn.* Ohio: Ohio State University Press.

Jameson, F. (1988). Cognitive Mapping. In *Marxism and the Interpretation of Culture,* eds. Nelson, G., Grossberg, L. Chicago: University of Illinois Press.

Jameson, F. (1991). *Postmodernism, or The Cultural Logic of Late Capitalism.* London: Verso.

Landow, G. (1991). The Rhetoric of Hypermedia: Some Rules for Authors. In *Hypermedia and Literary Studies,* eds. Delaney, Landow, pp.81-103. Cambridge, Mass.: The MIT Press.

Lynch, K. (1960). *The Image of the City.* Cambridge, Mass.: Tne MIT Press.

Mcknight, C, Dillon, A., Richardson, J. (1991). *Hypertext in Context.* Cambridge: Cambridge University Press.

Moulthorp, S. (1991). Reading from the Map: Metonymy and Metaphor in the Fiction of Working Paths. In *Hypermedia and Literary Studies,* eds. Delaney, Landow, pp.119-132. Cambridge, Mass.: The MIT Press.

Nelson, T.H. (1965). A File Structure for the Complex, The Changing and the Indeterminate. In *Association for Computing Macinery Proceedings of the 20th National Conference,* pp.84-100.

Nelson, T.H. (1987a). *Computer Lib.* Redmond: Microsoft Press.

Nelson, T.H. (1987b) *Dream Machines.* Redmond: Microsoft Press.

Venturi, R.. Brown, D. S., Izenour, S. (1972). *Learning from Las Vegas.* Cambridge, Mass.: The MIT Press.

14

Future Directions

Evolution proceeds in many waves, some brief by human temporal sensibilities and some lasting for centuries. Some changes in information seeking take place before technological investments are fully amortised (e.g., the latest CPU or software upgrade brings with it access to new information resources), and some take place over careers as strategies and pattern of use learned in school evolve based on new sources and tools. This final chapter examines one long-term change that computing technology brings to cognition in general and to information seeking in particular, considers how different domains interact to influence the evolution of information seeking, and concludes with some ideas about what types of systems we should strive to

Amplification and Augmentation

Applying computational power to information problems has been a research and design goal from the first days of computing. The dreams of language translation and cybernetic assistants have given way to dreams of artificial realities and intelligent agents, but our fascination with the manipulation of symbolic data and with interactivity remains a driving force behind much of the research in artificial intelligence and engineering. One way to consider how computation may be applied to information problems is to examine how it may be applied to amplify and augment intellect. Engelbart (1963) provided an early explication of how computing could be applied to amplify and augment the intellect and many of the developments he envisioned over 30 years ago have been fulfilled.

Amplification refers to an increase in an existing value or capability, and *augmentation* refers to the addition of a new value or capability. Electronic technology allows us to reach more people while seeking information and to scan or search more sources. Technology amplifies information seeking when it provides mechanical advantages for some of the information-seeking subprocesses, which in turn allows reallocations of time and cognitive load. As the mechanical advantage grows, it begins to change what is possible—a form of augmentation. Determining when there is enough amplification to enable new capabilities is a central problem in many fields (e.g., when velocity overcomes the force of gravity, when sufficient political dissatisfaction accumulates to force a parliamentary election, when multiple images become motion pictures). For information science, determining when speed and quantity of access enable new types of questions to be addressed is an important issue. One indicator that amplification has led to augmentation is in how our expectations change, such as when we come to expect as commonplace those things that were impossible or difficult beforehand. In turn, our expectations determine our actions, and the manual actions we amplified with technology eventually lead to entirely new actions. This chain of changes is one form of progress and is repeated for different technologies and different generations as part of the evolutionary process.

Lest this argument be overgeneralised, an important distinction must be made between changes in behavior and changes in thought. There is little evidence that basic cognitive and affective activity have changed because of any of the technological changes of the centuries, although many argue that television and video games have fundamentally altered attention spans. What has changed are the objects of thought and external tools for representing and transmitting the products of thought. Technological amplification leads to time savings that may lead to more thought and creativity (augmentation), or these savings may simply be filled with other, similar work—a menial productivity gain. One version of Parkinson's law tells us that jobs expand to fill the time available, and most of the productivity gains that technology provides suggest amplifications of behavior rather than augmentations of thought. An often-debated example of this distinction is the question of whether word-processing tools have improved the quality of writing or have simply created additional time for writers to perform clerical tasks and write more.

From an information-seeking perspective, an augmentation is indicated when the types of questions change. If factual access is less behaviorally demanding, then teachers, researchers, and workers can change assignments, problem focus, and tasks. A key decision is whether the diminished demands lead to more fact retrieval (amplification) or to interpretive information seeking. Some instructors who used Perseus in their teaching changed the types of assignments they gave to students so that the students explored primary materials and thought critically about them rather than studying textbook explications of what scholars wrote about those materials. This was an augmentation of the course, because it enabled new types of activity. Some students blossomed with the freedom to discover and invent their own theories; some floundered about without much effect; and still others complained that they missed the safety of scholarly interpretations. Clearly, these assignments took the place of traditional assignments and in many ways used time less efficiently.

Another way to address the distinction between behavior and thought is to consider specific tasks, the larger activity or job in which those tasks are embedded, and the general intellectual activity required for the job. When technology is used to amplify a specific task (e.g., get results faster, reach more people), the result is a gain in available time or a saving of effort. The time saved by the amplification can be used in different ways: for leisure activity, to perform more similar tasks, or to enable new types of tasks to be undertaken. When more similar tasks performed, a simple gain in productivity results may be considered an amplification of the job but have no effect on general intellectual activity. When new tasks are undertaken as a result of saving time, the job is augmented and intellectual activity may also be affected. For example, automating serials ordering in a library can save the time usually required to manually fill out and mail order forms. Time savings in this case may permit more attention to evaluation and selection and require different levels and amounts of intellectual activity. When amplification saves effort rather than time, productivity gains may not reflect more throughput but yield higher-quality products. For example, if an electronic search yields many more documents, more time may be required to examine them, but the overall quality of the solutions may be better. These examples illustrate a plausible chain of inferences regarding how amplification of tasks may lead to augmentation of the larger activity and possibly to augmentation of intellectual activity. Whether these inferences obtain is dependent on individual wills and institutional policies.

Interfaces are amplifications because they enable people to easily and effectively map tasks onto information resources. This book has argued that design should amplify human behavior rather than augment it directly. In regard to human performance, augmentation flows from amplification rather than from some external intervention. If we ever learn to be telepathic, it will come from learning about human physiology rather than from the invention of some device. Amplification evolves into augmentation only over a long time, largely because of the constraints of the physical and cultural environment. Humans evolve rather than transform, and the systems that support intellectual activity should amplify intellectual activity rather than directly transform it.

Communities of Perspective and Interdisciplinarity

Because information seeking is a generic cognitive activity, different communities develop views and strategies that are most useful for the knowledge and problems specific to their fields of interest. Although there has always been commonality of fields such as psychology, education, and library and information science, the advent of electronic information systems has broadened the overlap, extended the commonality to other fields, and led to increased collaboration and inter-disciplinary.

This book is aimed at communities interested in human-computer interaction and information science. These communities, in turn, draw theoretical principles and active participants from the fields of computer science and engineering, education, communications, psychology, philosophy, sociology, and library and information science. Each of these disciplines is concerned with seeking information and has developed particular views, languages, and techniques. Rather than a Tower of Babel, there is strength in this diversity of views, but researchers and practitioners must extend their reach beyond the comfortable confines of their discipline to cognate fields and perspectives.

Research results have demonstrated that information seeking depends on many interacting factors and is evolving in conjunction with developments in electronic technologies. Although much of the research on information seeking has focused on cognitive processes in the information seeker, much more remains to be discovered about how people formulate information problems, plan strategies, express those formulations, reflect on the results, extract and use information, and monitor the entire process. Little work has been done on the affective factors that influence information seeking, and so this seems to be a promising area for research. Although there has been considerable research on the physiological processes related to information seeking in manual environments, we need basic evidence on the physiological limits of human capabilities for scanning, recognising, and browsing in electronic environments. Thus, there is a need for research on the cognitive, affective, and physiological aspects of information seeking. These problems invite multidisciplinary teams of psychologists, information scientists, and sociologists.

Another research area focuses on the search system. Many engineering problems related to computational speed to process huge amounts of data on-the-fly, high-quality display, and novel input and output devices remain to be solved. More central to the concerns of this book, interface design and development have many challenges, including customizable interfaces for diverse user communities, new mechanisms for browsing and managing multiple views, the integration of analytical and browsing strategies into a common interface, rich and smoothly integrated representations for information objects at different levels of granularity, and a balance of user control with system help and documentation. These challenges invite interdisciplinary teams of engineers, computer scientists, and information scientists. Because information-seeking performance is also determined by the underlying information structures of search systems, computer scientists and information scientists must develop more powerful and more flexible data structures and indexes. Organisations that provide alternative, preprocessed views must be augmented by structures that allow on-the-fly views to be extracted according to information seekers' immediate and evolving needs.

The results of research thus far and the directions for the future have implications for practitioners. Designers of electronic search systems have a huge marketplace for their work and can best succeed by adopting a user-centered design philosophy and attending to the possible interactions among the information-seeking factors. In addition to task analysis, designers must know their user population and conduct formative evaluations. Just as most programming is maintenance rather than original work, interface work must increasingly aim at improving existing interfaces that have large installed bases. Thus, software engineering principles of reusability and incremental improvement should be adopted. Designers and developers should consider ways that browsing strategies can be supported while not losing the power and precision that analytical strategies provide.

Information specialists are perhaps most challenged by the evolution of information seeking because their roles are shifting to training and assisting end users who conduct their own searches, rather than conducting searches for them. Librarians and information specialists are more often collaborating with end users rather than serving as modular consultants on projects. These professionals have always been concerned with organising and presenting information, and these skills and experiences will be adapted to electronic environments. They have valuable contributions to make to interface design, especially in regard to conceptual interfaces. In addition, information specialists are increasingly active as information entrepreneurs, creating new information products and services that take advantage of electronic technology. Most important, information specialists should be engaged in the evaluation process. Information in many forms and in huge quantities must not only be organised for access but also judged for accuracy and value. Information specialists can coordinate the domain specialists who make such judgments and make sure that evaluative information is included at all levels of representation, starting with the bibliographic record. In addition, information specialists in the publishing industry should organise and disseminate digital multimedia representations in ways that provide a fair return to the creators yet ensure equitable access for all.

What Kinds of Information Environments Do We Want?

Given that electronic technology will play a role in most cases of information seeking in the future but has not yet reached levels of maturity that bring stabilisation and predictable growth, it is worth speculating on how we envision information seeking in the future. Several technological trends are candidates for improving the state of affairs.

Natural-language processing has developed through several stages, from early machine translation approaches based on brute-force algorithms to knowledge-based approaches depending on huge amounts of organised information and sets of inferencing rules (e.g., Lenat's CYC Project; Lenat, Guha, Pittman, Pratt, & Shepherd, 1990). Another promising stream of development uses common syntactic structures in different languages to create an interlingua that is used as the basis for machine translation (Dorr, 1992-93). Whether computers can "understand" human language is an issue for philosophers, but what is clear is that computers can recognise speech or typed text that adheres to regular patterns and has as their object the execution of some well-defined task. As the work on natural-language processing progresses, the ranges of patterns and tasks will certainly grow, and interfaces that apply human language will be more common. As is the case with all systems that support information seeking, people must still be able to articulate their information problem, make decisions about progress, and interpret results.

Intelligent agents have generated considerable interest, possibly because of the naive notion that we all can use personal secretaries or assistants in our professional and personal lives. Agents are reminiscent of batch processing, in which tasks are defined and the user goes on to another problem while the system executes the task. Two problems with agents for information seeking are apparent. First, the information seeker must articulate the task to the agent. This entails specifying where, what, and how the agent should search. It also requires that information seekers manage their agents—a requirement that itself could become time-consuming. Second, we have argued in this book that information seeking is a process, and so simply being involved with the input and output robs the information seeker of significant parts of the process. It is easy to imagine sending off agents to perform simple retrieval tasks, but it makes no more sense to believe that people will give up the experience of complex information seeking and learning to agents than it does to believe they would send their dog to the theater to see a play.

Another technology that generates considerable interest is virtual reality (telepresence). Visions of gliding through the bookshelves of virtual libraries and picking up animated volumes of information make for good conversation, but what real advantages can virtual reality offer? Information seeking is most often associated with nonfiction, with representations for abstractions related to reality. For virtual reality to be useful, it is necessary for designers to represent ideas and concepts as objects that can be observed and manipulated. This may be possible for spreadsheet values or database entries, but moving in and out of spaces of concepts and ideas requires that such spaces be defined and filled with appropriate information sources. This is the essential problem of classification systems (e.g., the Dewey Decimal System, the Colon Classification System). The problems of categorisation that such systems encounter are intellectual and interpretive, and any virtual representation is only as good as the underlying categorisations. Virtual reality seems promising for managing things, but it is unclear how it can help people manage words and ideas.

Virtual reality seems most appropriate to entertainment based on fictional contexts or to training simulations for complex systems (from which it developed).

Another technological trend that offers some interesting possibilities for information seeking is ubiquitous computing, in effect the aggregate advantages of having interconnected computers everywhere. Computers on the person (ranging from "Dick Tracy" communication watches to wearable robots) unite with computers in the home and workplace to provide constant access and control capabilities. Beyond the obvious possibilities of using commuting time to access and use remote information, having computational devices in the world around us offers new levels of control. If we consider putting computers into books and other information sources rather than simply putting books on computers, we may be able to invite information to come to us rather than having to go find it.

In addition to looking at specific technological trends, it may be instructive to consider global functionality. Do we want uniform information systems? Should everyone in the world be given a standardised device that enables uniform training and supports equitable usage? Although the final results from competitiveness in the telephone industries of the world are not yet in, there clearly seem to be some advantages to diversifying systems and services. A more idealised functionality is what might be called *information alchemy*. Given a potentially relevant information item, systems should be able to rerepresent it in a different form that better suits the needs of the information seeker. In the simplest case, a data set should be displayable in tabular or graphical forms. In the extreme, a text should be representable as a video. Rerepresentation is made possible by electronic environments, and many information-seeking innovations will come as we move from the simple rerepresentations toward the impossible extremes.

One way to encourage divergent thinking about possibilities is to consider some scenarios that use various technologies in problem contexts. The following three scenarios are meant to provoke thought about possible directions for future systems.

Scenario One: Multimedia Knowledge Bases

Deanna is a first-year engineering student assigned to a team that must design and build a windmill as a semester project. Cost constraints are provided; the model must be built and tested using reliable metrics; and a comprehensive written report that defends the procedure with literature and practice must be delivered. As part of the first group discussion, each member agrees to spend 2 weeks learning as much about windmills as possible before assigning specific tasks to individual members. Deanna accesses the Net from her dorm room and verbally describes her information needs to the system, at times reading phrases and sentences from the assignment provided by the instructor. A series of video descriptions appears. She does not even consider the virtual-world option, having long since decided that simulated experiences were best for entertainment. To determine which video to use, she chooses to see video clip summaries of 45 frames per second (she has learned through experience that 50% increases in display still allow her to get the sense of motion images—she envies her sister's ability to comprehend 75% increases) rather than to view the written summaries or hear the verbal summaries of each. Because she said she is looking for overview information at this time, the system presents 100 video summaries ranked according to statistical and knowledge-based retrieval analyses of her verbal problem statement. The fourth clip looks interesting and includes some spectacular views of the Utah desert area she plans to explore next summer. Her gesture freezes the summary window and begins the 30-minute presentation on windmills throughout history narrated by a prominent Japanese professor of materials science. As the video progresses, Deanna cuts and pastes single frames and short sequences into her notebook, in some cases including textual transcripts.

About 10 minutes into the video, she freezes the presentation and goes back to the summary window to scan through several more possible choices. After viewing one complete video and speeding through several more, she begins to focus on the trade-offs between the number of blades and production tolerances. Requesting blueprints for a two-blade optimal windmill for moderate wind conditions and for the traditional prairie design, she runs the simulations under different wind speeds to make sure that the two-blade design is superior. Fortunately, she noted that the narrator had commented on how critical blade balance was to the two-blade design and on the high costs of ceramic blades. She wonders what the cost-performance trade-offs will be given the group's inexperience with the manufacturing processes and their severe cost constraints. She types this problem (she found long ago that she can type as fast as she can talk), attaches it to her notes, and copies it to the rest of the group to get their thoughts on whether they should aim for an optimal design that they may not be able to implement or a more practical design.

Scenario Two: Intelligent Agents

Brian has 15 years of experience as a clinical psychologist in a state-run long-term care facility for the elderly and also has a thriving private practice. Because government services are increasingly contracted out to private enterprise, Brian has begun to consider opening a for-profit long-term facility. He has first hand experience with the needed services, and he has many colleagues who may be interested in joining his venture. He needs information about the administrative aspects of the concept, however, before he can begin serious discussions with others. Brian sits down at his workstation and begins to compose intelligent agents that he will send into the

Global Web. Although he does not have the latest agent-construction set, he does have experience using and confidence in Knowboty Better (Version 5.8.1, trademark Megasmart Inc.).

Brian defines an agent to gather information on local and state regulations for medical facilities, specifying the finest grain of detail (he wants regulations on all aspects of buildings and services) but the narrowest set of sources (he wants the regulations only for a single state and a few specific counties). He defines another agent to explore financial sources for investment costs, profit data, and competition in the long-term care field, setting broad parameters for sources and overview information (he knows he will eventually refine this agent to seek more specific data once he has gained a sense of the financial aspects). He requires this agent to report back daily and to include public-domain simulation models that he can use for analysing the data. He configures another agent to locate and organise coverage data for the various public and private health insurance options, specifying weekly reports. Another agent is defined to examine the availability of human resources in the region and typical credentials and salaries for physicians, nurses, attendants, social workers, and other health care workers. He suggests several professional jobline sources with which he is familiar and allows flexibility for the agent to consult others with high-similarity profile coefficients (including the newspaper want ads). Other specific agents are similarly constructed for topics such as the availability of buildings in the region, tax codes, and venture capital sources. A global agent is also constructed to gather medical and psychological case studies conducted at long-term care facilities. This agent's parameters are set to report back every other day and deposit cases in a database of psychological cases that Brian has constructed as part of his professional growth over the years (he views this as a sort of hedge, for even if he eventually decides not to develop a formal prospectus for the venture, he will have augmented his psychological database with some physiological cases that may help him in his work).

Scenario Three: Implants, Ubiquitous Computing, and Human-machine Symbiosis

Suzanne has a busy medical practice in a large metropolitan area. When she arrives at her office, she notes that the day wall displays today's appointments, most of which involve routine checkups or well-defined symptoms, but eight of them glow softly to indicate that some special preparations must be made. The first special case is a patient she has not seen in 2 years, a middle-aged man with little medical history who is coming because of persistent headaches and a low fever for the past 10 days. Suzanne selects one of the hundreds of implant modules displayed on the info wall and activates the radio link between the wall and her knowplant. Her knowplant (Real Intelligence Inc.) was recently upgraded to provide better visual/

kinesthetic fidelity and coordination, although she wishes she had invested the extra money to get the newly developed olfactory link.

In the milliseconds it takes for the module to come inmind (beyond online), she gasps at the visual/auditory burst, a sensation she has never quite gotten used to in her years of using her various implants. Although thinking about headache and fever will yield sensations and visual/auditory images of the latest causal probability diagrams with accompanying case studies, Suzanne verbalises the words as well. The Symbiosis Society has long debated whether multiple channel inputs improve the focus or the vividness of memories, but she has always found it reassuring to verbalise while thinking. As specific cases race through her mind, she turns her attention to possible diagnostic tests. Various instruments and monitors in her examination room snap to attention as she considers the data collection strategies she may want to use during her examination later that day. The various instruments are alerted by Suzanne's implant through signals sent to their internal computers and subsequently are updated from the patient medical record by the info wall.

Suzanne recalls her mentor from medical school, who told stories about searching huge bibliographic files just to locate paper journal articles that were then obtained through interlibrary loan. What was the name of that system? It never ceased to amaze her that simple fact retrieval was more difficult with knowplants because their organisations were conceptual in nature (top down from concepts to cases) rather than organised by discrete tokens like those old retrieval systems. As the first patient of the day arrives, it occurs to Suzanne that her patients believe they are coming to her office but that in many ways they are coming into her mind and enveloped by her augmented expertise disguised as an office.

Each of these scenarios offers some appeal and some repulsion. Although cast in positive contexts, each scenario could just as easily have presented the same technological perspective in horrific settings. It seems certain that aspects of each of these scenarios will come to pass, with the order of presentation likely correlating with the passage of time. Certainly, most of the technical components of scenario one would be available today if the cost constraints and the dilemma of technology/ database push-pull (if there were an installed base of hardware, the programming would come, and vice versa) could be ignored.

Scenario two represents an active area of research and speculation, and surely today's ability to send queries to multiple databases on a "canned" user profile basis will continue to become more sophisticated. A major problem here is "agent management": Controlling a group of agents itself requires time and effort, let alone making sense out of and integrating the fruits of their searches.

Scenario three is the least technically feasible, but research in monitoring and controlling electromagnetic and electrical activity in the, brain continues to progress toward mapping and understanding how the brain works. Moreover, the trends toward installing computing power in many devices rather than a single workstation is strong, positive, and irreversible. In fact, we should concentrate on putting computers into books rather than writing books on computers. The main problem here, of course, is not the technology but the failure to distinguish between brain and mind. We can conceive of a brain that contains all the external representations of knowledge in the world, but not amind that can survive without learning and interpretation.

More specifically, these scenarios do not obviate the importance of the information-seeking process. Information problems must be recognised, accepted, and defined. Although recognition and definition may be aided by external factors, acceptance is a strictly human factor. Moreover, recognition and definition must be driven by conscious attention and thought, and consciousness is the antithesis of machinery. Information problems must be articulated, and search systems selected. These subprocesses require mapping mental concepts to words, icons, or other physically represented tokens. System selection requires knowledge about alternatives and evaluative judgements of coverage and value. Evaluation and selection are perhaps the most critical elements of human information-seeking activity and are most directly applied during the subprocesses of system selection, examination of results, and reflection. In all these scenarios, the information seeker makes judgments about the possible relevance of high-level representations such as video summaries or memory modules. Relevance judgments regarding specific primary information related to the problem also must take into account applicability, accuracy, and expected value. These decisions in turn determine what is extracted and eventually used in solving the information problem. In sum, the technology may evolve beyond anything we can now imagine, but information seekers will always be required to think, make inferences and decisions, and develop confidence in these processes.

Conclusion

The aim of information seeking is to get relevant into one's head and either use it in conjunction with known information to take some action or integrate it into the knowledge base. This is accomplished by coordinating information-seeking factors in systematic and heuristic ways. Our personal information infrastructures are central to this process. Domain knowledge helps us determine where to look and what to look for; information-seeking skills help us to formulate queries and browse; and system knowledge allows us to manipulate the many devices that provide access to the various representations available. Search systems not only deliver information, but they also provide structure and format that guides and influence search. A critical need is for human-computer interaction research to address how electronic systems can enhance and go beyond the delivery and structuring techniques available in manual environments. Domains of knowledge are organised to distinguish themselves from other domains. These organisations and protocols guide information seeking for those familiar with the domain, but those systems used by domain novices must illustrate and make explicit such features.

There can be no doubt that we are immersed in a set of complex relationships with the environment. The things we do choose to think about are influenced by the world around us. Likewise, as part of the environment, we influence the world—sometimes in devastating ways. People are incredibly adaptable to positive as well as adverse conditions and also adapt the world to their needs. In the case of information environments, we have adapted to systems, collections, and organisations that have been put together in either haphazard ways or for the sake of efficiencies of scale. A more balanced, ecological, and sustainable view of information seeking in electronic environments is to design systems that amplify human capabilities and propensities so that the resulting augmentations will be positive and natural rather than sophisticated workarounds that we pass on to future generations of information seekers.

Our personal information infrastructures are constantly developing and changing throughout our lives. Systems designed principally for the convenience of the designer or the institution rather than the end user impede productive and satisfying work and inhibit the continued development of personal information infrastructures. What we have argued for in this book is design based on taking advantage of natural human capabilities and propensities rather than systems that magically or transparently think for users. This is particularly important to information seekers because information seeking is primarily an intellectual rather than a physical activity. We may like the thought of machines that can find the information we need, and in fact, we can observe systems that retrieve well-defined facts that we may need. What we cannot imagine and what we will not admit are machines that think for us. Somewhere in between is where most of information seeking falls. Information seeking is thinking in that most of the time we are not quite sure what we need—we are not quite sure what the information problem is—and it is the seeking itself that illuminates, informs, and assists us in defining, growing, learning, and succeeding. Directly hardwiring one's brain to a world encyclopedia database may ultimately facilitate more rapid associations and more broad-based associations, but ultimately it is our personal struggles with the problems, concepts, and abstractions of information that define not only intellectual tasks but also what we are as human beings.

Two principles obtain from this point of view. First, we should design systems that amplify and enhance natural capabilities. Second, we should pay more attention to the information-seeking process and the interactions among the information-seeking factors rather than to technology itself. An ecological point of view that bases design on how the different components interact with and influence one another is what is needed. The information-seeking process has become much more integrated, fluid, and parallel because of electronic environments, but most of the tools and techniques that have been developed focus on the query formulation and examination subprocesses. These are clearly needed, but what is more critical is attention to the problems of acceptance, definition, extraction, and use and, in fact, integrating the entire information-seeking process into the larger tasks of learning, working, and planning.

15

The Future in Computing

TOWARDS THE 21ST CENTURY

Over a century elapsed between Charles Babbage's first computing machines in the 1830s and the development of the first electronic computers in the 1940s. Since then, the pace of computing innovation has been progressing at an accelerating rate. Making predictions about where computing and information technology will move next is like trying to hit a fast-moving target.

In looking to the future, this chapter will examine some key *trends*. These are based on a report* produced, by a committee established in 1979 by the Japanese government to establish the main priorities for computing research until 1990; this has become known as the *Fifth Generation Computer System*. The committee sifted through current computing research and related it to what they defined as the main user and social requirements.

The Fifth Generation therefore represents a thorough analysis of the most likely shape of computing technology in the future. What is more, the Japanese government and industry decided to back the project when the committee published its report in 1981. They were followed by commitments from governments and companies around the world.

Even if some of the specific technologies identified in the Fifth Generation report prove to be red herrings, its user objectives will probably determine the route taken by computing and information technology on the way to the 21st Century.

THE FIFTH GENERATION COMPUTER SYSTEM

The Fifth Generation is really the first generation of computers to be defined by the user-oriented perspective recommended in Figure 9.1. *The first generation* were computers made with thermionic valves; the *second generation* introduced transistors; the *third generation* had integrated circuits; and the *fourth generation* was never clearly defined. It was spoken about in the early 1970s when computer specialists began looking at new forms of computer architecture to match real user needs; some of these new architectures matured to a point where they have been incorporated in the Fifth Generation Computer System. The use of VLSI technology has also sometimes been identified as typifying the fourth generation.

The Fifth Generation gives the highest priority to making systems that are easy and natural to use. Its other objectives relate to the types of technological support needed to support 'problem solving systems', according to the Fifth Generation Committee. In these systems, the Committee adds, 'Intelligence will be greatly improved to approach that of a human being. When compared to conventional systems, the man/machine interface will be closer to that of human behaviour'.

The Fifth Generation has three functional requirements:

— *ease of use* through computers with high 'intelligence' and natural human input and output mechanisms;
— *reliable and efficient software development* by languages, new computer architectures and systems software which overcome previous problems with software development;
— *improved overall functions and performance* aimed at making computers smaller, lighter, faster, of greater capacity, more flexible and more reliable.

It is these objectives which set the main themes for the future of computing, whatever techniques are used to achieve them.

FRIENDLY AND INTELLIGENT COMPUTERS

The notion of *user friendly* computers was picked up by computer marketing companies in the 1970s as a way of selling their systems.

The fact that systems could be sold on the basis of new-found friendliness was an implicit admission of the unfriendliness of previous systems. Many of the so-called user friendly systems were merely modifications of existing equipment which had not been subjected to the systematic human factors engineering discussed.

The Fifth Generation applies the human factors engineering approach to the total system, not just particular equipment or tasks. It recognises that the basic computer architecture and the system tools used to develop systems need to be tailored to meet human requirements and to provide an 'intelligent interface'.

The user/system interaction should therefore be in the method most natural for human communications. Special emphasis is given to the importance of automatic speech and vision understanding systems. It aims, for example, to develop a phonetic typewriter which prints directly from speech input; systems that can understand and respond to the voices of many speakers; and database information retrieval systems using picture and image information.

The Fifth Generation places stress on a number of developments which have arisen from *Artificial Intelligence* (AI) research. AI is the study of how computing can be applied to perform tasks which involve a degree of intelligence or communications ability which resembles human behaviour. Speech and vision understanding grew from AI research. AI has also been involved in robotics research which aims to produce robots which can see, hear, walk, talk, etc. The Fifth Generation identifies three particular areas of AI research, other than input and output techniques, which require special attention:

- — knowledge-based management systems;
- — logical problem solving and inference systems;
- — natural language processing.

The Knowledge Information Processing System

Human intelligence relies to a great extent on building up a base of knowledge, gained from learning and experience, and then applying reason to *infer* what course of action should be taken next. AI has developed expert systems which use *knowledge refining* techniques to distil the reasoned knowledge of experts into a computer program.

Traditional computer programs use algorithmic (procedural) techniques which define processes that need to be applied to data. The programming of expert systems is non-procedural. *Heuristic* techniques are used in AI, based on 'learning from experience' to solve problems rather than by applying predefined algorithms.

The developer of an expert system will talk to one or more experts in the specialisation or *domain* to be covered. Special *logic programming* languages are used to represent the knowledge in a systematic form. Once the expert system has been produced, it can be asked for advice as if it were a human consultant. The earliest expert systems could help provide medical diagnoses, explore for oil, assist computer engineers to find faults, solve problems and analyse chemicals.

The expert systems program will typically include statements such as:

IF x IS TRUE AND *y* IS TRUE THERE IS A z% CHANCE THAT *m* IS TRUE

This is very different to the type of code used in programming languages discussed.

The expert system statement above is a more systematic and quantified way of expressing the reasoning that, say, a doctor may use in diagnosing a patient. Through a question/answer dialogue and physical examination, the doctor gathers various elements of true or false observations. From these an inference can be made about the probability of the cause for the complaint

As the expert system is programmed in the way that represents human knowledge and reasoning, its 'code' can be understood directly. Following through the code is equivalent to sitting and listening to the expert explain the lessons drawn from experience. They are therefore useful training aids.

Knowledge representation and processing is regarded as the 'core' of the Fifth Generation. The whole project is sometimes known as the Knowledge Information Processing System (KIPS).

Logical Problem Solving

The traditional way of developing software has been to:

— specify the system in a natural language;
— translate this into a formal specification;
— translate the formal specification into detailed code.

Errors could be introduced at each transition. There is no way of showing that the specification is correct until after the coding is produced- and even then, debugging and testing can be a complex and untrustworthy process.

The Fifth Generation will use a language called *PROgramming in LOGic (PROLOG)* as its kernel language, ie as the language at the core of the system around which the architecture will be constructed. PROLOG uses a form of basic mathematical logic, called *resolution*, which was developed by Professor John Robinson of Syracuse University in the US. This provides a way of resolving problems by a series of logical inferences, similar in structure to the deductive reasoning of an expert system.

PROLOG has a number of advantages:

— it can be used to define both the formal specification and the program code;
— formal techniques can be applied to prove the correctness of a PROLOG specification;
— it can be used to represent a knowledge or database;
— it can be used as a database enquiry language, particularly for relational databases; Query-By-Example is a typical logical query language;

— it resembles the natural way of expressing problems and can be easily learnt by children.

PROLOG was developed in the 1970s at two main centres — by a team under Alain Colmerauer at the University of Marseilles and by a group at the Machine Intelligence Unit at Edinburgh University, where Robert Kowalski played a leading role.

The basic unit of a PROLOG program or database specification is a *Horn clause,* which could either be an *assertion,* such as

Fred works 38 hours a week

or an *implication,* such as

x is paid *y if x* works z hours *and* earns p

From these basic clauses, specifications of an information processing task or database search requirements can be produced. These specifications can also act directly as a program procedure or as a relational database enquiry. PROLOG therefore eliminates the gap between a specification and programming language and also between a programming and database enquiry language.

A popular but more limited example of a logical programming language is *LISt Programming (LISP).* It was developed in 1960 by a pioneer of AI, Professor John McCarthy of the Massachusetts Institute of Technology. As its name implies, the basic program structure of LISP is a list or string. Pure LISP (sometimes called S-LISP), represents lists within parentheses. For example, to add two numbers *(x* and *y)* together, the LISP statement would be:

(PLUS X Y)

where PLUS is defined as the function that adds two numbers together. As this basic structure can become difficult to understand for complex functions, versions of LISP have been developed which are easier to read. LISP is called a *functional* language because it includes functions like PLUS.

LISP is of particular interest because it can also be used as a means of specifying other languages and is known as a *metalanguage.* It has been used, for example, to create a language called. LOGO used for educational systems and for languages which enable algebraic expressions to be evaluated directly in the form that would normally be expressed by a mathematician. PROLOG can be used to do many LISP-type operations.

Logic programming languages are appropriate for writing expert systems.

Natural Language Processing

As indicated user/system interaction is aided by the ability to communicate in a natural human language rather than in the well-defined and restricted programming languages. The Fifth Generation will aim to extend the range and flexibility of the ways in which natural languages can be used. It will also give high priority to searching for techniques which will enable computers to be used in translating from one human language to another.

MACHINES DESIGNED TO SOLVE PROBLEMS

The traditional von Neumann architecture funnelled all information through a sequential processing channel. This may have been appropriate for the type of mathematical and scientific calculations which were the prime applications conceived of by Babbage, von Neumann and other early computer designers. As computing applications developed, the von Neumann architecture became a serious limitation. A central CPU of the typical mainframe systems of the 1960s and early-1970s, for example, had to cope with *all* database, communications and applications processing. Complex operating systems had to be developed to overcome the bottleneck at the CPU. Applications had to be squeezed into the sequential processing mould, whatever the real data structure and processing requirements.

This added significantly to the already complex difficult task of specifying and writing programs to solve real user problems. The Fifth Generation seeks to find new types of computer design and software aids which will provide an easier, more reliable and more efficient transition from the specification of a problem to be solved to the creation of a computer system to solve it.

The Fifth Generation has defined three main ways of lessening the burden of software generation:

— *automatic programming;*

— *new computing architectures* to overcome the von Neumann bottleneck;

— *aids to developing and verifying programs.*

Automated Programming

The Fifth Generation regards the ideal software development process as one in which a program is synthesised directly from requirement specifications described in a natural language. PROLOG is a step in this direction because the program specification in PROLOG can also be used as program code. PROLOG, however, is a formalised not a natural language.

Other techniques can be used to help automate software creation. The Fifth Generation will research, for example, the concept of an *intelligent programming system,* containing an 'algorithm bank' of proven procedures. This knowledge base would be used to synthesise programs directly from the specification of user requirements.

To achieve this, methods need to be devised to provide systematic and automated aids for the design, management, synthesis and verification of software. This will include the development of expert systems to advise on program design. Another aim is to develop a system which will help to automate the process of developing expert systems.

The potential for automatic programming was illustrated by Professor Ross Quinlan of the University of Sydney in Australia with a program called ID3, which is an expert automatic programmer. In 1979, Professor Quinlan got ID3 to generate a rule-based expert program to carry out a particular chess end-game. He did it by presenting various examples of the end-game positions to ID3 and indicating whether or not it would lead to a conclusion within three moves. From these examples, ID3 automatically identified about 50 key properties (such as the distance between knight and king) and related them to a set of logical rules. (The best program written by Professor Quinlan in LISP to do the same function took 17.5 milliseconds to run, whereas the ID3-generated program took 3.4 milliseconds.)

New Computing Architectures

One of the ways of breaking the von Neumann bottleneck is to distribute processing power around the system. Front-end processors to handle some communications tasks and back-end database processors were developed for this purpose. The problems of developing software can be eased when intelligence is distributed away from a CPU because programs can be divided into smaller and simpler functional units than the complex structure of integrated centralised systems.

The Fifth Generation proposals on new architectures include:

— *parallel processing.* The von Neumann architecture is designed for *sequential* processing, with instructions obeyed in the sequence dictated by the coding. Parallel processing gallows many processors to act at the same time on the same data for example in analysing an image) or for many processors to act on many similar items of data at the same time (say in processing all personnel data simultaneously in a payroll system). Parallel processing is faster, more efficient and more adaptable than sequential processing;

— *data flow architecture.* Von Neumann is an example of a *control flow* architecture where processing is directed by program instructions which manipulate data and control processing sequencing. Data flow architectures are driven by the flow of data from a *producer* to a *consumer* instruction, carried by a *data token.* When the required data inputs are available, an action is initiated, rather than actions being initiated by the instruction in a control flow architecture. Data flow architectures are suitable for parallel processing and the processing of knowledge bases which are important Fifth Generation goals;

— *distributed function architectures.* The overall architecture will be planned within a structured, modular blueprint with specialised machines to carry out specific functions. This will provide high reliability and availability of the system, easier adaptability to take account of new technological developments which affect specific functions, general systems efficiency and a powerful spread of capabilities. Specific machines and architectures will be developed to handle functions such as network control, databases (including a special machine to handle the algebra of relational databases), man/machine communications, high-speed numerical computations, logical programming languages like PROLOG, and parallel processing (including data flow architectures).

Improved Overall Functions and Performances

The Fifth Generation report highlighted six major capabilities which systems should possess to meet future computing requirements:

— *improved cost/performance value* which will enable computer systems to become economic for an increasing range of activities;

— *light and compact computers* which will make computer power more portable;

— *high speed and large capacity* to meet user demands. Specific targets have been set for each research project. For example, enhanced von Neumann architectures with ten million transistors per chip are aimed at. Other targets include a relational database machine with up to 600 processors and 1K Gigabytes of storage; a logical program machine that can process up to 1 Giga *logical inferences per second* (lips); a personal computer running LISP at 4 *million instructions per second* (mips); machine translation of 100,000 words at 90% accuracy; and speech recognition comprehending 10,000 words spoken by hundreds of speakers;

— *increased diversification and adaptability* through increased use of functionally modular subsystems and special-purpose machines;

— *high reliability* with automatic detection and repair of malfunctions and containment of uncorrectable malfunctions to avoid complete systems breakdown;

— *built-in security* to prevent computer crimes and unauthorised access to information.

In order to provide these improvements, various new technologies will be explored, such as video discs for storage, and Josephson junctions and gallium arsenide for processors. Other techniques not explicitly mentioned in the Fifth Generation report could also be used to improve future computing capabilities.

Biological and opto-electronic techniques could be used for processors. Biological material such as proteins, can be used to replace silicon in conventional processors and memories. Experiments have also been undertaken to 'grow' computers biologically from essential 'computing genes', in a similar way to how genetics evolve humans and other animals. Processing could also be carried out by devices which use combine optical fibres and microelectronics to provide processing capabilities using light pulses rather than digital electronic techniques.

Another important area of development not covered by the Fifth Generation is advanced robotics. The capabilities to understand speech and visual images would give eyes and ears to computers. The physical mobility of computers is being investigated in many research centres but is a difficult human function to simulate. The idea of a domestic robot which can do the washing up and dusting is therefore unlikely to happen until the 21st century, although some powerful advanced robots will appear before then.

COMPUTING: FOR BETTER OR WORSE?

Technology itself is neutral. The way it is applied, however, reflects the most powerful influences in the society within which it is applied. Computers could be applied in many ways that could have a positive or negative effect on individuals, organisations and society as a whole.

Computers could be used to enhance the quality of life, feed the hungry and cure the sick; or to dehumanise society, to intrude on people's privacy and to kill.

One of the dangers of computing is to assume that they can solve all problems. If the targets of the Fifth Generation are met, computers will be extremely adaptable and powerful devices. Their method of 'thinking', however, is currently different to that of human beings. Computers may exhibit many characteristics of intelligence but that does not make them equivalent to humans.

Many users of computers become cowed by the apparent invincibility of this 'rational superbrain'. Over-reliance is often placed on figures because they have been produced on a computer. Instead of getting computers to match human characteristics, there is a possibility that people will begin to match computing behaviour and assume that emotionless rationality is 'superior' to the 'irrationality and emotionality' of people.

All major technological innovations have created similar dilemmas- nuclear energy can be used for destruction or peaceful purposes; the motor car is a boon to mobility but is also a major cause of deaths and pollution. Computing and information technology pose a challenge on a wider and more complex scale than other innovations because they encompass such a diverse range of applications. Information technology is making these widespread impacts at a rapid pace throughout the world.

The increasing use of information technology is inevitable. This *does not* mean that there is any inevitability about the *way* it is introduced, who gains from its application — and who might suffer. By providing an understanding of the capabilities and potential of information technology, this book hopes to assist individuals, and therefore society as a whole, to decide for themselves the checks and balances needed to ensure that the 'information age' is of benefit to mankind.

Annexures

ANNEXURE - I

THE STORY OF INTERNET

BEFORE THE BEGINNING THE ARPANET AGE THE INTERNET AGE THE WEB AGE

BEFORE THE BEGINNING

1866

The first fully functional telephone cable is laid across the Atlantic, demonstrating the possibility of rapid communications between continents. Queen Victoria and President Johnson exchange messages across the cable

1943

Alan Turing builds Colossus, the machine used to decipher German communications in the second world war and one of the world's earliest programmable electronic computers.

1945

In a highly prescient article in the The Atlantic Monthly, entitled "As We May Think", Vannevar Bush, the first director of what eventually became the National Science Foundation, describes a machine he calls a memex. The microfilm-based memex would enable the user to link related pieces of information together for rapid retrieval. Almost 50 years before the Web, the ideas were there.

1948

Claude Shannon, a mathematician at AT&T's Bell Labs, publishes A Mathematical Theory of Communication. His theory enables the calculation of the information-carrying capacity of any channel. Shannon's work, which included the introduction of the word "bit" to describe a piece of binary information, underpins all information theory and all modern communications systems, including the Internet.

1958

Responding to the launch of Sputnik, the first Earth-orbiting satellite, President

Dwight D. Eisenhower creates the Advanced Research Projects Agency (ARPA) to oversee the development of space and military programs. ARPA's brief includes the creation of new computer and communications systems.

1960

J.C.R. Licklider, a researcher at the Massachusetts Institute of Technology (MIT) publishes "Man-Computer Symbiosis", a paper describing ways in which men and machines might co-operate to make decisions and save valuable time in solving problems.

1961

Leonard Kleinrock, a researcher at MIT, publishes the first paper on packet-switching theory, alerting ARPA scientists to the possibility of treating communications links in terms of passing active packages of information around rather than shovelling them through fixed circuits.

1962

Paul Baran, a computer scientist at the Rand Corporation working on the survivability of communications networks under nuclear attack, describes a distributed computer network for the fist time. His model, in which a network is built of a number of nodes, was revolutionary in its use of messages split up into blocks, each taking a different path to its final destination - in essence, a packet-based network.

1965

The word "packet" is used for the first time by Donald Davies, a British reseacher at the National Physical Laboratory (NPL), to describe a way of breaking up messages for transmission across new kinds of networks. Davies's work mirrored closely that of Paul Baran, although it focused on public communications networks rather military ones.

ARPA sponsors its first study of co-operatively networked computers, involving the connection of two machines in California and Massachusetts across a dedicated 2,000 bits per second telephone link.

Ted Nelson coins the term "hypertext".

1967

Larry Roberts, a computer scientist at ARPA, proposes a design for a fast, decentralised network built on dial-up telephone lines. In London. Donald Davies builds the National Physical Laboratory Data Network, an early experiment in packet-switching.

At the Association for Computing Machinery Symposium in October, Roberts presents the first paper on the proposed design for the "ARPA net" network.

Representatives of the three bodies researching packet networks (ARPA, RAND and NPL) meet for the first time.

1968

The contract to build the Interface Message Processors (IMPs) at at the core of the experimental ARPA network is awarded to Bolt, Beranek and Newman (BBN), a technical consulting firm in Cambridge, Massachusetts.

THE ARPANET AGE

1969

The first four ARPA network hosts, located at Stanford University, the University of California at Los Angeles (UCLA), the University of California at Santa Barbara and the University of Utah, are connected across 50kbps lines provided by AT&T. The first recorded network crash occurs in October, as the letter G of LOGIN is entered when trying to access the Stanford computer from UCLA.

At Bell Labs, Ken Thompson and Dennis Ritchie invent Unix, the operating system destined to become the bedrock of the Internet.

Compuserve starts life as a computer time-sharing service at an American insurance company.

Telnet, a program allowing people to log into and control computers from a remote terminal, is bom.

1970

AlohaNet, a system for exchanging data between computers on four Hawaiian islands, is created by Norman Ahramson.

1972

BBN's Ray Tomlinson writes the first e-mail program, and establishes the use of the @ sign in e-mail addresses. In July, Larry Roberts creates the first program which can list, forward and reply to messages—the first real e-mail client.

The first public demonstration of the ARPA network is held at the International Conference on Computer Communications in Washington's Hilton Hotel; 40 machines take part.

1973

The APRA network goes global, connecting machines in the United States to hosts at University College in London and The Royal Radar Establishment in Norway.

At Harvard, a PhD student, Bob Metcalfe, outlines the idea for Ethernet, a new and fast way of networking computers. His invention is tested for the first time on computers at Xerox PARC in Palo Alto, California.

1974

BBN launches Telenet, the first commercial packet-switched networking service. Vint Cerf and Bob Kahn publish the first specifications for their Transmission Control Protocol (TCP), a new way of managing the transmission of data packets across networks.

1975

Microsoft is founded by Bill Gates and Paul Alien to produce software for microcomputers. TCP's capabilities are tested across satellite links from the United States to Hawaii and the UK. The first mailing list, MsgGroup, is bom on Arpanet.

1976

Queen Elizabeth II sends the first royal e-mail from the Royal Signals and Radar Establishment at Malvem in the UK.

At Bell Labs, researchers develop the Unix-to-Umx Copy program, which later forms the basis of Usenet.

Whitfield Diffie, a cryptographer and privacy advocate, and Martin Hellman, an electrical engineer, invent public-key cryptography.

1977

Three researchers at MIT, Ron Rivest, Adi Shamir and Len Adleman, invent the RSA algorithm (the abbreviation is based on their names), a public key method for encrypting messages.

1978

The TCP protocol is split into two parts, creating the new Internet Protocol (IP). Networks that make use of this protocol become known as internets; the aggregate of these internets constitutes the wider Internet.

1979

Usenet is founded by Tom Truscott and Jim Ellis at Duke University and Steve

Bellovin at the University of North Carolina.

Emoticons, also known as smileys, are used for the first time on the Arpanet MsgGroup mailing list.

Richard Bartle and Roy Trubshaw, of the University of Essex in England, create the first multiuser dungeon software for role-playing games.

1981

IBM launches the first personal computer (PC), reshaping the computing landscape. It is equipped with Microsoft's DOS operating system, the source of the company's early fortunes.

The National Science Foundation (NSF)builds the CSNET backbone, a new network for use by academics and researchers with no access to Arpanet.

THE INTERNET AGE

1982

EUNet, the European Unix Network, is created to provide e-mail and Usenet services between the UK, Denmark, Sweden and the Netherlands.

The DOMAIN NAME SYSTEM (DNS) is established at the University of Wisconsin, bringing order to the previously chaotic addressing system on electronic networks. JANET, the UK's Joint Academic Network, is established.

Widespread development of PC-based local area networks begins.

1983

TCP is officially adopted by ARPA and the US Department of Defense as the core Internet protocol.

1984

The term "cyberspace" first appears in William Gibson's novel Neuromancer.

The Well, one of the Net's most famous communities, is started by Stewart Brand, Larry Brilliant and others. It quickly becomes an important forum for electronic discussion.

The first Macintosh computer appears.

1985

The NSF builds on its CSNET idea with the creation of NSFNET, a new high-speed backbone connecting five supercomputing centres in the United States. The arrival of NSFNET triggers an explosion of smaller networks.

America Online (AOL) begins life as Quantum Computer Services.

1986

The Internet Engineering Task Force (IETF) is created to co-ordinate technical developments on Arpanet and key Internet gateway systems.

NETP. the Network News Transport Protocol, arrives and begins to replace UUCP on Usenet as the standard way of exchanging newsgroup data.

1987

UUNET, a commercial organisation providing access to Usenet and other network services, is founded

Bill Atkinson writes HyperCard for the Apple Macintosh, the first tool for creating mass-market hypertext and hypermedia applications.

1988

Robert Morris, a computer science graduate at Cornell University, releases a self-replicating program on to the Internet. This so-called worm eventually brings down 6,000 hosts, 10% of all the machines on the network.

Internet relay chat (IRC) is developed in Finland by Jarkko Oikarinen.

1989

In Germany, the Fraunhofer Institute patents the MP3 music compression algorithm.

The World (world.std.com), the first dial-up Internet Service Provider (ISP), is founded in Massachusetts.

1990

Arpanet officially ceases to be a research tool and becomes just another network.

In July, John Perry Barlow and Mitch Kapor found the Electronic Freedom Foundation (EFF).

1991

A team at CERN, Europe's particle physics laboratory, releases the first text-only "browser" for use with the HTML mark-up language and HTTP protocol that it has developed to allow far-flung researchers to collaborate. Tim Berners-Lee later posts the first public Web software on the alt.hypertext newsgroup.

Linus Torvalds, a Finnish student, starts work on writing the operating system that will eventually become Linux.

The first version of Pretty Good Privacy (PGP). a software package that uses the RSA algorithm for encrypting the contents of messages, is released by Phil Zimmerman.

Commercial traffic is permitted to use the NSFNET backbone for the first time. By March, traffic passes 1 trillion bytes and 10 billion packets per month.

Gopher, a program for finding information of the Web, is released by the University of Minnesota.

1992

CERN releases its World Wide Web software into the public domain.

The number of Internet hosts passes I m.

THE WEB AGE

1993

The first graphical browser, Mosaic for X, written by Marc Andreessen, is released by the National Centre for Supercomputing Applications (NCSA). Traffic on the World Wide Web expands by over 300,000%; by contrast,Gopher usage grows at a mere 997%.

InterNic is created by the National Science Foundation to direct the management of Internet registration services.

CERN announces that the Web and its supporting technology will be freely available to all.

1994

Marc Andreessen and Jim Clark start Netscape, releasing the first version of the Navigator browser in the autumn. Linus Torvalds unveils version 1.0 of the Linux kernel.

The World Wide Web Consortium is formed to steer the development of Web technologies, with Tim Berners-Lee appointed as its director.

Laurence Canter and Martha Siegel, two American lawyers, become the most despised people in Internet history after flooding Usenet with advertisements for their green card lottery services, thus becoming the first spammers.

Pizza Hut starts taking orders over the Internet. The first Internet bank, First

Virtual, opens in the United States, Wasting no time, Vladimir Levin, a Russian computer expert, becomes the first Internet bank robber, stealing millions of dollars from Citibank.

Traffic on the NSFNET backbone exceeds 10 trillion bytes per month.

1995

The Web constitutes the bulk of Internet traffic. Sun Microsystems unveils Java. The first version of the RealAudio audio streaming product appears. CompuServe and AOL hitherto proprietary networks, provide dial-up access to the Internet for the first time.

Netscape goes public after only 14 months of existence, offering 5m shares to the public on August 8th at an initial price of $28. Shares close at $58.25, valuing the company at over $2 billion and earning its co-founder, Jim Clark, $663m on the first day of trading. In December the share price hits S170.

Jeff Bezos opens his online bookstore at Amazon,com. The Web-based eBay auction house accepts its first bids.

Digital launches its AltaVista search engine, the first serious attempt to index the Web,

Microsoft releases Windows 95, the long-awaited upgrade to its popular Windows program. The first version of the company's Web browser. Internet Explorer, is released; based on code licensed from Spyglass, it is sold as part of an add-on package for Windows 95.

NSFNET announces that it will no longer provide direct access to its backbone, farming out responsibility for managing access to private companies. Charging for domain names begins, with each costing $50 per year.

Compuserve removes access to 200 pornographic newsgroups after pressure from Bavarian government officials, attracting the ire of free-speech campaigners and anti-censorship activists.

1996

The browser wars begin in earnest as both Microsoft and Netscape each launch the third version of their browsers.

Despite widespread opposition the controversial US Communications Decency Act (CDA.), designed to control the distribution of indecent material over the Internet, becomes law in the United States.

Internet telephony, already years old, comes to the attention of American telecommunications companies. America's Carriers Telecommunication Association (ACTA) files a petition to the Federal Communications Commission (FCC) seeking to ban IE telephony products, arguing that they should be subject to regulation. The FCC disagrees.

1997

NASA's home page generates 46m hits in one day as people log in to watch the broadcast from the Pathfinder spacecraft on Mars.

.com and .net addresses disappear for several hours as human error at Network Solutions causes the DNS table for .com and .net domains to become corrupted, making millions of systems unreachable.

The DES private key encryption system is broken by a collaborative effort between thousands of Internet users, after testing 18 quadrillion possible key combinations. The challenge, set by RSA Data Security, was to decrypt a message which was eventually found to read "Strong cryptography makes the world a safer place".

The Communications Decency Act is overturned by the US Supreme Court, which pronounces it unconstitutional.

Netscape launches version 4 of its browser just ahead of Microsoft. The US Justice Department files its first complaint against Microsoft, on grounds of breaching anti-trust regulations with its browser distribution.

1998

Netscape announces that it will give away not only its browser but the browser's source code as well, an unprecedented move by a software company. A separate division, Mozilla.org, is set up to create products based on the open source element of the business.

Network Solutions registers its 2-millionth domain.

The Microsoft anti-trust trial begins in October. Originally predicted to last eight weeks, the proceedings continue into 1999 as the scope of the trial expands to *cover* Microsoft's broader exclusionary practices.

AOL and Netscape announce their intention to merge in a $4.2 billion deal, a move seen as a betrayal of Netscape's ideals by Web purists. Many Netscape employees resign.

The first portable MP3 players arrive, enabling people to play back pirated digital music. The Secure Digital Music Initiative, designed to prevent this kind of music piracy, is announced by a consortium of music and technology companies.

Portals become big business on the Web. Major search engines and ISPs re-engineer their sites to add customisation, chat and auction features.

1999

Day traders operating from home PCS seize opportunities to capitalise on the boom in Internet and other stocks. Charles Schwab, an American stockbroker, specialising in electronic trading, sees its market capitalisation rise to $25.5 billion at the end of the financial year, valuing it more highly than many old-style brokers such as Merrill Lynch.

The Melissa virus, carried in Microsoft Word documents, attacks e-mail networks all over the world, replicating itself in enormous numbers and swamping mail servers.

AOL and Microsoft come to blows over chat software, as AOL tries to prevent users of Microsoft's product accessing its huge user base. Microsoft pushes for open standards in the chat market.

Microsoft's Web-based e-mail service, Hotmail, is cracked, leaving its 40 million accounts open to access without the need of a password.

In November, Judge Thomas Penfield Jackson rules that Microsoft harmed consumer interests and distorted competition in Internet markets, fuelling speculation about the future of the company and its strategy.

The number of Internet users passes 200 million.

2000

AOL announces a $150 billion takeover of entertainment giant Time Warner, creating the world's biggest media company and gaining access to over 100m subscribers. The Indium global satellite communications network goes into liquidation after its failure to turn a $5 billion investment into a viable business. Plans are made to pullthe company's 66 satellites out of orbit.

Some of the world's biggest websites, including Yahoo, Amazon and eBay, suffer denial-of-service attacks by malicious hackers, forcing them offline for several hours and renewing concerns about the security of Internet businesses.

The UK's Queen Elizabeth becomes the first royal dot-com millionaire following an investment in Getmapping.com, a site reproducing the Domesday Book with digital aerial photographs.

AT&T's wireless communications division raises $10.6 billion on the first day of public trading of its shares, setting a record for the biggest IPO in American history. The company's valuation hits $70 billion at the end of the day's trading.

Judge Jackson rules that Microsoft broke American antitrust laws, using "technological shackles" to prevent rivals from competing with its Internet Explorer browser. Microsoft shares plummet in value, causing a new wave of volatility in the valuation of high-tech stocks. Cisco's market capitalisation creeps ahead of Microsoft's, making it the world's most valuable company.

Metallica, a rock band, forces the Napster music distribution network to remove 300,000 users, which it says pirated its music using the MP3 format. An American federal judge rules that MP3.com broke copyright law by collating 45,000 commercial CDs into its database, prompting the site to shut down its popular MyMP3 web-based distribution service.

Despite the warnings following 1999's Melissa virus, the I Love You virus causes havoc on computers around the world, flooding e-mail networks and deleting users' music and graphics files. Microsoft is widely criticised for security holes in its Outlook e-mail program, said to be responsible for allowing the virus to propagate and destroy information. As interest in wireless communications technology grows, the British government auctions off third-generation wide-spectrum bandwidth licences to mobile operators, raising £22.5 billion in the process. Germany announces plans to follow suit.

Boo.com, one of Europe's highest-profile online retailers, goes into liquidation after its widely criticised marketing strategy and complex design fail to create a profitable market for its sportswear and fashion goods. Valuations of European e-commerce companies fall rapidly as confidence among high-tech investors evaporates.

The total number of web pages reaches 1 billion.

ANNEXURE - II

BSNL LAUNCHES NETONE (INTERNET @10 PAISA PER MINUTE)

"NETONE" is Account Less CLI-Based Internet Service which will enable all Lucknow BSNL Landline Customers to Access internet and Pay as per use@ 10 paise per minute plus normal local pulse rate.

First time user needs to connect to registration site http://netonelkw.bsnl.co.in by dialing 172222. with Username ("netone") and password ("netone").

• After registration connect by dialing I72222,with your phone no. as username and password as filled during registration.

General Information

Account Less Internet Access is a new method of accessing the Internet. The solution provides the support for automatic authentication to any PSTN access on the basis of CLI.The authentication will be done at Radius and it will generate the CDR of the access and based on that user will be billed.

NETONE

- No Form Filling, Hassle Free.
- USE FIRST. PAY LATER
- No pre commitment of minimum hours of usage
- No need to purchase Internet Account
- There is no chance of Account being misused
- Free Online Registration
- Get your full usage report from the feature My Account
- Get the Internet bill along with your Telephone Bill.

ANNEXURE-III

A BRIEF HISTORY OF THE NET

From a Four-node Network to Many Millions

Let there be light, said the Lord. And then in six days he created the Universe. On the seventh day he rested. It has not been this easy for the creators of the Internet. The Internet was not created in six days, nor have its creators been able to rest on the seventh, satisfied at a job well done.

It has been a long haul indeed. The Net has evolved slowly to what it is today, and even as you read this, that evolution continues, in many directions, simultaneously. Some of them will the out. Some will sustain, without anybody really knowing about how or why they came about. And some, like the Web browser, will totally revolutionise your lives.

Let's take a walk down the memory lane, looking at some of the revolutionary changes that have molded the Internet into what it is today.

How old is the Net? Two years? Four? What about 37? That's how old the Net is. Surprised? But, before that....

Before the beginning....

1961: Packet switching is devised. The earliest models of networking used circuit switching. This required an unbroken connection between the communicating hosts. Leonard Kleinrock at MIT came up with packet switching which was not dependent on a single unbroken line of communication. Circuit switching was not flexible and the connections had to be maintained once made. But packets could, in case of a broken connection, route themselves through other available routes. Packet switching is at the core of the Net as it exists today.

1962: Galactic network—the Internet's first Idea document by JCR Licklider. This can be found at http://memex.org/ licklider.pdf (there are even a few neat diagrams). He predicts that it will one day become the chief medium of communication.

1968: The US department of defense gets Interested.A RAND Corporation study shows the "no single outage point" facet of packet switching. That is, with packet switching you are not limited by the existence or otherwise of a specific network route for communication. The US DoD gets interested and calls for contracts to build the IMP (interface message processor) for such a network. BBN Bolt Beranek and Newman get the contract to build the IMP The RAND study is available at www. rand.org/publications/RM/RM3420/

Also, the NWG (networking group) is formed. The NWG went on to develop protocols for the infant Net.

1969: ARPANET, the first usable packet switched network. *That is part of the Internet folklore.* However, there was an earlier attempt at packet-switched networks, the NPL network in Middlesex, England (1967). ARPANET had three universities—University of California, Santa Barbara, University of California, LA (UCLA), the University of Utah—and the Stanford Research Institute (SRI), as its nodes. Bolt Beranek, and Newman Inc built it, and the first message was sent from UCLA to SRI.

1970: The first of many protocols for the Internet, NCP (network communication protocol), is released by the NWG. The NCP over the years became increasingly unfeasible as more machines joined the "Net".

1972: E-mall, the first "killer app" for the Net Is born. Applications like this will increasingly drive the Web's growth. The Net is still limited to scientists and academicians within computer sciences faculties. The open networking model is also proposed in this year to get over the problem of differences between the protocols developed by different agencies.

1973: First International connections to the ARPANET from Norway and UK. Other sidelights include the arrival of FTP and the Ethernet. More and more small networks will make use of this to become a profusion of small networks within offices and local areas. This is also driven by a deliberate policy to keep these networks off ARPANET'S backbone.

1974: First part of TCP/IP—TCP arrives. Later they would find that TCP needed to be split into two, TCP and IP, for error control and efficiency at the packet level.

1978: TCP splits Into TCP and IP.

1979: ICCB, the Internet Configuration Control Board, is formed. These boards become increasingly necessary as variants of technology emerge, and coordinating between them requires continuous effort.

1983: NCP makes way for TCP/IP. The Internet is formally ushered in on January 1,1983. NSFNET is the first network to start off in life as a pure TCP/IP network. The internet becomes the Internet—with the capital I.

MILNET splits off from ARPANET

IAB, the Internet Activities Board, formed. It later on becomes the Internet Architecture Board.

1984: Domain Name System is started to get over the problem of remembering routes and network numbers.

1988: The Internet faces its first major security incident with the **Internet worm**. It made one tenth of the Net go down in its wake. The worm attacked the distributed nature of the Net itself. For more information see www.eos.ncsu. edu/eos/info/ computer_ethics/dengler/ wvt/internet_worm/index.html.

1989: Two more boards formed under the IAB: the **IETF** and **IRTF**. The IRTF is to be the Web's premier research agency, and the IETF is to take care of coordinating the architecture of the Internet.

1990: ARPANET dies happy. Networks proliferate and ARPANET feels not necessary for it to exist and provide services. **Archie**, an easier way to find files on the Net arrives. In fact, it seems like easier ways of using the Net are going to be the rage.

1991: Commercialisation of the Internet arrives and the commercial use of the Net is no longer restricted. CX(com-mercial Internet exchange) is formed. **The age of the general user arrives.** WWW is released at CERN, and MOSAIC, a graphical browser for the WWW, is also released. I can use the Net now! **Gopher**, another easy way of finding information on the Net, is also released

1992: The Internet society is launched in 1992, and the IAB comes under ISOC.

1995: Commercialisation becomes visible. Internet addresses are no longer free. In fact, all the time there's the whisper that one could make money on the Net. More and more people get thinking about e-commerce. Sites multiply. And security becomes a big problem. Going online is the operative word, and even the Vatican goes online. So do governments, and anybody and everybody.

1999: Internet 2 is here. A network that operates at a hundred to a thousand times the speed of the Internet, and enables live video and 3D. Currently restricted to US universities, its operation reminds one of the early days of the ARPANET, restricted to academicia. Is history repeating itself?

SEARCH THE NET

Make Your Search Effective by Using the Right Keywords in Search Engines

Some search engines are designed for specialised searches. These search for a particular topic only. For instance, "dejanews.com" is a search , engine, which searches exclusively for newsgroups. "devSearch.com" and "NetSearcher.com" are search engines particularly for Web developers and Internet professionals. "Filez.com" is for searching files on FTP sites and "mwsearch.com" al-lows you to search within a number of medical sites. "Mp3.com" lets you find mp3 files and "arribavista.com" lets you search for images.

Looking for a good book, a new job, an old friend or someone to chat with over the Internet? Well, these searches involve using a search engine. Many of you must be using these quite often and at times must have ended up wasting precious time, following useless URLs which didn't lead you to the right place.

To avoid this, you've to know what you're looking for and how to get it.Do you want to gather all possible data on a broad subject say, "fine arts in Asia" or are you looking for a specific topic like the "award winning paintings of Asia"?

If you are looking for a broad subject, the best place to look for is a search engine, which is in the form of a Web directory like "yahoo.com" or "hindustan.net" (for Indian Websites). And for something more specific, go to one of the specialised search engines.

How Do Search Engines Work?

Finding relevant data not only depends on search engines but also on the type of keywords you search for. To do an effective search, knowing about how search engines operate helps.

Most of the search engines share some common features. One of the most common feature, is that all of them follow a basic approach of relevance ranking. This means that the engine will present the results so that the first site on the list is deemed the most relevant, and the relevance decreases as you go down the list. This can be helpful, but remember you can only tell what is relevant by looking at it.

The other consequence of relevance ranking is that there may be nothing at all on the Web which answers your query, but the search engine may still find a large number of results. This is because the search engines will not insist that all your keywords are present in the resulting Websites. If even a single word occurs in a Website, that site will be brought back to you as a result. The first few results will hopefully contain all your keywords, but that may not be the case always. If no sites contain all your words, then the best available will be presented to you as the most relevant site.

Ways to an Effective Search

There are many ways to narrow down your search.

Boolean logic is one of the most common and effective way and involves using AND, OR, NOT, and ( ) parentheses for grouping. For example, "computers AND pc NOT mac" will only list links containing pc computers and exclude links regarding macs.

You can also use the "+" sign in your statements. For example, "Indian+cinema" will give you more focused results than "Indian cinema". Similarly, you can use the "-" sign to exclude certain words.

You can also give your statement enclosed in quotes if you want it to find the pages where the words appear next to each other like in "job vacancies".

Multiple words give more refined results than using a single word. Also, use similar words when you search— the more synonyms you get the more chances of getting results. For example, if you want to search for things to buy say, "buy purchase order shop" in the search text box instead of using only one of these words.

Also, lowercase words will match any case. For example, typing next will return documents containing the words next, Next, and Next.

Use the pipe (I) key to refine your search results in a one-step search. For example, using "delhi restaurants" tells the search engine that you are searching within the broad category of Delhi for the specific subject of restaurants.

If you are trying to look at multiple forms of a word (like woman and women), you can indicate it with a symbol, for example, wom*n. Search engines have different symbols for truncation. The "help" link on the search engine will tell you the symbols to use in truncation when you are constructing your search.

Most of the search engines offer their "advance search" where you have all these options and more listed in pulldown menus. But all search engines don't offer similar options.

www.yahoo.com

Yahoo! is an extremely popular search engine, which is in the form of a Web directory and looks for keyword matches in its titles and categories. There are options to limit your search-within Yahoo! categories or to search other Websites too. You can also search through the Usenet for relative newsgroups. Yahoo search supports exact phrase matching using quotation marks, wildcard matching, boolean logic, plus and minus signs and field search. Giving "t:indian cinema" will restrict the search to document titles only whereas "u:intel" will restrict the search to URLs. You can restrict your search to documents that are more recent than a certain date. You can also adjust the number of search results displayed on all the result pages following the summary page. Both these features can be accessed from the "search options page" in the advanced search.

www.excite.com

Excite also has a number of categories, though not as many as Yahoo. It uses both full text and abstracts of Web pages when conducting a search, using Intelligent Concept Extraction (ICE) to find relationships that exist between words and ideas. So enter more than one word to get better results. It also supports exact phrase matching, plus and minus sign and boolean search. For your search, you can choose among the World Wide Web, Selected Websites, Current News, Excite Germany, Excite France, Excite UK, Excite Sweden, and Usenet Newsgroups. You can also control the number of results to be returned and the type of content you want to search against.

www.infoseek.com

Infoseek's database houses the complete text of every home page it catalogs. Info-seek looks at the full text of each page before providing results to the seeker. Infoseek allows boolean search, field searches, exact phrase matching, plus and minus sign and pipes. Apart from searching within Infoseek's select sites, you can also search through WWW, Usenet, timely news, company directory, e-mail addresses and World Wide Web FAQs. "Advance search" includes interesting features like location search, limiting the number of search results and options for phrase matching in the document.

www.lycos.com

Lycos, one of the oldest search engines on the Web, has one of the largest databases. Lycos search is based partly on the popularity of a given site, that is, how many other links point to that site. Search results will list the most popular sites first. Moreover, Lycos database doesn't house the full text of every Web page, it works from abstracts of pages, that is, headers, titles, links and keywords in the first paragraph. It also supports exact phrase matching, plus and minus signs and boolean search. The advance search allows you to search in various languages, match URLs, titles, and so on.

Most of the search engines have the option to add your Web page or a site to a search engine, but if they don't, you can do so through a site called "submit.com", which takes URLs and adds them to most of the search engines. You both have a free service and a paid service in this site. The free service adds to most of the above mentioned search engines.

Field searches allow you to create specific searches. A field search can be done with commands like file, link, site, uri, title, alt, etc, in lowercase, followed by a colon and then the search term without a space. For example "link: pcquest.com", will list the Web pages that link to pcquest.com, "file:.vbrun" will find you files with this extensions.

www.altavista.com

AltaVista is another popular search-engine and its popularity stems from its reputation of speed. Also, it has some innovative search features, such as, you can ask a question and it'll search for an answer. Searches like, "Where can I find books on Internet?" will find you answers not only within AltaVista database, but also give you numerous links to other sites.

Infoseek and AltaVista offer search services—"Express" and "Discovery" respectively— for faster and easier search. These software are available on this month's PCQ CD. They run within your browser and can search various search engines at a time for information, files, images, and so on.

Apart from a list of usual search categories, AltaVista also offers AltaVista Family Filter, AltaVista Photo Finder, AltaVista Finance and many more features. The AV Family Finder reduces the chance that you'll view objectionable material when searching the Internet. The AV Photo Finder helps you find millions of colorful and imaginative pictures from the World Wide Web.

AltaVista supports exact phrase matching, plus and minus sign and also some features which narrow down your search like "anchor:text" which will find pages that contain the specified word or phrase in the text of a hyperlink. Say, if you enter anchor: "Click here to visit Alta Vista", it'll find pages with "Click here to visit AltaVista" as a link. Use "domain:org" to find pages from .org domain. In its boolean search, it has a new option, near or -'. This finds documents containing both specified words or phrases within 10 words of each other. AltaVista also has a "range of dates" option for limiting search results.

If you Want to search for friends or people around the world, you can try many especially designed search engines. Bigfoot.com, Four11.com (Yahoo! People Search), WhoWhere.com, Infospace.com are a few examples. All of these are listed in the "Find" option of your "Start" menu in Win 9x and you can use them to find someone through the "People" option or you can go directly to their sites and search from there. Some of them even al-low you to enter telephone numbers and addresses to search.

When you see the result list displayed, click on the "Refine" button. You'll see the List View of the Refine screen. Click the "Graph View" button and a map of expandable topics appears. The percentages given at the right of each word in a topic indicates the probable relevance of that word to your search. The higher the number, the more relevant a word for your search.

www.hotbot.com

HotBot is another very efficient search engine. The home page offers you properly divided categories and sub-categories. Also you can specify the search options right in the beginning to narrow your search like matching of words, limiting results by specifying their lime, number, language, and so on. It also offers a large number of areas where the search can be done like within Usenet, e-mail addresses, classifieds and many more. It supports, boolean search, wild cards, case-sensitive search and field searches.

www.askjeeves.com

This search engine offers the easiest way to search. It does an "English search", that is you just have to ask a question in plain English and click on its "ask" button. Not only will it list out the answers but will also provide you various links in pull-down menus from other search engines. For example, if you enter, "where can I find a tutorial on Win 95?" and click on the "ask" button, it'll provide you answers by searching its database and also various links in pull-down menus by other common search engines.

More and more search engines are now incorporating Web directories and are characterising themselves as "portals" or "hubs". They have various categories that are further divided into sub-categories. All you have to do is to click on any and search within them. As a result, searching is becoming a relatively easier process than before. They not only offer you all the categories to search in, they offer you ways to locate your friends from all over the world, chat with different people on various topics, Find relating Websites and so on.

Some more search engines

www.dogpile.com
www.electricmonk.com
www.google.com
www.msn.com
www.opentext.com
www.galaxy.com

Some Indian search engines

www.khoj.com
www.123india.com
www.cyberindian.com
www.SAIR.com

www.Indiaexpress.com
www.Indiatime.com
www.hindustan.net
www.indiaconnect.com

All of the engines also provide help features for users and make it easy for a novice to search. So the most important factor that goes into choosing a search engine is personal preference and your needs. For instance, if you're not sure about a particular topic you would find it easier through a Web directory like Yahoo!, or if you want an easy way to search you would like to use Askjeeves. If you want to search data regarding India you'll find it faster with the Indian sites. If you are searching for something more specific you'll find it easier and faster with the specialised search engines.

Sara Hassan

MISS MANNERS ON THE NET

Cyberspace is really a new culture. And it's one where we're still trying to find our feet. The past few years have hurled the world headlong at breakneck speed, into a degree of connectedness and accessibility which is changing the way we do, almost everything. Who's in charge?, What are the rules? No one—and we have to make the rules as we go along unless we want to interact in a chaotic, anarchic, unpredictable dimension for the next few foreseeable years.

Netizens have been putting together the rules of appropriate behavior on the Internet for some time now. They fondly call it Netiquette. Try sending a seasoned Net user some e-mail typed in ALL CAPS. The response will be immediate—a sharp online rap on the knuckles informing you that All Caps amounts to shouting in the online world. And you thought it would make things more readable. Such rules already run into pages and pages (found online with simple searches) and aren't restricted to how e-mail is used but extend to the way Websites are made, messages are posted to newsgroups, chain mail and more. These rules cannot be ignored. Especially not by businesses that plan to work online, using e-mail and Websites. Here are some of the most important for working, e-mailing people.

You've got mall: Using e-mail and the Internet is going to be critical to the very survival of businesses around the world. The sooner you get to grips with online communication the better. Used effectively, e-mail can cut down on time and costs—so meet your colleagues halfway by staying in touch. If you're a techno-phobe, get over it. The fact that you get mail electronically is no excuse for ignoring it. Reading work e-mail is a professional responsibility just like answering your phone at the office. If someone you're e-mailing doesn't respond, use the return receipt feature on your mail system. If you send important mail and it's not read in a reasonable amount of time, follow up with a phone call. If you still get nowhere, send another e-mail note and copy to your own boss (if you just want to keep yourself out of trouble) or the other person's boss (if you want to get the other person in trouble). Warning: Copy a manager only when it's really important that your information gets through. It's a technique guaranteed to make you unpopular with the person.

Mail to the world: You may well think sending mass mail is a good business tactic. In reality, it's one of the rudest things you can do online. And it's called Spam. Consider what you're doing—sending mail to someone you're not sure wants it, giving the person no choice at all. If you think your one little message won't make a difference and it can always be deleted, think again. Add up all similar messages and that's quite a lot of deleting to do each day. Sending unsolicited mail is also a violation of privacy. A better business strategy is to make sure those who are looking for you find you.

Who are you anyway? An anonymous sender, a suppressed list of other recipients, no subject. That's a quick way to ensure your mail and whatever proposal or offer that goes with it, is not taken seriously, if at all. Depersonalised and inconsiderate, such mail only says: I don't care who you are and you don't need to know who I am, you have to go through my entire message to figure out why I'm sending this to you—but pay me good money.

With a lot of attachment: Consider this—you have a few minutes to download your mail before you rush off for a meeting; you're waiting for an important file to come through; you're not able to think straight from the phone calls coming in. But just when you're in a steaming hurry, your mail is taking forever to download. Bad connection? Or bad sender? Respect others' bandwidth as you would have them respect yours. Next time you send out an attachment with your mail, stop to double check if: a) the recipient really wants it. b) you can lighten the load—for instance, reduce a fat BMP to a JPG or GIF. Never send an unexplained attachment. A message that says "Dear friend, please see attachment" with no further ado, should be hurled straight into infinity. It could be a virus. Politely explain what the attachment contains and why you're sending it. When sending attachments to colleagues, restrict this to those who are not on the same network. For coworkers on the same network, send a filename and path instead.

Fifty e-mail addresses! Almost every e-mail program lets you send e-mail via blind carbon copy. This is a very good tool if you are going to send e-mail to multiple individuals. The problem comes when you e-mail something to a whole bunch of people am. their addresses appear in the headers of the e-mail. Not only is it annoying to have to go through address after address it also fails to protect people's privacy.

And I quote... When responding to other users, it's very useful to quote some of what they've said in order to provide context for your response. However, it's not at all useful to quote their *entire* message unless you are responding to the whole thing. Furthermore, it's completely unnecessary to quote someone's signature unless you're responding directly to it. It's also really not at all fun to see an entire 100-line message quoted only to see "I agree" at the end of the message.

Look before you...oops! The Internet abounds with horror stories of e-mail disasters (try cnet.com). All because people were a little bit too hasty with the reply, reply to all, or forward buttons. Nasty wisecracks about a colleague have gone out to company-wide addresses, extra-marital but in-house affairs have been laid bare before an unsuspecting world and people have been fired forthwith because of their legendary clicking speed with the mouse. Interestingly, everyone thinks it's something that can only happen to someone else.

One for you, and one for you, and one for you: A colleague says something that totally gets your goat. What's the best way to get back? Embarrass him nice and good by copying his message and your clever answer to the rest of the company. Easy enough to do—and very difficult to undo. In one instant, you'll have earned yourself enough mistrust to last you a few months, inhibiting further interaction. Don't Waste your colleagues' time by copying them notes that don't affect them. On the other hand, do keep them informed about projects they're working on. Don't assume that they already know what's happening.

What's this about? Many people just don't bother with putting anything in the subject line of their e-mail. Or they'll put in something generic and vague because it just seems too much effort to think of a subject. Put in intelligent subject headers and not something like "message from admin" which is obvious enough to begin with. Smart headers will help colleagues identify messages quickly later when they need to act upon them. It's specially important to put in meaningful headers if you're exchanging a lot of mail on one subject. Rather than having to go through fifteen messages that say "3rd quarter results" your colleagues should be able to identify what is it that you're saying about those 3rd quarter results. Stick to the point and avoid irrelevant history and material in your work related mail.

Other rules:

- Use a short, polite auto-response if you're away and will not be able to check your mail for a certain time.

- Think before you give out someone else's e-mail address.
- Respect other people's time—send mail only when it needs to be sent.
- Don't come free with the e-mail. A peculiar trend in offices is to send someone mail and then to bound into their offices to inform you've just sent them mail. Or call them up, wasting some good phone time. If you think the message you're sending looks so unimportant that no one will read it, send a note explaining why it's important. If it's not important, don't send it.
- Try not to send a string of related messages in a row because you forgot an important point (for example, the time or date of a meeting), or re-send the same document several times because you corrected an error. But remember that it's easier on your readers (as well as making you look better) if you get it right the first time.
- If your mail is not being stored locally on your hard disk, make sure you delete it periodically.
- If you're sending mail that shows your company name, be sure to remember you're representing your company. Don't send anything that you feel opposes company opinions and policy.
- Avoid company related gossip on newsgroups and mailing lists. This can be an area of potential and large scale disaster.

Mala Bhargava
<malab@cmil.com>

LOG ON TO IRC

Get Chatting with a TCP/IP or Shell Account

Some useful IRC commands

Command	*Purpose*
/list	Lists channels.
/join <#channelname>	To join the channel "channelname".
/ping < nickname >	Finds the time taken for a message to get to that nick.
/me < message >	Substitutes your nickname before the message.
/nick <newnick>	Changes your <nick to <newnick>.
/msg <nickname>	Chat privately with "nickname".
/join < new channel name>	Create your own chat room. The "new channel name" is unique, and you have your own channel and are its channel operator.

For the complete list look up the help section of your chat client.

Using a TCP/IP Connection

1. Install a chat client such as Pirch, Mirc, etc, and connect to the Internet.
2. Register a nickname for yourself, which will be your identity on the chat service you log onto. Some chat sites don't have this facility, so you don't have to worry about it there. Others like TalkCity (www.talkcity.com) offer free nickname registration. Upon registration you get a password and some of them even offer free Web space.
3. Fire up your chat client, and choose the chat server to which you have registered yourself. Enter your nickname and password and hit the "connect" button. The chat site verifies your identity and togs you" in.
4. Use the /list command with parameters like -min 25 or -max 25 to list only channels with less than 25 or more than 25 users.
5. Use /join <#channelname> to join a channel that looks interesting to you. In case you are using a graphical chat client you can double click on a channel name to join it.
6. Once you have joined a channel you can see the list of all the people in the channel. Whatever you type will be visible to all users logged in. Go on say "Hi" to people, introduce yourself and start chatting! You can also chat privately by typing /msg < nickname > before your message. In graphical chat clients just double click on the nickname you need to chat privately with.

Using a Shell Account

In case you use a shell account, things are a bit different. Most ISPs provide a default chat server that you can connect to, for example, VSNL's default is Talkcity.

To chat from a shell account do the following:

1. Go to the Unix shell prompt.
2. Type: ire <nickname> <servername: port> :server-password.

   Here < nickname > is the nickname that you have registered at the Website of that chat service and NOT your VSNL login name. Port number by default is 6667.
3. Once you're logged in, just type the message in your chat client and press "enter". Public messages are visible to everyone on the channel.
4. To send private messages, type "/ msg < nickname >" in front of your message. If you don't want to repeatedly type /msg nickname, you can also type "/query <nickname>" which will send all your subsequent

messages to the specified nick. Issue a /query without any parameters to end a private chat session.

There is one disadvantage of using IRC on a shell account. Any user on IRC can do a /whois of your nickname and find out your ISP login name and even your IP address. To prevent this type in the following commands at the Unix shell prompt:

1. IRCNAME = "It's a secret" [Enter]
2. Export IRCNAME [Enter]

After doing this, log on as explained above. Now when someone does a / whois of your nickname, he/she will see "It's a secret" instead of your login name.

Devi Prasad Misra

USING IRC

Make Friends and Influence People Across the Globe with Chat and Messaging Services

When Jarkko Oikarinen set out to make a replacement for the Unix "talk" program in 1988, he had no inkling thai this program which he began writing as a hobby would become so popular and widely used today. Nor did he ever think that his creation would be used as a crucial means of communication in crunch situations such as the Persian Gulf War of 1991 and the Soviet coup of 1993. His creation today is popularly referred to as IRC (Internet relay chat).

IRC is a service on the Internet that lets people converse across the globe. People come together on various IRC channels or virtual places to discuss topics of common interest, either in groups or on an one-to-one basis. Some channels have a topic of discussion, while others are simply dedicated to small talk or idle chat.

IRC conversation is done by typing messages and transmitting it over the Internet to a chat server. The server in turn passes the messages to all the users logged into it. In order to chat you need a client program to log into the chat server. Mire, Pirch, and Comic Chat are some popular chat clients for Windows.

There are a host of chat servers that your chat client can connect to. Among them TalkCity, Efnet, DALNet and Undernet are the more popular ones. These servers have lots of channels where people with common interests join together and talk.

Every channel has a chanop, short for channel operator. A chanop is identified by an @ symbol that precedes his nickname. These chanops moderate and manage a certain channel. They can ban offensive users, decide upon discussion topics on a channel and schedule events such as celebrity chats or group discussions.

Direct Chat

A smarter way to chat is DCC (direct client chat). Using this, two parties can communicate directly with each other rather than going through the IRC network. DCC allows you to send and receive files too. It has several advantages and disadvantages. Because the DCC connection bypasses the IRC servers and the IRC network as a whole, they are generally considered more secure. You also are not limited by the data transfer rate of the IRC network. You connect at the speed of the other parties' network setup and the quality of the network connection. The disadvantages are that you can't perform special IRC commands such as using the/ me command within a DCC communication.

IRC Ethics

There are some unwritten codes and ethics on IRC that must be followed at all times, or you might just end up irritating people as well as getting yourself banned from a channel. This code of ethics doesn't only apply to IRC, but any data that you transmit over the Net, be it via e-mail, chat, or some other messaging service.

Using all capitals in a sentence is the equivalent of shouting, so use all caps only if you want to convey something that is very important or urgent. You may use accepted standard short forms such as ROTFL (roll over the floor laughing) to keep your message short and crisp. As a general rule, be polite and friendly to everyone and never say anything that you would say to anyone in person. Never keep repealing a sentence or message (known in IRC parlance as "scrolling"). Most IRC servers provide a detailed code of conduct and ethics on their Websites.

Instant Messaging: A Smarter Alternative to Chat

IRC is great for chatting with friends and keeping in touch with people who have common interests; but outside of these fairly constrained boundaries it's limited in its practical use. When you log off, you are effectively cut off from the whole IRC community. You can't find out when a friend comes back online nor can anyone else send you messages until the next time you log on.

The IRC Lingo

IRC is a wonderful way to communicate ideas, thoughts and viewpoints. But often, chatting by typing down messages can be extremely tedious and dull. Especially when messages are long. Due to these reasons, smiley faces or emoticons are used. These keep your messages short and crisp. The official definition of an emoticon according to the "New Hacker's Dictionary" is: An ASCII glyph used to indicate an emotional state in e-mail or news. Some smileys and short forms for popular phrases are as follows:

IMHO	In My Humble Opinion	ppl	People
ROTFL	Roll Over The Floor Laughing	pls	Please
ASAP	As Soon As Possible	tnx	Thanks
F2F	Face To Face (as to meet in person)	ic	I see
RTFM	Read The F*@#ing Manual	:-)	Smile
LOL	Laugh Out Loud	:-D	Laughing
AFK	Away From the Keyboard	:-]	Smirk
BRB	Be Right Back	:-(	Frown
J/K	Just Kidding	;-)	Wink
BTW	By The Way	:-X	Close-mouthed
FYI	For Your Information	8-)	Wide-eyed
a/s/l	Age/Sex/Location	:-O	Open-mouthed

A more suitable alternative, therefore, would be something that maintains a virtual presence even when your connection is not active. It could also take care of any messages that other users want to send when you are not logged on; simultaneously offering a powerful search engine that would enable you to contact users sharing a common interest. This is what instant messaging offers.

There are a number of options available such as 1CQ (I seek you), Yahoo! Pager and AOL's Instant Messenger. These programs can be configured to load automatically at system startup and when you log onto the Internet, inform the paging service that you are online. You can enter the list of friends whom you wish to chat with (of course, they must also be using the same service). Now when your friends log on, you can be alerted and vice versa. This whole process works in the background so you can surf the Net or up/download your mail at the same time.

Certain paging services offer lots of other features too. ICQ, for instance, lets you send messages and files to other users. You can play certain games online with them as well. Yahoo! Pager on the other hand can keep a track of your stock portfolio and alert you when your stocks cross certain limits.

Devi Prasad Misra

ONLINE GAMING

Multiplayer Gaming Lets You Play Against Your Friends Over a Local network or the Internet

Though games have become more life-like with stunning visuals and sound effects, they still lack the sense of live challenge. The enemies though more powerful are less than intelligent. In fact, the monsters in certain early versions of DOOM didn't attack you till you fired at them. So you could safely walk past them and they wouldn't even know you were there.

To quench this thirst for challenge, multiplayer games were created. The same stages to clear, but instead of dumb computer opponents, you've to beat other humans, like or better than you. What could be more challenging and satisfying than disemboweling a human opponent (in the game of course)! Multiplayer games also introduced the concept of cooperative effort, where you could pool in your skills and fight against common computer or human opponents as a team. And no, multiplayer games are not limited to role-playing games. One can choose any genre of games—simulations, shoot 'em ups or board games.

Most Multiplayer games run on any network—a LAN or the Internet, on TCP/IP or IPX. They can also be played over a dial-up link, provided you get a good connect (at least 28.8 k). On your LAN, one of the users needs to create a virtual server first, to which others may dial up and connect. Most shareware games have their multiplayer options turned off. So you'll need to get the full version of the game. You can also make some games multiplayer by downloading patches from the Internet.

Configuring most games for online play is easy, as the basic options remain the same. First get the game running. Now connect to the Internet using your modem. Choose "multiplayer" from the opening menu. Then choose "favorite servers". You'll be presented with a series of servers that you may choose to connect to. Out of these, Mplayer.com is one of the most popular, meaning lots of people to play against. Most of the new games make this very simple, but for older games you may need to tweak around with your modem settings. If you really want to have fun, then join in after a lot of practice, maybe over a LAN with a few opponents. Beginners can get slaughtered. You can also dial a friend's phone number using your modem and have a head-to-head battle.

When configuring for game-play over a LAN, choose the IP address of the game server to connect to. Next choose the game mode (co-operative or death match), and finally whether you want to join in a game or start a new one. Some of the new-generation games' make connecting to or starting a network game even easier. Just select multiplayer game option, and the software browses the LAN to find all running servers and joins a server of your choice.

While starting a server (to which all other players will connect) a few choices need to be made. These vary from game to game and relate to the rules and conditions of play, such as presence of computer enemies, time limits, etc. While playing a game on a LAN, it's a good idea to have a dedicated server because that improves performance and ensures a level playing field to all the players.

Keep a few important things in mind while playing a multiplayer game. Most games can be played across a network only if all players have the same version of the game. Make sure that you've a good connection, otherwise be ready to get slaughtered. In case the same familiar levels and situations become too boring and monotonous, you may download (from the numerous official and unofficial gaming sites) and install "maps". This adds additional levels and functionality to games, and makes them even more interesting. Read your game manuals for information regarding installation of maps.

A final word of caution: multiplayer games can be highly addictive and engrossing. You can run, but you, can't hide!

Devi Prasad Misra

A NAME FOR MY WEBSITE

The Internet Naming Conventions Help People Find You on the Net

Computers on the Internet identify each other by their IP addresses like 209.194.84.59. But remembering numbers is a gift only few of us possess. The way around has been names like pcquest.com.

The Internet is divided into a number of registries or top level domains (TLDs). The sidebar lists the currently available top-level domains. Additions to this list have been proposed and have been under active consideration for some time now.

Internet naming conventions call for the type of Website to be identified by the registry—the part after the dot in the name. For example, sites that come under the .com registry are commercial sites or sites belonging to commercial organisations. Similarly, .gov is supposed to indicate government bodies and .org represents non-profit organisations, societies, etc. But unfortunately, that's not always the case. The .com registry has been by far the most popular, and everybody seem to opt for .com by default.

Take for example, Delhipolice.com!

Delhi Police, a business organisation? Or is there more to the name, than just a mistake? It's not just the funny side. The registries are an important pointer to people looking for particular Websites. For example, anyone looking for PC *Quest* Website will automatically look for pcquest.com and not pcquest.mil or pcquest.edu. Now suppose someone is looking for the site of Reserve Bank of India. What are the URLs that you would guess at? reservebank.gov or reserve bank.gov.in are possible options that you would try. And you would not succeed in reaching the Reserve Bank site. Yes. You have to try reservebank.com to get there.

Guess the Website of the finance ministry? And the Indian President? And the Indian Parliament? Yes. They all have Websites. But you won't find them at addresses you can easily guess. The Finance ministry is at (www.nic.in/finmin/), and Rashtrapathi Bhavan is at (http:/ alfa.nic.in/rb) but one has to go through the Parliament's site (http://alfa.nic.in/).

Why? What's wrong with loksabha. gov.in? Or finance.gov.in? Why hide these splendid sites in these strange subdirectories at NIC? Do we have a paucity of names? Or are we ashamed of announcing these to the world?

And, that's not all. Look at the absurdly long site addresses and e-mail addressees that we sport. Almost all e-mail and ISP services in this country give you addresses that are a-half-mile long. me@giasmdl01 .vsnl.net.in! you@satyam. net.in! someone@somecompany. sprintrpg.ems.vsnl.net.in! Give me a break. Why can't we have short e-mail addresses that are easy to remember? VSNL has finally woken up and have started giving shortened vsnl.com addresses. What are the others waiting for?

Are your site and e-mail addresses all right? After all, others are going to use them to find you. If they can't they will take their business somewhere else, as if you never existed.

Krishna Kumar

Top-Level Domains

Domain	Indicates	Example
com	Commercial organisations	pcquest.com
edu	Educational institutions	aiims.edu
mil	(US) military	nic.mil
gov	(US) government	nasa.gov
org	Other organisations	un.org
net	Other networks	usa.net
int	International organisations	tpc.int
in, fr, sk	Country the site is registered in	ernet.in

A MAILING LIST

It's a Great Offline Discussion Forum—and Also an E-mail-Merge Medium that Saves Vandwidth and Precious Internet Hours

Sending all your friends individual e-mail with the same text is a major problem.

You'll soon start wondering where all those 500 hours of your VSNL account have gone. Using the bulk mailing facilities some mail clients give you (or sending a cc to each person) is foolhardy, leaving every person on this list with their e-mail ID in plain view, a bonanza for the spammer who gets hold of such a list. You and everyone else on this kind of a list are likely to have your mailboxes deluged with junk mail advertising everything from unbelievable discounts on software products to magic drugs which beat Viagra hollow.

The best solution is to set up a mailing list. Any message sent to a common e-mail address (say mylist@listprovider. com) is automatically sent to all members of the mailing list "MyList".

There are many kinds of mailing lists.

Announcement lists: These are used to distribute information about a product, a service, an event, or other noteworthy information. In most cases, the organisation that runs the mailing list controls what information is sent out. If you join such a list, you can't post to it, only receive messages posted by the list manager. Keith Dawson's TBTF <www.tbtf.com>, Microsoft's SBNWire <www.microsoft.com/ sbnmember/ default.asp> .and Website Journal <www.websitejournal.com> are excellent examples of such a list.

Open discussion lists: Anyone who is a member of the mailing list can submit information to be distributed to the entire group. Such lists are interactive groups for several like-minded people to share information on topics of common interest.

Moderated forums/discussion groups: These combine the best features of the two types above. In such lists, members of the group can submit information to be distributed to the entire group. However, all messages are first routed through the list manager, who can forward it to the mailing list at his discretion.

List servers

List servers like Lyris <www.lyris. com> can also be used to create auto-responders. These are e-mail "robots" which reply to incoming e-mail with a specific document. For instance, sending info@company.com will send back a reply with a brief thank you note, along with a corporate profile and other essential data about the company.

Even a year ago, setting up and maintaining such a list was next to impossible for the common man, requiring as it did the necessity of delving into the mystic world of list servers. These are difficult to set up and maintain and commercial list providers will generally charge you an arm and a leg.

Some of the most popular mailing list servers include:

- ListServ by Eric Thomas—now produced by Lsoft <www.lsoft.com>
- Listproc from CREN (Corporation for Research and Educational Networking)
- Brent Chapman's Majordomo
- Some other popular list servers are Lyris <www.lyris.com> and MajorDomo (a list server for the Macintosh)

  All this has changed now, thanks to several free Web-based mailing list providers. These now offer several advantages over the old mailing list servers, including:

- A simple Web-based interface for managing the list.
- Ready-made forms for joining the list which, you can put up on your Website.
- List archives (all messages posted on the list) on the Web indexed by name, date, and frequency of posting.
- Easy, automated subscribing and un-subscribing facilities for list members.
- Anti spam filters to ensure that spamming can be minimised and easily blocked.

  ... and many more.

Setting up a free e-mail list is now ridiculously easy. Just point your browser at one of these sites for more details. EGroups—www.egroups.com, List-Bot—www.listbot.com, WebSite Post Office—www.websitepostoffice.com.

All these and other free list providers in return place a discreet ad or two at the bottom of every message posted to the list.

Setting up a Mailing List

To set up a mailing list on ListServ, ListProc, or MajorDomo, just contact the system administrator, who will set up the list for you. Setting up a Web-based list like eGroups or ListBot is a breeze—as easy as filling out a form which asks for your name, your e-mail, and postal addresses. You then specify a name for your list and a password for you to identify yourself as the list owner on later visits. If the list name is mylist, a list <mylist@egroups.com > will be created for you. You then fill in another form, which sets policies for your list—things like:

1. [All/Only You/Members Only] can post to this list
2. [All/Members Only] can read list archives on the Net.

   .....and others

These policies are essential for your running a good list, and the form usually has the default values displayed. These default values are generally the best settings for a well-regulated mail list. Too tight a control on the list (say specifying that all posts have to be routed through you) can be a major problem, especially when the traffic on the list starts becoming something like twenty messages a day. Too loose a hold on your list (setting "all can post to this list") renders your list a haven for spammers, who can then gleefully latch onto your list and flood it with junk mail.

Now, let's get down to brass tacks, Just what do you **really** do to set up a mailing list?

Set a Topic

This can be anything—a club newsletter, a daily set of jokes, etc. One such list is QuizNet (www.angelfire.com/or/ masthana/quiznet.html)—a large list which, reaches Indian quizzers around the world. Remember, the only criterion is that sufficient people must be interested enough to join your list and actively participate in it.

Get Some Members

This is not as easy as it sounds, because most people have a rooted objection to wasting precious Internet time on something they feel doesn't interest them. So, ask your friends if they are interested in joining such a list. Remember, eGroups and other similar providers do offer you the facility of adding a whole lot of e-mail addresses to your list. However, netiquette (net + etiquette, by the way) demands that you first ask a person before you subscribe him to a mailing list and start bombarding him with unsolicited messages.

Plan Some Content

A mailing list will soon the a natural death if the list topic is not something all members are genuinely interested in. Your list will survive if and only if it's participative, with members frequently posting to the list and getting replies or feedback from the others on the list.

Lay Down Some Basic Ground Rules

This is necessary to avoid clogging up each member's inbox (including yours) with a load of junk mail. *(Refer "Miss Manners on the Net" in this issue).*

In conclusion, let me repeat: getting a mailing list of your own is quite easy but demands considerable personal attention from you.

Suresh Ramasubramanian

<savitr@hd2.dot.net.in>

FREE-E-MAIL SERVICES

Chose Your Kind of Mail Account—POP3, Web Mail or Forward

After the phenomenal success of Hotmail—the world's first free e-mail service—a lot of other free e-mail service providers joined the bandwagon with more features, better interface, filtering, address hooks, and so on.

Today, mainly three types of free e-mail services are being offered on the Net: POP mail, Web-based e-mail and mail forwarding. A fourth kind called IMAP service has also started gaining ground in the free e-mail world.

In POP mail, a user can download messages from the mail server using a mail client like Outlook Express. Since all the messages are stored on a user's computer after downloading, a user can refer to these messages at any time without connecting to the Internet, thus saving precious online time and money. A disadvantage of POP mail is that it downloads all messages at one go. So if you're on a slow connection and one of the message has come with a huge attachment, you have no choice but to download the whole message.

In Web-based e-mail services, the mail resides on the mail server and can be accessed using a Web browser. The user has to log onto the site to access his e-mail. Most Web-based free e-mail service providers give added functionality to their users like online spell-checkers, personal address books, etc. The advantage of this is that you don't need a mail client to check your mail, so the hassles of creating a mail account are not there. The disadvantage is that you can check your e-mail as long as you're online.

Some free e-mail service providers act as "mail forwarding" services. They give you an e-mail account, but don't store your messages on their servers. Instead, they only pass the e-mail coming to this account to another account that you specify. Therefore, you must have an e-mail account (POP or Web-based) before you sign up with a mail forwarding service.

Mail forwarding services have the advantage that you don't have to stick to one e-mail account. If you get a new e-mail account, you just have to change the configuration of your mail forwarding account to point to the new account. This way, the mail forwarding account acts as your permanent e-mail account.

A fourth kind of mail service—IMAP—is now being offered by some mail service providers. It's better than POP3 in that it just shows you the header and subject fields of each e-mail message, from where you can choose the messages you want to download.

Free E-mail Services on the Internet

E-mail services	Internet address	Disk Space	Web based	Mail forwarding	POP3	Pickup*	Mail filtering	Auto responders	Address book	Signatures	Attachments	Reminders
123India	www. 123india.com	2.5 MB	√	√	-	√	√	√	√	√	√	-
Ame-Mail**	www.ame-mail.com	5 MB	√	√	-	√	√	√	√	√	√	-
Ape-Mail***	www.ape-mail.com	3 MB	√	√	-	√	√	√	√	√	√	√
BigFoot	www.bigfoot.com	+	-	√	-	√	-	√	√	-	-	√
Email	www.email.com	5 MB	√	√	-	√	√	-	√	√	√	-
EudoraMail	www.eudormail.com	4 MB	√	-	-	√	√	-	√	√	√	-
FasterMail	www.fastermail.com	5 MB	√	√	-	√	√	√	√	√	√	-
Fetchmail	www.fetchmail.com	5 MB	√	√	-	√	√	-	√	√	√	-
FlashMail	www.flashmail.com	3 MB	√	√	√	√	√	-	√	√	√	-
Hotmail	www.hotmail.com	2 MB	√	-	-	*	√	√	√	√	√	-
HotPop	www.hotpop.com	+	-	√	√	-	-	-	-	-	√	-
Iname****	www.iname.com	4 MB	√	√	√	√	-	-	√	√	√	-
IndiaSite	www.indiasite.com	5 MB	√	√	-	√	√	√	√	√	√	-
Mailcity	www.mailcity.com	4 MB	√	-	-	√	√	√	√	√	√	-
Maile-cite	www.maile-cite.com	4 MB	√	-	-	√	√	-	√	√	√	-
Netscape	www.webmail. netscape.com	5 MB	√	-	-	√	√	√	√	√	√	-
RediffMail	www.rediffmail.com	5 MB	√	-	-	√	-	-	√	√	√	-
RocketMail	www.rocketmail.com	3 MB	√	-	-	√	√	-	√	√	√	-
USA.net	www.netaddress.com	5 MB	√	√	-	√	√	√	√	√	√	-
Yahoo!Mail	www.yahoomail.com	3 MB	√	-	-	√	√	√	√	√	√	Y
ZDNetmail	www.zdnetmail.com	4 MB	√	-	-	√	√	√	√	√	√	-

* *This allows the mail service* to *pick up messages from other mail services that support POP3*

** *This is powered by USA.Net*

*** *This mail service has comprehensive users manuals*

**** *Allows you to choose from over300 domain names*

\+ *Forwarding services*

CHOOSE YOUR MAIL SOFTWARE

Six E-mail Clients and Two Mail Utilities Reviewed

There are lots of e-mail clients around, some of which are small and fast, some big and slow. Some are friendly, other's rather cryptic. Here we look at the most popular mail clients and tell you what each one does and how well.

FoxMail 2.1

FoxMail supports multiple POP mailboxes, HTML message preview (in IE 3 or 4 browser component) and a really cool remote mailbox tool that lets you kill huge attachments right on the mail server. Filters help you sort mail into user created folders or dump spam into your trash mailbox based upon the contents of the From, To, CC or Subject lines. The address book lets you import Eudora or Netscape address books. However, it's not possible to export a FoxMail address book to some other e-mail app. FoxMail also lets you import and export messages to and from Exchange and Outlook. The standard features such as signatures, labels and message sorting are all available. It has some minor bugs. Sometimes you can't copy text from an HTML formatted message to the clipboard. The cursor doesn't land up in the To text box when you compose a new message.

Eudora Light 3.06

Eudora Light is the only mail client around that supports shell accounts in addition to TCP/IP This app has all the standard features—filters, address book, signatures, etc. You can check periodically for mail, skip large messages over a particular kB limit and use filters to look for text and copy or move a message to another folder or change the priority of the message. Rich text is supported but HTML rendering is far from perfect. So what's wrong? Well, Eudora Light hasn't seen an upgrade for quite some time.

FoxMail 2.1

A free e-mail client.

Features: Multiple POP3 accounts, remote mailbox administration, mail filters, HTML message preview.

Pros: Simple Interface.

Cons: No shell account and MAPI support, some minor bugs.

Source: www.aerofox.com/fox (520 kB download).

Eudora Light 3.06

A free e-mail client.

Features: Shell account support.

Pros: Fast, powerful and easy to use.

Cons: Doesn't support multiple mailboxes, dated interface.

Source: Qualcomm. www.eudora.com/ eudoralight (5 MB download).

Netscape Messenger

Netscape Messenger is the Mail and News client that comes as part of Netscape Communicator 4.x, It's a simple but robust mail client with few frills. You can do all the standard stuff such as sending attachments, filtering mail, etc. Some neat features include the ability to bookmark your messages. You can find people in online directories such as Four 11, WhoWhere, or Bigfoot without leaving Messenger from the address book. There's also a notification tool that checks your mail in the background, without requiring you to open Messenger. While Messenger isn't exactly bursting to the brim with features, it's a solid and usable mail and news client.

Netscape Messenger

A mail client that's part of Netscape Communicator.

Features: Supports filtering, HTML messages, IMAR

Pros: Reliable and easy to use.

Cons: Doesn't support multiple POP accounts.

Source: Any Communicator distribution on the *PC Quest* CD.

Eudora Pro 4.1

If you like Eudora Light but want a little more power and a more up to date interface, Eudora Pro 4.1 could be for you. But keep in mind that unlike most of the apps reviewed here, Eudora Pro is a commercial software and has to be bought for Rs 1,950. Other than the new interface, Pro has more powerful filtering options than Eudora Light, a better address book (you can enter the fax, phone, address and other details). Pro can check several e-mail accounts. A new account wizard leads you through setting up your e-mail account. You can import existing settings, e-mail and address books from Outlook, Outlook Express or Netscape Mail. Eudora Pro 4 supports HTML mail using either an internal HTML viewer or IE 4. Eudora Pro can also work with IE 3 but its built-in HTML viewer is better. The tabbed Win 95 taskbar style interface for navigating your mailboxes and filters is really nice. Eudora Pro has IMAP support that lets you view your e-mail at the server. Using LDAP you can query any of the popular e-mail address databases on the Web (Four 11 , etc), for finding a person's e-mail address. A spell checker and a dockable and customizable toolbar round off this powerful and elegant app. You can download the standard edition from ftp://ftp .qual comm.com/eudora/eudorapro/win dows/english/demo41/cp41demo.exe.

Eudora Pro 4.1

An e-mail client. Rs 1,950

Features: Advanced filtering, full HTML preview. Supports IMAP and multiple accounts.

Pros: Very powerful and still easy to use.

Cons: It's not free.

Source: Avda Comptech, 443/40/2,9th Cross, Mahalakshmi Layout, Bangalore 560086. Tel: 80-3322624 Fax: 3322624 E-mail: avda® giasbg01.vsnl.net.in RQS# E04101

Outlook Express

If you've got IE 4 installed on your PC, you've probably also got Outlook Express. This is MS's replacement for Internet Mail. Outlook Express is cute and has enough bells and whistles to keep even the most feature happy user busy for ages. The app comes with almost every feature you'll need including support for multiple POP accounts, an elegant interface, powerful filters and a functional spell checker. However, the fancy stationary can make it tough for other people to read your mail. If you like IE 4 you'll probably like Outlook Express.

Outlook Express

An e-mail client that comes with IE 4.

Features: Supports multiple POP accounts.

Pros: Powerful filters, functional spell checker.

Cons: Tends to hang when you cancel a mail download that's taking too long.

Source: www.microsoft.com/ie or any IE 4 distribution on the *PC Quest* CD.

Cwebmail

Cwebmail lets you check your Web-mail account at Hotmail or Yahoo mail using a regular e-mail client such as Eudora. You just need to configure your SMTP and POP server information to Cwebmail's servers (hotmail.cwebmail. com and yahoo.cwebmail.com). The help file has instructions on configuring Outlook Express, Outlook, Eudora and other popular mail clients. The app works quite well though it's a little slower than using a plain old POP account.

Cwebmail

A mail utility. $10 registration.

Features: Lets you check your Hotmail or Yahoo! mail account using a POP3 client.

Pros: Saves Internet hours.

Cons: Not free.

Source: 30-day free trial from http:// cwebmail. com/

Magic Mail Monitor

This is a program that sits in your system tray, monitoring all your POP accounts for new mail. It's very configurable and lets you set the time interval after which new mail is checked and alerts you using a sound or just by popping up a window listing the new messages and so forth. Magic Mail even lets you view (using Notepad) or delete messages directly from the server. The Quick Reply option lets you reply to the mail in your default mail client.

Magic Mail Monitor

Tray POP-mail checker. Free.

Features: You can check all your POP accounts from a single app that runs in the background.

Pros: Saves you the trouble of launching your mail client, handy in deleting spam.

Cons: None.

Source: www.geocities.com/SiliconValley/Vista/2576/magic.html

Pegasus Mail 3.02

Pegasus Mail is very powerful with options such as multiple users, network support (using NetWare) and encryption. Unfortunately it also has a confusing and complicated interface. Pegasus supports MAPI, rich text, HTML messages (not too well) and can be set up in single or multi-user mode (here each user has to enter a username and password to log into the mail client). It supports rules based filtering to keep out spam. A Finger tool is part of the mailer as is LDAP support. The switchboard feature lets you create a local "newsgroup" on a shared network folder.

That's the good stuff. The downside is that Pegasus has a rather old-fashioned interface that reminds you of a badly designed Windows 3.x application. The screen is cluttered and confusing with enough options to frighten the average user.

Pegasus Mail 3.02

A free e-mail client.

Features: Supports encryption, multiple users with passwords, network "newsgroups".

Pros: Good for e-mail on LAN.

Cons: Hard to use, very confusing interface.

Source: www.pegasus.usa.com/dl/

IMAP

The Internet Message Access Protocol lets you view your e-mail at the server treating the server mailbox as an extension of your computer. You can view, delete and search for mail on the server.

LDAP

Lightweight Directory Access Protocol is a set of protocols for querying information directories including popular e-mail databases on the Web, such as Four 11 for finding a person's e-mail address when you aren't sure about it.

Prashant L Rao at PCQ Labs

UNDERSTANDING NEWSGROUPS

You Need an E-mail Client or Newsreader to Access These Online, Category-Based Discussion Forums

You are trying to configure the latest palmtop that your friend got for you from abroad. No one else you know has a similar model. And calling up the companies help desk abroad is going to be terribly expensive. So what do you do?

Search the newsgroups—an online discussion group or a virtual community of people with similar interests. More likely than not, someone somewhere would have faced the same problem and might have posted a solution. If not, find a newsgroup that discusses a similar topic and post your question. Chances are that you would get your answer pretty soon.

Origin of Newsgoups

Usenet News (User Network News), as newsgroups are officially known, was born in 1979 when two graduate students—Tom Truscott and Jim Ellis-thought of connecting machines for the purpose of information exchange among Unix users. They set up a small network of three machines in North Carolina. Today, there are over 20,000 different newsgroups organised around every topic imaginable. Humor, movies, culture, news, computers, creativity, books, music, science, research, environment, business announcements, animals... you name it and there's at least one newsgroup covering it.

Common categories of newsgroups

alt	For alternative. Anybody can start a group under alt. This is perhaps the largest and the most varied in terms of the subjects covered, alt.humor is a newsgroup where you can read and post jokes, "alt.movies.indian" is where you can find people's opinions and comments on Indian movies and so on.
biz	This is about business. For example, "biz.comp.hardware" is the place to advertise for selling computer hardware.
comp	This group is related to computers. "comp.edu.languages" is a group of people interested in different computer languages.
news	This is related to Usenet and all sorts of announcements, advice regarding newsgroups can be posted and received from here.
soc	This stands for "social", "soc.culture.indian" is the place to talk about Indian culture.
sci	This is related to science, "sci.research" is the group where you can find discussions about various researches going on in the field of science.
rec	This is for recreation and you can talk of music or your pets or anything recreational. For example, "rec.music.indian.classical" is, as the name suggests, for taking and being heard about Indian classical music.
misc	Anything which doesn't fit anywhere fits in this group. For example, in "misc.books.technical" you can read and write about all sorts of technical books.

In order to make them easily recognizable, newsgroups follow a standard naming convention. The name of a newsgroup starts with a category type, followed by a dot and a subject, which can be followed by any number of sub-categories, each separated by a dot. For example, "news.announce.newusers" is a group in the category "news" featuring announcements for new users, while "alt.movies.indian" is a subgroup of the movies newsgroup dealing with Indian movies. This falls under the category "alternate"(see the box "Common Categories of Newsgroups").

Newsgroups can be divided into two categories—discussion groups and electronic journals. Discussion groups allow multi-directional postings and anybody can join in any time. Most of the newsgroups listed above are discussion groups. Electronic journals allow oneway communication only and only the person or the organisation that starts the newsgroup can post messages to it. No individual postings are allowed. The "americast" hierarchy is an example of e-journals.

Newsgroups or Mailing Lists?

Newsgroups differ from mailing lists in number of ways.

- You receive *all* the messages posted to a mailing list. But in case of a newsgroup, the subscriber can choose his topic of interest, and thus the messages to browse, without receiving each post.
- Mailing lists messages exist in your mailboxe, newsgroup posts get sent to your news server, you can then enter a group, and the newsreader down-loads just the message headers in the news folder. The messages themselves, however, are not on your machine. As you access a particular message, the newsreader gets it from the server at that moment. When you finish reading a message, it's not stored on your machine, unless you save it specifically.
- Unlike mailing lists, in a newsgroup, if you use a "threaded" newsreader, then the messages in it show up in a logical order—replies to a particular post show up under that post, in a thread.
- You can post a message to either the newsgroup, reply to the author of a message or to both simultaneously. But in a mailing list, you,can only post messages to the entire group.

Newsgroups through Internet Explorer

1. Open Outlook Express and select Go > News.
2. The "Internet Connection Wizard" appears and asks for a name by which you would like to be known while posting to a newsgroup.
3. Type a name and in the next dialog box type an e-mail address where you would like to receive replies from the newsgroup members.

4. In the next dialog box type in the name of your news server like, "news.vsnl.net.in" if VSNL is your Internet provider.
5. After this, it'll ask for a friendly name for the news server, by which it'll appear in your Outlook.
6. The last dialog box asks for your connection type giving you a choice between a phone line, a LAN and a manual connection.

That is it. You'll now see the friendly name of your news server added to the bottom of your Outlook Express's folder tree.

Now to subscribe to a newsgroup, right click the news server folder and select "newsgroups". This will tell you that you're not subscribed to any newsgroup and will ask whether you'd like to subscribe to one. Click on OK to start the downloading process.

Once the list is downloaded, click on any newsgroup and the "subscribe" button to subscribe to it.

To post a message to a newsgroup, select the newsgroup from your news folder. Select the header of the message to which you want to reply to, open the Compose menu and select from: reply to author, reply to newsgroup or reply to newsgroup and author. You can now send your message just like an ordinary mail.

Another way of classifying newsgroups is according to the type of control—as moderated or unmoderated newsgroups. In moderated newsgroups there is a moderator who goes through all the messages posted and decides whether they are eligible to be forwarded to the group or not. Obviously, this becomes impossible for large groups with heavy volume of messages. Unmoderated newsgroups are open to all and anybody can join and post whatever they want, and no moderator checks the messages here. The "whatever they want" is not strictly true as members of newsgroups invariably set up informal rules of decency and topics that can be posted. The "alt" hierarchy is a typical example of this type. Some newsgroups are "by invitation only". That is, only the invited people (by the moderator) can join in.

Servers called "news servers" host newsgroups and keep a record of the messages posted on them. NNTP (Network News Transfer Protocol) is the protocol used by the servers and the news clients. News servers are also known as NNTP servers, for example, "news.vsnl. net.in" is VSNL's news server. This is the place from where you can download the list of newsgroups. Subscribe to a few and soon you'll be flood-ed with postings from all corners of the globe. So be careful and don't just go on selecting every other newsgroup for subscription.

By now, it should be clear that newsgroups are about opinions than about news as in newspaper. To access a newsgroups, that is to read all messages posted to the group and to post message yourselves, you need a software called newsreader. The latest versions of major browsers, suh as IE and Netscaper have built-in newsreaders.

You can use search engines, such as *infoseek.com* and *yahoo.com,* too to subscribe to newsgroups--click or any newsgroup listed in if, *dejanews.com* is also good for the purpose. It's set up just like a Web search engine, except that it searches exclusively for newsgroups and their contents. Here you can also sarch for a message or a keyword across the varius newsgrups. For india-related newsgroups use khaj.com and *indiatime.com.*

A NEWSGROUP IN YOUR OFFICE

Set up a Newsgroup for Your Intranet on a Linux or Win NT 4 Server

Companies can set up private newsgroups within their intranets to serve as a whiteboard, where users can share different ideas and exchange information. They have an edge over e-mail as you can categorise them based on the topic. Companies can create newsgroups for their various projects, which can then be used by members of the respective project teams. The team members can put in new ideas and refer back to old ones in the newsgroup. They don't have to sit together,to discuss matters, which reduces the time spent in holding meetings, thus enhancing productivity.

Newsgroup on a Win NT 4 Server

Setting up a newsgroup in Win NT is easy and a few minutes job. It's a part of the Internet Information Server 4, and gets installed by the name of Default NNTP Site. Open your Internet Service Manager to see whether the news service is already installed. If it's not there, then you can add it by running the IIS 4 setup program.

Once you've installed the NNTP service, you'll need to create a new Virtual Directory on the Default NNTP Site. This directory will hold all the news postings. So start your Internet Service Manager and click on the Default NNTP Site. Now right click and choose new Virtual Directory. This will invoke a wizard that'll prompt you to enter the name of the newsgroup that'll store the files in this directory and its physical path.

There are several options under the Default NNTP Site. These are expiration policies, Directories, and current sessions. The Directories option will list the newsgroup you just created.

You can add more newsgroups on the Default NNTP Site by going to its properties. The window that pops up contains six tabs. One of these, called groups, lets you add more newsgroups. You can also set security permissions on this newsgroup by going to the directory security tab. Here you can limit access to the news site to specific IP addresses, groups of computers or Internet domains.

That's all you need to do. Use a newsgroup client like Outlook Express to create a newsgroup account that'll access this news site.

Another option in the News Service, expiration policies, let you remove content from the newsgroups that is older than the number of days you specify.

Newsgroup on a Linux Server

The March issue of PC *Quest* carries InterNetNews (INN), a complete USENET system for Linux. However, this package can also work as a local news server on your company's LAN.

INN is undoubtedly a very complex piece of software. Fortunately, setting it up is just a matter of installing the correct RPM and making a few changes to some configuration files. Your system should be connected to the local network and running Red Hat Linux.

INTERNET EXPLORER 5

The Latest Version of Microsoft's Famous Browser has Improved Search, and Enhanced Offline Browsing and Auto-Complete

This new version of Internet Explorer has many enhancements over the previous one. You can download it from www.microsoft.com/windows/ie/download. The Website checks the current version of Internet Explorer running on your desktop, and prompts you for an upgrade. Here's a glimpse of some of its new features.

Improved Search

IE 5 divides your search into several categories: It has a wizard to help you find e-mail, street addresses, Websites, and places. It also has an advanced search facility to find specific articles from an encyclopedia, or search a newsgroup for a particular topic.

Offline Browsing

You can mark specific Web pages to be made available offline in your favorites folder and schedule updates for them. You can also select the content you want offline from a particular Web page. What's really new is: you can save all the contents of the Web page, graphic etc, onto another directory on your hard disk for later viewing.

Auto Complete

This feature works with the browser, the Windows explorer, and the Start menu Run command. If you enable this feature, then IE 5 will remember your keystrokes so that next time you want to go to the same location, it'll automatically fill the complete path after you punch in a few initial keys. You can also optionally enable this for remembering passwords. So next time you go to a particular site that requires a password, it'll automatically place it there the moment you enter your username. But beware, this feature can also auto-complete your password for someone else.

Multiple Connections

The browser gives you the option of adding multiple dial-up connections. It has an Internet connection wizard that lets you specify whether you'll be accessing the Net using a modem, or through your LAN. In dial-up, you can define multiple dial-up settings if you're using more than one Internet account.

Anil Chopra at PCQ Labs

DIGITAL CERTIFICATES

Authenticate Sender Identify for Secure E-transactions

Security has never been Internet's strong point. A hacker with malicious intent and a bit of luck can intercept sensitive data sent over the Net. He could then use this information to carry out forged Internet transactions. So, if this use of e-commerce is to become widespread, a reliable method of identity verification is required. That is why digital certificates are being more commonly used by various authentication techniques.

A digital certificate is a software object that guarantees the identity of the sender. It's given by a third party called a Certificate Authority (CA) to anyone who wants to engage in secure transactions over the Net. It issues a certificate only after verifying the party's identity. This is done by various means including checking the validity of e-mail addresses or verifying credit accounts. In some cases the CA even checks the certificate holder's relationship to his company or organisation.

Who Needs a Certificate?

Companies conducting business Over the Net can use digital certificates to engage in secure Internet transactions. Moreover, traditional business activities like banking are now shifting to the Internet. To take advantage of these new services, security and privacy over the Net is essential. Without a certificate you risk being impersonated on-line.

For instance, if you need to withdraw Rs 10,000 from your bank account over the Net, the bank will allow the transaction only if you have a certificate. Likewise, servers running vital business activities also need certificates. With a certificate, users are assured that the server is indeed being run by the organisation it claims to be affiliated to.

Uses of Certificates

Certificates are used in a number of techniques and by various applications. One of the techniques called the Public Key Infrastructure (PKI) uses public/private key algorithms and digital certificates to verify the authenticity of all parties involved in an Internet transaction.

A public/private key algorithm generates a unique set of keys—a public and private key—for the user. The individual distributes his public key to all those he sends messages to. His private key is secret and kept only with him. The way the keys are generated, it's not possible to decipher the private key from the public one.

While engaging in, a digital transaction, the sender encrypts a message with his private key. The recipient uses the sender's public key to decrypt it. If the message decrypts properly, the recipient can be sure that the mail has been sent by the sender, and not by any other party.

What happens if the recipient doesn't have the sender's public key? If he does manage to get the key from somewhere, how does he verify the sender's identity? This is where the PKI mechanism comes into picture.

Authentication Process with Digital Certificates

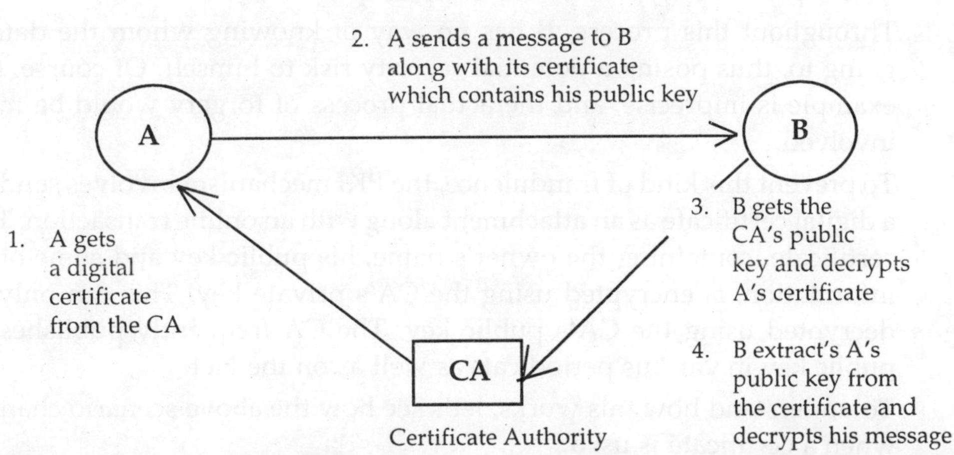

AUTHORITIES FOR DIGITAL CERTIFICATES

Certificate authority	*Website*	*Service*	*Charges*
VeriSign	www. verisign.com	Digital certificates and enterprise PKI solutions	Class 1 digital ID: $9.95 per year or free 60-day trial edition
Thawte	www.thawte.com	Digital certification products services, and solutions	Free mail certificate Basic certificate: $20 per year Premium certificate: $100 per year
IBM	www.ibm.com/security	General security solutions	As per the solution
Entrust technologies	www.entrust.com	General security solutions	As per the solution

The PKI Mechanism

To understand why public/private key algorithm alone is insufficient for an online transaction, and how the PKI mechanism overcomes its limitations, let's take a simple example.

- There's a computer B that wishes to send some sensitive data to A.
- B sends a request to A asking for A's public key.
- An impostor intercepts this request and sends a forged and encrypted reply back to B along with his own public key to decrypt it.
- The imposter also asks for B's public key.
- B then sends the imposter his public key, thinking that he's sending it to A.
- B sends the sensitive data encrypted with his private key to the imposter.
- The imposter decrypts the data with B's public key.

  Throughout this process, B has no way of knowing whom the data is going to, thus posing a potential security risk to himself. Of course, this example is imprecise, and the actual process of forgery would be more involved.

  To prevent this kind of fraudulence, the PKI mechanism involves sending a digital certificate as an attachment along with an online transaction. This certificate, containing the owner's name, his public key and some other information, is encrypted using the CA's private key. This can only be decrypted using the CA's public key. The CA frequently publishes its public key in various periodicals as well as on the Net.

  To understand how this works, let's see how the above scenario changes when a certificate is used.
- Computer B sends a request to A along with its certificate.

- Now even if the imposter intercepts the message, he cannot impersonate A, as he cannot forge a certificate.
- Therefore A receives the request, and decrypts it with the CA's public key.
- A knows that the message is from B, and not any imposter.
- A replies back to B with his own certificate.
- B receives the answer from A, and verifies the identity through the attached certificate.
- The online transaction can thus take place safely.

Certificate Authorities

What happens if you don't trust the certificate authority? In that case you check the certificate on its certificate, which is issued by another organisation. This way a hierarchy of trust is set up, with the CA depending on other organisations and these organisations in turn depending on their governments for authentication. However, most of this trust hierarchy is still not in place. Currently a certificate issued by 2 CA is considered trustworthy and no further verification takes place.

There are several CAs (see the box) whom you can contact to obtain digital certificates. Some of them even assist in setting up a complete company-wide public key infrastructure.

Vivek Kumar

JARGON BUSTER

A Glossary of Commonly-used Internet Terms

Archie: A search tool for use with FTP that searches an Archie site (a database of filenames) for a specific filename.

ARPANET (Advanced Research Projects Agency Network): The predecessor of the Internet, in use between 1971 and 1990, connecting military and academic institutions. Officially dismantled in 1990.

Certificate authority: An organisation that issues digital certificates. A CA is responsible for guaranteeing a certificate holder's identity.

CGI(Common Gateway Interface): A specification for transferring information between a Webserver and a CGI program. The programs cam be written in any language like C, Perl, Visual Basic, Java, as long as it conforms to CGI specifications. CGI makes it possible for Webservers to dynamically interact with users. The most common use of CGI is seen in online forms.

Client: When you access a service on a computer, then your computer is the client, while the other one is called the server. Services include file and print, e-mail, Web, etc.

Digital certificate: An attachment sent along with a message for authentication purposes. A digital certificate verifies that the user sending the message is *who* he or she claims to be.

Directory service: A service that stores information on the network in a hierarchical format for easy accessibility. It can store information about applications, equipment, and users on a network.

Domain; A group of computers that function under common, rules. On the Internet, it's put as an extension in a host name for identifying the type of host. Various domain types have been identified. These include .com (company/commercial), .edu (educational institutions), .gov (government), .mil (military), .org (organisation). Outside the US, she domain name is a 2-letter country code (.in for India).

DNS (Domain Name System): A system used on the Internet to translate IP addresses into easy to remember names. The service that does this translation is called DNS. DNS servers are connected with each other over the Internet. So, if one DNS server doesn't have an IP address translation in its table, it queries other systems running DNS to find out.

Download: To copy a file from a remote machine, for example, with anonymous FTP, or when you want to copy a program from a Website and save it to your hard disk.

DHCP (Dynamic Host Configuration Protocol): A protocol used for dynamically assigning IP addresses to clients that request for it. When configuring a DHCP server, a pool or range of IP addresses has to be given. The server then uses DHCP to assign the IP addresses from this pool.

DHTML (Dynamic HTML): Refers to Web pages, that change their contents depending on client requests.

Finger: A standard utility that is part of the TCP/IP protocol stack that lets you determine who is a valid user and who is logged into a system you have access to. It's used in UNIX based systems. The syntax is finger username@domain. name, or fingei@host:

Firewall: A system to prevent unauthorised access to a private network. A firewall is used on a network directly connected to the Internet to prevent outside internet users from accessing it.

Freeware: Software that is distributed free of charge, but often without customer service or much documentation.

FTP (File Transfer Protocol): A simple program to transfer files over a network from one computer to another. Many FT? servers allow you to download files without having an account on the machine, by using anonymous or FTP for a user name and your e-mail address as a password. This is a major means of distributing software and info on the Internet.

Gateway: A device that is connected to the Internet, and allows other machines inside a company's network to access the Internet. In other words, it's the connection point between a LAN and the internet. The device can be a specialised piece of hardware like a router, or it can be software installed on a computer.

GIF (Graphics Interchange Format): A standard graphics image format used on the Internet.

Gopher: A menu-based system for organising and distributing information on the Internet. It's similar to FTP as it lets users browse or download files and directories. A key feature of Gopher is the ability to include menu items that connect the user to other Gopher servers. Gopher is no longer in popular use.

Hacker: Originally, this term referred to crackerjack programmers and computer experts and connoted respect. Though this meaning is still in use, this word is now also used (especially by the media) to refer to people who deliberately try to penetrate the security of other computers. The computer user community prefers to call these people crackers.

Header: Information in the beginning of a piece of data being sent over a network that describes its content, the destination address, etc.

Homepage: An HTML document that serves as the main access point to a company's Website.

Guest: When you connect to or log onto a remote computer on which you don't have your own account, (perhaps using a special account for guests) you are referred to as a guest or visitor.

HTML (Hypertext Markup Language): A simple and easy to learn programming language that Web documents are written in.

HTTP (HyperText Transfer Protocol): The protocol used on the Internet to transfer HTML documents. All Web browsers use this protocol to read the Web pages.

Hypertext: A new concept for organising information made possible by computers, where keywords or phrases can be used not only to reference additional resources, but also serve as software links to these resources.

IMAP4: The Internet Message Access Protocol lets you view your e-mail at the server treating the server mailbox as an extension of your computer. You can view, delete and search for mail on the server, and only download the ones you need to your local machine.

Interface: The manner in which a user provides information to a computer program. Some examples are GUI for graphical user interface, and CLI for command line interface.

Internet: The Internet is the Grand Daddy of all networks. It's a collection of computers and computer networks across the world that communicate across dedicated high-speed phone lines using a single protocol family called TCP/ IP.

IP address: A unique set of four numbers between 1 and 254 separated by periods, such as 209.194.84.60, used to identify every machine connected to the Internet. As these numbers are very difficult to remember, they are mapped to an easy to remember name, which is called the host name.

IRC (Internet Relay Chat): A program that allows multiple users to conduct typed conversations in real time over the Internet.

ISO (International Organisation for Standardisation): An international body made up of national standard bodies from over 75 countries. It's engaged indefining Standards. The most popular computer standard defined by ISO was the OSI model.

ITU (International Telecommunications Union): An international body engaged in defining telecommunication standards.

JPEG (Joint Photographies Expert Group): A standard (compressed) format for color images commonly used on the Internet. They use the JPC or JPEG extensions.

Jughead (Jonzy's universal gopher hierarchy excavation and display): A powerful gopher search tool written by Rhett "Jonzy" Jones.

Kermit: A simple modem protocol for transferring files between Macs and/or PCs, or from these to bigger computers. Since TCP/IP was adopted as the official Internet protocol in 1983, most PC software has abandoned Kermit. However, Kermit and its cousins X-, Y-, and Z-modem are still needed in the absence of an ethernet or SLIP connection.

LDAP (Lightweight Directory Access Protocol): A set of protocols for querying information directories. There are various directory services on the Internet that can be queried for information. LDAP is being used in operating systems like the upcoming Windows 2000 and NetWare for querying their directory services. LDAP is a simpler version of the X.500 directory service standard.

Lynx: A text only Web browser.

Mailing list: A mechanism for simultaneously distributing e-mail messages to a group of e-mail users who have subscribed to the list. A common use of mailing lists is in newsletter subscriptions.

MIME (Multipurpose Internet Mail Extensions): A way to encapsulate binary file attachments, such as images and sounds into e-mail messages. The method was originally suggested in RFC-1341.

MP3(MPEG1 Layer 3): A new format for storing audio information that is becoming very popular on the Internet. It achieves very high compression ratios, and gives high quality playback. Some shareware MP_3 players are available on the Internet. There is an upgrade to the Windows Media Player that also supports this standard.

Mirror site: A site that is the exact replica of another site. This is used by various anonymous FTP sites to reduce bandwidth bottlenecks, so that more users can access it.

Multilink PPP: A protocol that combines the bandwidths of multiple PPP links to give greater throughputs.

Netiquette: The etiquette of communicating over the Internet. The Internet community follows various conventions when transmitting information over the Internet. For example, sending a message in all caps is the equivalent of shouting.

Newsgroup: A UseNet discussion group or bulletin board. Users can subscribe to newsgroups, and then see all or post messages on it.

NSFNET: The backbone of the Internet since 1990 when ARPANET was dismantled. It originally linked six supercomputers through high-speed phone lines.

Online: A standard terminology that indicates whether an Internet connection is live or not.

PINE (Pine Is Not Elm): A sophisticated e-mail utility that can send not only text files, but also binary files, such as images and sounds by using MIME.

Ping (Packet Internet Gopher): A utility that checks whether a host on the Internet is accessible or not. It's mostly used to troubleshoot connectivity issues on the Internet.

PNG (Portable Network Graphics): A new graphics format that is becoming popular on the Internet.

Port: A 16-bit number used by a server to identify itself to clients. A client connecting to a computer uses an IP address as well as a port number to talk to a particular server.

PPP (Point-to-Point Protocol): A protocol that dynamically assigns an IP address to a computer, so that it can access the Internet.

Public Key Infrastructure (PKI): A technique that uses digital certificates to verify the authenticity of all parties involved in an Internet transaction.

Public/private key encryption: A cryptographic algorithm which uses two keys, one to encrypt and the other to decrypt the data.

Push technology: A technology being used on the Internet in which a server sends out information to the client without the client requesting for it. The most common use of the technology is seen in subscribing to newsletters, where news is sent to the registered clients without requesting for it.

Pull technology: The opposite of Push technology in which information is only provided when a client requests for it. The Web functions on pull technology where a browser sends a request to a Website for information.

RFCs (Request For Comments): The working notes of the committees that develop the protocols and standards of the Internet, including proposed changes. These documents contain a great deal of info about the Net and are maintained by the Internet Activities Board (IAB).

Shareware: Software that is distributed for a small fee. There is a large shareware community that is philosophically opposed to selling software for profit.

Socket: A software object that connects a program (process) to a network protocol. A socket allows a software program (process) to converse with other processes over a network. Sockets use different numbers, known as ports to communicate with each other.

TCP/IP (Transmission Control Protocol/ Internet Protocol): A family of protocols used over the Internet. This family includes protocols for handling data transport

(TCP, UDP), routing (IP, ICMP, RIP, OSPF), addresses (ARP, DNS, RARP), user services (BOOTP, FTP, TELNET), gateways (EGP, GGP, IGP), and other services (NFS, NIS, RFC, SMTP, SNMP).

Telnet: A utility to log onto a remote computer.

Tunneling: A method used to connect two points using the Internet as the channel. VPNs use tunneling to establish connections between different computers. The tunneling is done using various tunneling protocols like PPTP, L2F, IPSec, etc. These protocols encapsulate the data inside the TCP/IP protocol so that it can be sent over the Internet. Some of these protocols like IP Sec also encrypt the data before sending it for security.

URL (Universal Resource Locator): The mechanism used by the Internet to find a particular page, image, or sound. Simply speaking, it's an address for the page.

UseNet (Users' Network): A text-based mechanism that supports discussion groups known as newsgroups, that allow users from anywhere on the Internet to participate. Contrary to the name, it's not actually a network but a service available on the Internet.

uuencode (Unix-to-Unix encoding): A UNIX utility for converting binary files to ASCII for transmission via e-mail between UNIX machines. On the receiving end, uudecode is used to convert back to binary.

Veronica (Very Easy Rodent-Oriented Net-wide Index to Computerised Archives): A search tool for use with Gophers (a rodent).

VPN (Virtual Private Networking): A technology that allows interconnectivity between networks or between mobile users and a network using the Internet backbone as the media for transferring the data.

W3C: The World Wide Web Consortium is an international organisation involved in creating and maintaining most Web-based standards.

WAIS (Wide Area Information Servers): Using keywords supplied by the user, WAIS servers search their databases for any files which contain a match. WAIS goes Beyond Gopher, FTP, and Archie searches, but is somewhat similar to WebCrawler.

Web browser: An application for browsing the Internet. These browsers can read both HTTP and FTP Websites. There are many popular Web browsers around like Netscape Communicator, and Internet Explorer.

Web page: A page written in Hyper-Text Markup Language that's available on the Internet through the HTTP protocol.

Website: A site consisting of various Web pages that can be accesses by anyone connected to the Internet.

WWW (World Wide Web): Now more commonly known as the Web. It's a system that lets users graphically browse through sites on the Internet, and follow pointers (called links or hyperlinks) to other documents that can be anywhere.

XML (Extensible Markup Language): A new scripting language being developed by the W3C (World Wide Web Consortium) which provides more functionality than HTML.

X.500: An ISO and ITU standard that defines how a directory service should be structured.

DDR SDRAM

In the SDRAM used today (JEDEC SDRAM), there's a design limitation of 125 to 133 MHz bus speeds. Clearly, bus speeds will need to increase well beyond that so that memory bandwidth can keep up with future processors. Emerging standards that look promising require other changes: special pin-outs, smaller bus widths, and so on. For now, "Double Data Rate" SDRAM looks very appealing. This design allows the activation of output operations on the chip to occur on both the rising and falling edge of the clock; in conventional SDRAM, only the rising edge signals an event to occur. Thus DDR can effectively double the speed of operation—up to 200 MHz.

There is already one Socket 7 chipset that has support for DDR SDRAM, and more will follow if manufacturers decide to make this memory available.

Goodbye, EDO

EDO (Extended DataOut) RAM is fading out, but it's still supported by the largest number of PCs around, so it's worth mentioning here.

Also called Hyperpage mode, EDO added 40 percent or greater improvement in access time to the older DRAM, with the same amount of silicon and the same package size. EDO works well with memory bus speeds up to 83 MHz. If the chips are 55 ns or faster, EDO can be used even with a 100 MHz memory bus. One of the best reasons to use EDO is that all of the current motherboard chipsets support it with no compatibility problems, unlike some of the SDRAM modules now being used.

However, EDO is difficult to get (it's now more expensive than SDRAM) because of limited production.

Your PC's motherboard probably has room for both EDO and SDRAM (check out the boot-up information, which should then list both types). If you already own EDO memory, there is no real reason to upgrade to SDRAM unless you require bus speeds above 83 MHz. With a typical EDO timing of 5-2-2-2 at 66 MHz, there is almost no noticeable improvement with SDRAM over EDO, and at 83 MHz it's still negligible. If you require 100 MHz bus operation, EDO will lag far behind current SDRAM in performance.

With information from Intel.com,
www.tomshardware.com, and other
sources on the Internet

NEWSGROUPS THROUGH NETSCAPE NAVIGATOR

Netscape Nevigator 4.05

1. Newsgroups are called discussion groups in the Netscape Navigator. Select Communicator> Collabra Discussion Groups.
2. In the "Netscape Message Center" window click on "subscribe" in the toolbar.
3. Click on the "Add Server" button and type in the news server like, "news.vsni.net.in" if VSNL is your Internet provider.
4. This will start downloading a list of newsgroups form your news server.
5. Once the list is downloaded, you can click on any newsgroup then click the "subscribe" button.

Netscape Navigator 4.5

1. Select Communication > Newsgroups.
2. Right click the News folder that appears in your folder tree.
3. Click on the Subscribe to newsgroups option.
4. Click on Add Server button in the window that appears and select News Server from the Add Server dialog box and click on Continue button.
5. Enter the news server name, that is, "news.vsnl.net.in" and click OK.
6. This will start downloading a list of newsgroups. Click on "subscribe" button to subscribe to any newsgroups you want.

To post a message to a newsgroup, double click a group from the list in your news folder an select the mail you want to reply to. Click on the Reply manu and select form: reply to sender, reply to group, or reply to sender and group. And send the message as an ordinary mail.

GET THE MESSAGE?

With Myriad E-mail Services Freely Available on the Web, Choosing One Can be Difficult. Here are Some Services You Could Choose From

Sangeeta Kulkarni

Electronic mail has given a new dimension to communication—it is fast, is capable of multimedia content and usually elicits prompt response. With dozens of providers offering free Web-based e-mail, it is for the user to judiciously decide and settle for the ideal service. Believe us, choosing the right mail service can make a big difference. Managing half a dozen accounts while sub-scribing to a dozen newsletters can prove cumbersome for any user, not to forget those gigantic 2 MB attachments your friends love to bomb you with.

Hot Favourite

This is the one that started it all. Hotmail, the world's most popular and preferred mail service, is looking better than ever. Sadly, it still takes ages to load.

The new 'Passport' feature promises added security from hackers, and its' single sign-in facility allows you to access Clockwise from top: The Big Four among free Web-based e-mail services an Hotmail Yahoo, iName and usa.net your Hotmail account from other participating Passport sites.

This is especially advantageous when you are required: to furnish your personal details such as home and company address, e-mail and telephone number etc repeatedly for different sites. Passport provides the necessary information, with your prior consent of course. Also, While making e-purchases, Hotmail's Wallet feature allows you to shop online, receive updates and subscribe to free newsletters.

Hotmail can be added to your office mail client (such as Outlook Express) for archiving messages into your hard drive. You can; opt for up to four POP accounts with your Internet; service provider or your company.

It is also possible to receive mail from Hotmail in your Outlook Express inbox. But this is possible only if you are online. Hotmail also allows you to check spam by using mail filters.

Something to Exult About

Yahoo! provides you with 3 MB of storage space and can be used to access POP3 mail as well; it can be used to read Eudora mail, for instance. A registered user can specify up to three POP mail servers. The Messenger facility informs you if you get new mail. Among other features are a calendar, an address book, a search option and voicemail.

Yahoo! too allows you to block up to 100 addresses, to help you avoid spam. Once this option is enabled, junk mail arriving from specified addresses will be automatically deleted. Or you could divert such mail into another folder.

The 'TrueSync' free facility synchronises Outlook, Palm and Windows CE devices with your calendar, address book and 'to do' list. The fax and voicemail facility allows you to route faxes and voicemail directly through your mailbox. You can configure your mobile phone to receive or check your e-mail messages, and also send faxes at low rates.

Your Virtual Abode

www.netaddress.com gives you a file storage space of 25 MB, with a link to www.driveway.com (an online storage account) and 5 MB of space for mail. Its unique print feature allows you to print messages in pure text format, without visuals or graphics. Other primary services include collecting mail from POP3-compliant mail accounts and blocking junk mail with a 'Junk mail blocker'.

However, premium services come at a price. These include POP access, extra storage, paging, advertisement suppression, scanning and faxing. E-mail forwarding is another feature that permits you to forward all Netaddress e-mail to an existing e-mail address.

This is especially beneficial when you change ISPs, or move, and your Netaddress e-mail can be treated as a primary address. Besides, Netaddress also facilitates easy downloads and transfer of large files, unlike other services.

POP Goes the Mail!

You can use your e-mail client to retrieve mail from multiple accounts without actually.logging on to the internet. Many e-mail clients like Outlook Express, Netscape Messenger and Eudora enable you to access multiple POP (Post Office Protocol) accounts. The number of POP accounts may vary in accordance with the kind of service your mail provider offers.

POP accounts offered by ISPs are usually accessed through e-mail software and not a browser. You can easily set up a POP account by configuring your mail client and providing necessary details such as username and password. The main advantage is that you save costs by reading mail offline. This is because you get to read downloaded e-mail without actually logging in.

Setting up a POP Account

Most mail clients have similar methods of setting up POPS accounts across free Web-based e-mail services. All you have to do is feed the necessary entries in a required format. If use Outlook Express 5, here's how you can do it;

1] Under the Tools button in the File menu, choose Accounts
2] Click on Mail, select the Add button and choose 'Mail' again
3] You'll be prompted to enter your name (if you haven't already) and specify the account address in which you would like to receive mail.
4] Make the following entry in your Incoming mail dialog box: POP.mail.yahoo.com (if you've chosen Yahoo!) and SMTP.mail.yahoo.com in the Outgoing mail (SMTP) server.
5] Enter a password for your account ?name.

You now have an active POP account that will redirect your Yahoo! mail to your account. Of course, do make sure that you have an account with Yahoo!, or ' another free Web-based e-mail service, prior to setup.

It's in the Name

www.iname.com adds a personal touch to an account holder's identity by providing a range of dynamic, job-specific and casy-to-remember domain names such as writeme, cheerful, accountant, archeolo-gist, comic, deliveryman and gardener. The site has more than 300 personalised domains to choose from and more are added every three months.

However, names are not all that iName has to offer. A registered user is permitted storage space of 3 MB and attachments are limited to 500 KB, while MailPRO customers have a 4 MB limit for sending and receiving mail and 20 MB of storage space. Moreover, there is a forwarding facility that permits you to forward messages, irrespective of the ISP you subscribe to. So, if you move to another city or change your ISP, all you need to do is modify the forwarding address, rather than writing to everyone in the address book.

With 5 MB storage space for mail and a 2 MB limit for sending and receiving messages, www.postmark.net has recently introduced a POP service that allows users to download and read mail using POP3 compliant mail software.

Postmark currently does not host an SMTP server for outgoing mail, but users can temporarily use the SMTP server of their ISP to overcome this. One of the prerequisites for using Postmark is that you should have a Web browser that is set to receive cookies. This is easy enough if you have Internet Explorer or Netscape Communicator.

Other Options

Described as the most secure Web-based fully encrypted mail system, www.hush-mail.com comes with a 1024-bit encryption system.

Hushmail is comparatively faster than other services, since users are not required to load new Web pages while navigating. It uses a patent-pending process called 'Public Key Cryptosystem with Roaming User Capability' which, ensures that your message is delivered only to the intended recipient.

Different Options

Want to earn money and have fun doing it? Visit www.chequemail.com, a service that actually pays suffers for frequent usage. Conceived and launched by Manish Desai, Himanshu Ashar and Ambrish Desai, this unique service aims at integrating customer relationship with their business model. Instead of spending money on advertise-ments and excessive promotions, they have devised a system where any user accessing their service 30 days a month is eligible for a cheque, amounting to a certain percent-age of the profits earned by the company. They also give away free gifts.

www.epatra.com allows you to send e-mail in nine Indian languages—Hindi, Marathi, Gujarati, Punjabi, Malayalam, Assamese, Bengali, Tamil and Telugu. They also plan to incorporate Kannada and Oriya soon. You don't need to know how to type in the regiional language—you can compose mail in the English script, and an applet transliterates the characters phonetically into the script of your choice. Of, course, some tweaking is required before your letter is ready, and the process can be a little slow. However, e-patra does make It easy for you to communicate with those who would not otherwise be able to read and understand mail in English.

www.tntsb.com/anymail, an efficient mall service, checks your e-mail and notifies you of new mail. Another feature, though not secure, allows you to access your mailbox directly without having to retype your user-name and password.

www.zeenext.com, as the name suggests; is Zee Telefilm's new venture for providing free mail service. The site has links to other Zee Interests such as television, news, events, education and Zee Premiere. Anoth-er feature Is the request for demographic data from users, which Is used by advertis-ers for targeting their niche market..

So if you e-mail a non-user of hushmail, the message is not secure and you receive a message informing you of the same. The encryption radio button also remains unchecked during this process, confirming lack of security. Users can set a 'passphrase' of their choice for accessing their accounts. Hushmail provides 3 MB of storage space for mail and up to 1.5 MB for file attachments. Another feature allows users to create nicknames so that they don't have to key in the entire address everytime.

For Techles Only!

If you breathe, eat and sleep technology, a subscription to www.techemail.com is a must. Techemail honours techies (and wannabe techies) by adding an appropriate tag to the domain name. And so, you have domain names such as TechEmail, PCGeek, PCTechni-cian, TechieGuy. After registering , you can access your inbox directly through mail.techemail.com. You also have access to POP accounts, 5 MB of disk space, voicemail and fax.

www.myownemail.com offers 20 megs of free online space for registered Users. It also gives you a choice of 200 domain names, www.mystartingpage.com offers the latest headlines and cool downloads. The page is easily customisable.

You can be patrotic and go in for an Indian mail service if you wish. Perhaps the most popular is Rediffmail.com, which claims to offer blazingly fast access times. ;

There is also www.indiatimes.com, from the Times of India group. Other sites (especially portals) that offer free e-mail, abound, and offer a fair mix of features and services. ,

All said and done, there are some aspects that certainly cannot be overlooked, irrespective, of the kind of mail service you use. Most mail services have a size limitation, which means you have to be particularly careful while sending large e-mail attachments.

Reading the terms of service while registering with a mail service provider might not sound very appealing, but it is essential. Receiving notices of discontinuance or a 'threat' to delete some of your mail at random is not a pleasant experience!

MAKE YOUR PC HACKER-PROOF

By Jeff Sengstack

Our Test of 6 Personal Firewalls Finds the Best Ones for Keeping uninvited Guests Out of Your Office or Home System

IT WAS GETTING LATE, so Jim Jar-rard, president of Ginenet, a stock film footage company in Simi Valley, California, decided to leave his computer on overnight to finish downloading a big file. While Jarrard was gone, a hacker accessed his PC over its DSL Internet connection and loaded a program giving the intruder power to commandeer Jarrard's computer, steal valuable film files, and erase the system's hard drives.

Allan Soifer, an Ottawa, Ontario, electronic mailing list administrator, didn't realise a distant hacker had been scanning his home PC for hours. The hacker had found a way in and needed only a password to access Soifer's files. So he pelted the machine with computer-generated words, hoping for a lucky match. Fortunately, neither of dip hackers got the goods.

Jarrard escaped catastrophe because a frozen system and an error message the next morning told him something was wrong, He spent two weeks investigating the problem (and learning more than he wanted to know about hacking) before realising that he would have to back up his data files and reformat the hard drive to delete the hacker's self-replicating program. Finally, he installed personal firewall software to guard against future attacks.

Soifer was luckier. Before the attack, he had visited Shields Up "(www.grc.com), a website dedicated to Internet security advice. Soifer followed its recommendation to download and install ZoneAlarm, a free personal firewall program. ZoneAlarm alerted Soifer to the flood of incoming passwords and helped him identify the hacker's ISP—in Anchorage, Alaska. The ISP cut off the intruder's service, hut the miscreant could likely open an account with another ISP and continue his misdeeds. And law enforcement is unlikely to take action on any but the largest, most prominent computer crimes.

Hackers come in all flavors. Many are simply curious folks who want to find out how a program or system works. They may not do any harm, and some even provide a service by discovering programming bugs and helping fix them. But malicious or criminal hackers use their skills for devious purposes. Criminal hacking incidents can range from obnoxious to destructive. The latter category includes "denial-of-service" attacks—like those that shut down Internet sites EBay and Yahoo last February when hackers bombarded the sites with data and caused the companies' servers to crash. Is your PC likely to suffer such a massive attack? If you're an individual or small-business user, probably not.

Hacking individual PCs remains a fairly rare phenomenon. Your chances of suffering some type of Internet vandalism are rising, however, especially if you have an uninterrupted, dedicated connection like DSL or cable modem. Fortunately, you can take some simple steps to protect yourself. For most Internet users, changing a few settings, installing a good personal firewall, maintaining updated antivirus software, and using common sense will provide reasonable protection for a small cost

Many Ports of Entry

How do malicious hackers cause damage? They have access to increasingly sophisticated automated software tools that scour the Internet for vulnerable PCs. The tools locate an individual machine by its Internet Protocol address, a unique number that identifies a computer on the Net. Most computers equipped with dial-up connections have dynamic IP addresses: The Internet service provider assigns them a new IP address each time their users log on. By contrast, most highspeed connections, like DSL and cable modems, use constant or "static" IP addresses. In the unlikely event that a hacker decides to target you specifically, such a static address makes it easier to track you down.

An IP address identifies a computer but doesn't provide a way inside. To get in, the hacker must find an *open port,* or connection point. Think of an IP address as a computer's switchboard number and a port as an individual phone extension. Software on your PC creates ports to allow specific networking functions. Web access, for example, generally uses port 80, while FTP runs through port 21. Once they've targeted an IP address, hackers scan the machine for open ports, as happened to Allan Soifer.

Malicious hackers may also trick users into opening ports by sending *Trojan horses.* Mimicking the tactic invented :by the wily Greek Invaders of Troy, Trojan horses hide damaging cargo within a seemingly benign shell—in this case, an e-mail attachment or a download. When you double-click and open the shell, the hidden program sneaks out to wreak havoc on your computer. One of the best-known Trojan horses is "Back Orifice." (The name is a play on Microsoft's BackOffice network administration software.) Back Orifice surreptitiously opens a port on your PC that a hacker can then exploit to take control of your machine remotely.

PC Defenders

Personal Firewall	*Street price (6/2/00)*	*Security settings (default in bold)*	*Automatically blocks file sharing*	*Asks permission for Internet applications*
Aladdin Knowledge Systems ESafe Desktop 2.2 800/562-2543 www.eAladdin.com/esafe	Free[2] $40	Extreme, Normal, Low Block Everything. Filter	—	—
McAfee.com Personal Firewall 408.992-8100 www-eAladdin-com/esafe		Traffic. Allow Everything	A	
Network ICE BlackICE Defender 1.9 650/532-4100 www.networkIce.com	$40[4]	Paranoid, Nervous, Cautious, Trusting	A	—
Sybergen Networks Secure Desktop 2.1 510/742-2600 www.sybergen.com/products	$30	Ultra, High, Medium, Low	—	A
Symantec Norton Personal Firewall 2000 version 2 800/441-7234 www.symantec.com	$50	High, Medium, Minimal	A	A
Zone Labs ZoneAlarm 2.1 415/547-0050 www.zonelabs.com	Free	High, Medium, Low	A	A

A Yes
Best Buy No

1. As tested at default setting.
2. Free to home users; the price for business customers depends on the number of users.
3. Caught by the product's built-in virus scanner.
4. includes updates for oneyear; . update fee is $20 per year thereafter

CLOSE THE WINDOWS

So how can windows users protect themselves? Before you install any new software, you should perform some simple housekeeping on, your operating system to make it safer. The first step is to check the Microsoft website for security updates and patches. If you have Windows 9.v, Windows NT, or Windows 2000 Professional, point your browser to windowsupdate. microsoft.com and follow the links there to find the updates for your particular operating system.

In addition, David Ursino, Microsoft's product manager for the new Windows Millennium Edition, recommends disabling the File and Printer Sharing option that provides other computers access to a machine running any version of Windows. Go to *Start Settings Control Panel* and double-click the *Network* icon. In the dialog box that opens, search the list of installed network components for "File and Printer Sharing for Microsoft Networks." If this item is present, highlight it and then click the *Remove* button beneath the list of components.

Another way you can protect yourself is to use software that blocks Trojan horse programs. Any good antivirus package is designed to identify Trojan horses, but you must keep it up-to-date to defeat the latest subterfuges. You should also make sure your e-mail program is not set to open attachments automatically. And never open an attachment that you don't recognise or that comes from an unknown source.

These measures alone, though, will guarantee security for only a minority of PC users. "Unless you've installed your system from scratch, there's no way of knowing just how secure it really is," says Stuart McClure, coauthor of *Hacking Exposed.* Security breaches can occur on many fronts, typically through Inter-net software—like PC Anywhere, Net Meeting, or ICQ—that opens ports hackers can subsequently exploit. Even Microsoft's Ursino sees the need to add another layer of security. "If I were a user who had a home network with a persistent Internet connection," he says, "I would choose to have a firewall."

GOOD FENCES MAKE GOOD NEIGHBORS

Personal firewall software goes a step beyond the basic precautions. Like expensive and complex corporate-level firewalls, these affordable and simple products promise to repel intruders by monitoring incoming and outgoing Internet traffic and alerting you to possible dangers. To learn more about how firewalls function, see "How It Works: Personal Firewalls" (www.pcworld.com/ how_it_works/firewalls). We looked at ten personal firewalls and chose the six strongest contenders for more detailed testing. This is a new kind of software product, and it shows. The firewalls' performance, usability, and interface quality run the gamut from effective and accessible to weak and incomprehensible.

The perfect personal firewall would be inexpensive and easy to install and use, would offer clearly explained configuration options, would hide all ports to make your PC invisible to scans, would protect your system from all attacks, would track all potential and actual threats, would immediately alert you to serious attacks, and would ensure nothing unauthorised entered or left your PC. Only two products come reasonably close to meeting that ideal: Network ICE's $40 BlackICE Defender 1.9 and Zone Labs' ZoneAlarm 2.1, which is free for home users and nonprofit organisations. Though neither package is perfect, each has strengths that will make it attractive to particular users. Ultimately, we decided that these two products should share the title of Best Buy.

McAfee.corn's Personal Firewall and Symantec's Norton Personal Firewall 2000 version 2 fall into the second tier of products. Sybergen Networks' Secure Desktop 2.1 performed unimpressively in our tests and didn't provide sufficient feedback (or even an indication that it was running). And Aladdin's free ESafe Desktop 2.2 fared poorly because it is essentially an antivirus product with what our tests showed to be a kludgy, leaky firewall tacked on.

FEATURES COMPARISON

Detects TSAdbot	*Blocks Back Orifice*	*Puts openports into stealth mode*	*Detects port scanning*	*Repels denial-of-service attack*	*Comments*
—	A	—	—	—	Poor performance and confusing configuration. Comes with built-in antivirus utility and filter to block obscenties in Web content.
A	A	A	A	A	Easy configuration and good interface, but event log is difficult to access. User must configure firewall to run automatically at system startup.
—	—	A	A	A	Easy installation and configuration. Clear, easily accessible event log. Best documentation of the products we tested. Identifies type of attack and attacker.
A	—	—	—	—	Poor performance. Provides little feedback and no indication that it is running, but it does have a good, readily accessible event log.
A	A	—	A	A	Provides good protection, but interface is overly complex and controls are clumsy. Also includes filter to block obscenities or objectionable Web content.
A	A	A	A	A	Easy to install and set up. Provides solid protection and plenty of feedback-sometimes too much. Scans e-mail attachments for potential viruses or Trojan horses.

5. Network ICE does not consider TSAdbot to beharmful.
6. Blocked Back Orifice at its "Nervous" security setting.
7. Includes updates for one year; update fee is $7 per year thereafter.
8. Free to individuals and nonprofits; licensed at $20 per seat per year for business users.

Four other products that we examined—Digital Robotics' Internet Firewall 2000 ($40), Delta Design's Net-Commando 2000 ($30), Plasmatek Software's ProtectX 3 Standard Edition ($25), and Tiny Software's Tiny Personal Firewall ($29)—failed to get past our preliminary cut because they exhibited more-serious flaws, such as incomprehensible instructions, weak documentation, or limited functionality.

We assessed the six contending products on three criteria: User-friendliness, ability to work with common programs that access the Internet, and prowess at repelling hacking attempts. In each case we independently installed the firewall on an otherwise unprotected Quantex QP6 350 M2X, a Pentium 11-350 machine equipped with 64MB of RAM and running Windows 98 SE.

The best configuration process should be comfortable for a neophyte while giving an advanced PC user the opportunity to tweak the settings. Most of the products we tested offer only three security settings: Block, all traffic, allow some traffic, and provide no security at all. This scheme works fine if you just surf the Web and check e-mail, but it's too limiting for many users. BlackICE Defender and McAfee.com Personal Firewall have the best configuration options and default settings. BlackICE has the simplest, best-explained security options, and it offers four levels of security for finer adjustment by the user. McAfee.com defaults to a middle "filter" security level that is an excellent starting point for most users. ZoncAlarm ranks near the top, too, but we thought it would have benefited from offering a fourth level of security between its high and medium settings.

Even the best documentation for the firewalls we tested is scarcely adequate, especially since hacking remains a mysterious aspect of computing for most PC users. In particular, none of the products we looked at fully explains its advanced configuration features. If you take into account its reasonably clear and organised online help, BlackICE Defender scores highest in the documentation category. But in this case that's a small honor.

THINGS THAT GO 'BUMP,'ON THE NET

The ideal firewall would also work quietly in the background but alert the user to anything worth reporting, and provide comprehensive logs of events. Unfortunately, most of these products tend to overwhelm the user with data. Firewall novices may be stunned at how often someone "touches" their PC. Most of that contact, however, is innocuous traffic that security expert Steve Gibson calls IBR—Internet background radiation. According to Gibson, who maintains the Shields Up website, "All firewalls overreport, and they don't do a useful job of discriminating between IBR and actual attacks."

Security Checklist

NO COMPUTER connected to the Internet is 100 percent safe from hiking. But take heart: These five easy steps can make *a* PC running Windows virtually impervious to online attacks.

Check Microsoft's website regularly for the latest Windows security updates and patches.

Remove File and Printer Sharing for Microsoft Networks under the Network Control Panel.

Use up-to-date antivirus software to block Trojan horse programs. Exercise caution when deciding whether to open e-mail attachments, even from trusted senders.

Install personal firewall software. We recommend BlackICE Defender for users not interested in becoming security experts and ZoneAlarm for those who want to know all the details about their Internet connection.

If you maintain *a* persistent Internet connection, and you really want to play it safe, then just shut down your system whenever you will not be using it.

Spikes of IBR occur for various reasons. For example, Internet services like WebTV sometimes send data to the wrong IP address when they attempt to contact users. A firewall might interpret that activity as a port scan. Internet privacy and security guru Simson Garfinkel, author of *Database Nation*, criticizes the misinformation typical firewall products generate. The most frequent complaint ISPs receive is no longer about spam, he says,;but about firewall alerts of attempted scans. "Lots of people are going to scan you," he says. "You just can't react every time."

Of the products we examined, BlackICE—using carefully crafted reporting windows—provides the clearest, most useful information. The program notes the source of any probe, and it's the only personal firewall we tested that automatically looks up IP addresses and provides contact information about whoever "touched" your PC. An honorable mention goes to Norton and Secure Desktop, which log events in accessible text windows. But ZoneAlarm went a bit overboard: We finally turned off its endless stream of pop-up alert windows, relying instead on its comprehensive event logging for detailed information. However, only ZoneAlarm effectively alerts you in real time to all potential threats—a level of detail that may appeal to some hands-on users. (For more on using ZoneAlarm, see www.pcworld.com/ heres_how/zone.) Most firewalls simply flash an icon in the system tray when they detect something, but you won't see it if your system tray is covered or if you're not looking for it.

COMPATIBILITY TEST

We ran each of the six firewalls through a number of scenarios to check its compatibility with other applications and its responsiveness to a potential Trojan horse. Compatibility is an important concern with applications that access the Internet: A poorly designed firewall might misconstrue as hacking attempts such legitimate activities as opening ports for Internet communication, and it may mistake legitimate programs for *malware*, or malicious software. Some firewalls will ask the user for permission to run applications, while others will allow or block the apps without providing feedback. In overall compatibility, BlackICE Defender had nearly flawless results, and McAfee.com finished close behind. Norton and ZoneAlarm worked well in most instances; Secure Desktop and ESafe performed poorly.

A good firewall can distinguish between network traffic related to trusted applications and malicious traffic from a hacker or Trojan horse. Some firewalls focus on applications, while others focus on data traffic. In the first case, Norton uses a lookup table of preapproved applications. BlackICE Defender, on the other hand, doesn't note what apps are running. Instead, it scrutinises all dara passing to and from the computer for suspicious behavior, or *signatures*. BlackICE has an extensive, updatable signature file of known hacking techniques, so it can often identify and explain exactly what is happening to your PC.

In our tests, we connected to the Internet over DSL and evaluated each firewall's ability to work with common applications that access the Internet: Microsoft Internet Explorer and NetMeeting, WS-FTP LE (a file-transfer program), ICQ (a messaging program), Napster (MP3 music search and download software), PC Anywhere (a program that aII6ws remote control of one computer by another), and RealPlayer (music and video player software).

Sometimes the biggest challenge was determining whether the firewalls were working at all. For instance, in its default installation, McAfee.com does not launch at system start-up or appear in the system tray. You must select those options in the program's configuration. And even though Secure Desktop launches automatically at start-up, it runs entirely in the background—there isn't even an icon for the program in the system tray.

Secure Desktop did ask for permission to run some applications, but when operating at its highest security setting, the program would not allow other applications—ICQ, Napster, or NetMeeting—to run at all. MoAfee.com and ZoneAlarm worked fairly smoothly, asking permission for each application. Norton automatically configured rules to permit some apps, but in other cases it made us walk through an overly detailed, six-screen Q&A to manually configure rules for future use of the app. BlackICE doesn't scrutinise applications per se, but it accurately monitors the types of data they send and receive.

Finally, we ran a not-so-trusted application: The freeware version of PKZip (file-compression software). This download includes a built-in application called TSAdbot, which acts as a conduit for advertisements from the Internet and displays them while PKZip is running. TSAdbot is not a malicious program, but it does function similarly to a Trojan horse and thus tests the firewalls' sensitivity to these intruders. McAfee.com, Norton, Secure Desktop, and ZoneAlarm detected TSAdbot and asked us for authorisation. ESafe failed to react; BlackICE did not recognise TSAdbot's behavior as harmful. When we asked Network ICE about this result, spokesperson Robert Graham said, "Currently, Network ICE does not consider adbots to be malware." But he added, "Maybe we should reconsider our position."

SPARRING MATCH

We then hit each firewall with three simulated hacks: Installing and accessing the Back Orifice Trojan horse, running a port scan, and conducting a denial-of-service attack. We ran each test at the programs' default security settings. (Some default to the highest security setting, while others default to the second-highest.) If a firewall failed a test, we tried it again at a higher setting.

In the Back Orifice test, BlackICE did not stop the attack at its default security setting. However, it did stop the Trojan horse when we bumped the security up a notch. (The. newest BlackICE version, not available in time for our comparison testing, does stop Back Orifice at its default setting.)

Three products--McAfee.com, Norton, and ZoneAlarm—identified Back Orifice by its file name, Umgr32.exe, and asked permission to run it. Not many PC users have heard of Back Orifice, let alone Umgr32.exe, so they might not know whether to block the app or let it run. ESafe's built-in virus checker identified the Umgr32.exe file and asked whether we wanted to delete it. Secure Desktop failed the Back Orifice test—and all other attack tests—even at its highest security setting.

We next hit our test PC with a port scan, having deliberately left two ports open to see how the firewalls would handle them. The first port, called NetBIOS, is opened when printer and file sharing are enabled. The second port was opened for our Back Orifice Trojan horse. (Some firewalls look for standard ports used by Trojan horses, but we upped the ante by choosing a nonstandard port.) A personal firewall can hide your PC by putting ports into stealth mode so they will not respond to a hacker's prot scan; the ports will thereby offer no evidence that your computer exists.

A HACKER'S GLOSSARY

INTERNET security is a complex subject. Here are some key terms and concepts for PC users to know.

- Denial-of-Service (DoS) Attack: Flooding an IP address with data, causing computers to crash or lose their connection to the Internet. Most DoS attacks are aimed at large Web servers, with the objective of rendering the target site unavailable to other visitors.
- Distributed Denial-of-Service (DDoS) Attack: Using multiple computers to launch a DoS, attack. A hacker commandeers several outside computers and uses them as platforms to launch the attack, magnifying its Intensity.and cloaking the hacker's identity.
- Hacker: Someone who deliberately gains access to other computers, often without a user's knowledge or permission. Malicious hackers do this to steal valuable information, disrupt service, or cause other damage.
- IP (Internet Protocol) Address: The identifying number of a computer or other device. Two machines Connected directly to the Internet cannot have the same IP address at the same time. Computers with static IP addresses (most systems with DSL or cable modem connections) always use the same IP address; those with dynamic addresses (most systems with dial-up connections) are assigned a new IP address each time they log on to the Internet.
- Personal Firewall: Software that keeps unauthorised users from accessing a standalone PC. It also prevents malicious programs from sending data out.
- Port: An electronic connection that allows data to travel between a client PC and a server over a network.
- Port Scan (or Port Probe): Data sent by a hacker over the Internet to locate a PC or network and determine whether it has open ports that will accept a connection.
- Stealth Mode: A protective setting that hides a port so it isn't visible over the Internet. A port that has been put into stealth mode will give no reply to a port scan, thereby providing no evidence that a computer exists at the scanned IP address.
- Trojan Horse: A malicious program masquerading as something harmless, usually an e-mail attachment or a download that you open and run. A Trojan horse opens your computer to incursions by a hacker.

At their default settings, BlackICE, McAfee.com, and Zone-Alarm put the two ports into stealth mode, but ESafe, Norton, and Secure Desktop failed to hide the ports we left open.

Finally, we ran a miniature denial-of-service (DoS) attack, hitting each firewall with a flood of meaningless data intended to confound the operating system. In the real world, a DoS attack overwhelms your Internet connection, making it difficult or impossible to access the Net. It can also crash your system. Malicious hackers can increase the pressure by launching a distributed-denial-of-service (DDoS) attack, in which multiple computers are commandeered and used to launch an attack. Such assaults are usually directed against major websites and the servers that support them. In the unlikely event your PC is targeted for a full attack, a good firewall may block the incoming data packets and prevent your machine from crashing, but no firewall can ensure that your Internet connection will remain open.

At their default settings, four of the firewalls we tested—BlackICE, McAfee.com, Norton, and ZoneAlarm—prevented a crash, although BlackICE was the only product that correctly identified the nature of the attack. Norton gave no indication an attack was under way. We were disappointed that ZoneAlarm repelled the attack only at its default (High) setting, and Secure Desktop and ESafe failed to prevent a crash even at their highest settings.

Play it Staff

According to Murphy's Law, anything that can go wrong, will. People are putting more sensitive data (such as financial records) on their PCs, and sending other sensitive data (such as credit card numbers) over the Web. They're also switching from dial-up modem-based service to broad band connections, with continuous service and fixed IP addresses. Meanwhile, hackers are acquiring more devious software tools and putting more potential victims at risk. Hacking will inevitably increase. But the good news is, you can protect yourself now.

Jeff Sengstack is a freelance writer who contributes regularly to PC World. *Test procedures were designed by Elliott Kirschling of the PC World Test Center. Steve Gibson, a software publisher and security advocate, consulted on this story.*

INTERNET TOMORROW

1995--the Internet for us in India was mostly a distant dream. And for the lucky few who had access, it was all about ASCII text and e-mail. Mostly e-mail. Barely five year later, most of us can hardly imagine a world without the Net.

From a small network exclusive to the American academia and military, the

Internet has today become an intricate part of our everyday lives, and has indeed changed the way we look at, understand, and assimilate things. Way back in 1995, who would've imagined online chat or e-commerce?

But the fact is that even more revolutionary things are happening. Things that could totally change the way you and me use the Internet and maybe, even understand it. What are they? How are they? How are they going to affect you? And when are they going to happen?

BROADBAND

The World Wide Web is often referred to as the World Wide Wait. Who among us hasn't had to undergo the frustration of waiting those agonisingly long minutes while a Web page loads? This is more often than not caused by a lack of sufficient bandwidth—either from your end to your ISP, or from your ISP to the Internet backbone. The solution is obviously to increase bandwidth. And broadband is being seen as the savior.

Almost everyone today talks about broadband. But what exactly is it? Simply put, broadband is what baseband is not. Computers traditionally use baseband to communicate. With baseband, you can have only one channel of communication on a media (read wire), as in a telephone line. As opposed to this, broadband offers multiple channels at the same time, like with cable TV. It isn't as if broadband for computers is a new invention. B-ISDN or Broadband ISDN was perhaps the first broadband carrier for computer networks. But it never got popular, largely because it worked only with fiber, and fiber was a rather costly option all these years.

It isn't the multiplicity of channels that attracts the Net towards broadband. Rather, it's the high bandwidth possible. The availability of multiple channels makes it all the more sweeter, allowing you to have Internet and TV and God knows what else, all delivered by the same wire. Higher bandwidths would enable multimedia-rich content to reach users. Forget music and animation, multimedia-rich Web content and video is where the excitement's going to be.

There are four carriers of broadband Internet—, DSL, cable TV, fiber optic cables, and wireless. One of the limitations of wire-based broadband is that the end user has to be pre- tty much near the control or distribution centers of the ISP (or service provider) because the quality of the signal degrades fast. Or, as is the case with fiber optic cables, the media is very costly to layout, and it may not be possible to take it to every possible nook and cranny. That's where wireless broadband offers an alternative.

Of these, DSL—Digital Subscriber Line—is perhaps the easiest. It works over existing copper cables used by conventional telephones. There are actually different types of DSL—like ADSL and HDSL. DSL typically offers much higher bandwidths downstream to the user's computer, than upstream from the user's computer to other machines on the Net. So, DSL is good for home or individual use, where you draw more content from the Net than you would provide to others. By the same token, it's unsuitable for uses like Website hosting.

For setting up a DSL service, you need to set up special equipment at the back end or at the exchange, and near the subscriber's premises. Subscribers also need a DSL modem. DSL services have already reached Indian shores, and Dishnet has started offering them in Bangalore.

The next option is to use the existing cable TV network:—in effect, converting your neighborhood cablewallah into your ISP. Here, the Internet connect comes through your TV cable. So, you have the choice of having a TV set-top box and getting Web pages and mail on your TV, or opting for a cable modem that'll connect to your PC. Here again, downstream speeds are many times more than upstream speeds. By its very nature— cable TV connections are typically to homes and not to offices—broadband over cable is more suited to homes and small offices than to larger corporates. But there are attempts on in Mumbai to use cable to give Internet access to corporate offices. For more information on how the back end works, refer to "A cable modem network", PC *Quest* April 1999, page 92.

Like DSL, Internet over cable is also available in many cities in India, even outside the metros. Ask your cablewallah for more information.

That brings us to fiber. Both the previous options used existing media— the telephone connection or the cable TV connection. Fiber requires significantly large investments just to lay the cable. But the advantage is that fiber provides tremendous bandwidth in both directions, and the Internet isn't the only thing it can carry. It could well be the single media that you need for telecommunication, Internet, TV, and whatever else the future may throw up. The problem, as I mentioned earlier, is the very high initial costs for laying the fiber network.

But even that seems to be giving way, faced with the consistent onslaught of the Net. Spectranet is currently wiring up Delhi (the service should have been launched by the time you read this). More cities are expected to be covered soon.

What about areas where you can't draw a wire to, for whatever, reason? Or, if you as a service provider, don't have the right of way for drawing cable? For.., that, there's wireless broadband. You put up a dish antenna at the receiving location and beam data and TV to it from towers, much like today's terrestrial TV transmission or microwave transmission. Going a bit further, there are plans to beam broadband Internet down from satellites, much like Indium wanted to do with telephony. If the plan really works out, who knows, you may soon have mobile broadband, the ultimate Viagra for any Internet junkie.

To sum up, broadband access would make the Internet more media-rich, and all-pervasive like TV and telephone is today. Broadband could even help the Net replace the telephone and the TV. Many of the other trends that we'll be discussing depend on broadband happening. The good news is that broadband is indeed happening somewhere very near you.

THE INTERNET ON YOUR CELL PHONE

Cell phones are about communication. Of being able to communicate to anyone from anywhere. Right? And the Internet? That's again about communication—one-to-one as in chat and e-mail, and one-to-many as when you browse a Website.

So, it's only natural that some bright spark comes up with the idea of marrying the two. Thus were bom cell phones with built-in Web browsers. The most famous of these were perhaps the Nokia communicators. Unfortunately, Web pages were not exactly designed to be viewed on the small screens that cell phones offered. In general, navigation turned out to be quite a pain. Also, cell phones were not the only mobile communication devices around. There were quite a few of them indeed—pagers, wireless systems, two-way radios. Would it be possible to bring the Internet to al) of them in an easy-to-use way?

So came WAR the Wireless Application Protocol. Though cell phones are the most visible users of WAP, the protocol is such that it can be used by any wireless device. To access the Web, these devices use embedded microbrowsers—small footprint software that can operate in the limited memory that these devices offer. WAP is scalable from text-based browsers—for devices like pagers that can display just two lines of text—to full-function color and multimedia smart-phones. WAP supports HTML and XML too,out WML (an extension of XML) is specifically devised for small screens and numeric keypad-based navigation.

While WAP is yet to catch up in India, Indian software companies are strongly on to the WAP bandwagon, working hard to be on the forefront of the Net revolution's new wave. Silicon Automation Systems and Integra Microsystems are two companies that have already made significant headway in the WAP world.

Even without WAR you can still access parts of the Internet on your cell phone.

Many cell phone services in India now allow anyone to go to their Website and send any of their subscribers an e-mail message, which will be displayed on their cell phone. Many give their subscribers access to stuff like news and scrip prices. , Expect more to come your way, and not just to your cell phone.

THE NAME GAME

Any site on the Net is identified either by a number—its IP address, or its name, like pcquest.com. I won't go into the mechanics of how these are allotted, as we've covered it often enough in these pages. The problem is that both the names and numbers come from a finite set of possibilities, and both run the risk of getting exhausted soon.

Let's look at IP addresses first. We're currently on what's called IPv4 or IP version" 4. It's been estimated that all possible IP addresses available under IPv4 would be exhausted by 2010. And that estimate was made before the current Internet boom. Does that mean that after some time there won't be any more new sites possible?:Has nobody thought of a way out?

Yes, people have been working on a solution for some time now. The answer to the problem is IPv6 or IP version 6. IPv6 offers a whole host of new features, but what's important for us is that it increases the number of available IP addresses beyond any imaginable number. You could give every gadget and electric outlet on this earth an IP address, and still have a vast reserve left over.

Unfortunately, these things work by committee, and as you know any committee takes Its own time doing things. So, IPv6 has been some time in the making. Jokes about committees apart, IPv6 is not an easy task, what with having to ensure that all current systems remain compliant with the new setup. No wonder that it's taking so much time.

That brings us to the name part. The name of a site is in two parts—the name itself as in "pcquest" and the registry as in ".com" There are any number of registries, including country specific ones like ".co.in". Unfortunately, by far the most popular is .com, and an overwhelming majority of Websites have a .com address—so much so that most short combinations of characters in the English (and in native) languages have been registered with .com extensions. To quote the' ICANN (Internet Corporation for Assigned Names and Numbers), "in April 1999, a survey found that of 25,500 standard English-language dictionary words, only 1,760 were free in the .com domain".

So what do newcomers do? Twiddle their thumbs and give the internet up as a lost baltle even-before they started? Here again, alternatives have been thought of. An additional set of international registries have been proposed. The current plan is to add six to ten new generic Top Level Domains (as they're technically called), evaluate how things work out, and then proceed further. The exact process of rollout is being worked out.

Given the current Internet craze, with dozens of sites sprouting up everyday, one thing is for sure. You'll see additions in both areas—IP addresses and top-level domains faster than you think. So, fasten your seatbelts and get ready logo beyond dotcom.

AN ELECTRIC NET

You connect to the Internet over telephone, or over network cables. Nothing new in that. What about accessing the Net through your electric socket? Shocking? Read on.

So far, the Net has been very much a computers-only service. That is, you need to have a computer for Net access, or looking at it from the other side, the Net could reach only computers. As we saw earlier, cell phones and other wireless devices are now trying to enter this space. But they aren't the only ones in the queue. A whole lot of gadgets and appliances would like to connect and communicate over the Net.

Let's look at some standard examples. What about your microwave downloading settings for that new dish you want to try out, from the Website you downloaded the menu from? Or on the same token, what about your washing machine downloading the settings for that expensive dress, right from the online shop where the dress was bought? Makes life simple. Right?

Again the bright sparks are at work, Internet-enabling all sorts Of gadgets and devices. That's the easy part. Now comes the question. How do you connect up all the appliances in your home—refrigerator, washing machine, food processor, microwave, computers, radio, TV...—to the Net? Face it, we're talking of a full-fledged network at your home. Obviously, you can't use individual telephone dialups for each piece of equipment. So, you need a network. There are two major options for doing this. One camp argues that home networking is best done with telephone cables. This is along more or less familiar routes. The other argues that you should use already existing connections—the electrical outlets—for home networking. Companies are already at work, developing standards and technologies for routing the Net over electricity lines and through your electric plugs. Wait a year, or even less, to see the early results of their efforts.

ENTERTAINMENT FIRST

The growth of the Internet has been associated with certain killer applications—applications that made people flock to the Net in droves. The first killer application was e-mail. It was e-mail—instantaneous, personal, and almost free—that made the Net a success in its early days. Then came chat. The leap from one-way e-mail to two-way chat made the Net a real-time media, rather than just a faster and cheaper post office. The third killer application, which happened almost simultaneously, was e-commerce. Millions were drawn to the Net by its lure— the lure of being able to shop from home, of being able to trade in stocks from home, and of being able to conduct a garage sale from your desktop. The fancy discount schemes and the high voltage ad campaigns of online businesses added fuel to this fire in no mean measure.

But the killer application of them all is yet to come. And that's going to be entertainment.

Consider this. There are mor eTV and radio sets than there are telephone instruments or PCs. There are more TV and radio stations than there are telephone companies and ISPs. And entertainment—sports, movies, drama, and of course, news—has always been big business. So what better than to marry the Net and entertainment? The opportunities are mind-boggling.

So what's holding it back? The lack of bandwidth at the user end. Movies and even plain audio take up huge amounts of bandwidth, and it's virtually impossible to get good results over analog dialup lines. Here too, it isn't as if the technology and the services don't exist. There are streaming news and music services currently operating on the Net. But you get to see them only on miniscule windows, and that too with at least an ISDN connect.

Broadband, when it happends will alter the scene completely. What would make the Net a full-fledged entertainment medium is broadband, and what would make broadband viable is entertainment services. It's a Catch 22 situation, but the logjam should be breaking sooner than later.

WILL THE NET BE YOUR COMPUTER?

By and large, when we talk of a computer, we mean the PC. That may soon be a thing of the past, and the Net may well become your computer!

I don't mean that you'll use the huge servers on the Net to create a supercomputer that'll do your work taster, the scenario I'm outlining is totally different.

Basically, your PC carried out three functions—it stores data, processes data, and displays stuff. Now, there's no reason why all of these should be on the same machine, or even at the same place.

Already, the Web is offering to store your stuff for you. And that too, not just e-mail. Today, you can maintain your fifes and your schedules on various Websites. Now, what if all your files are always stored on the Web, and you can access them over broadband connects? Then, you just need a device that can do the minimal processing required at the front end and display the stuff for you. Add a WAP-enabled gadget, and bingo! There goes the need for a PC Another possibility is to have display-only devices with Net connects available all over, and wherever you are, you plug in a smart card into the nearest one to access your "PC" from the Web.

Sounds futuristic? Parts of it are already. in place. Apple has a service called iDisk (available at www.itools.mac.com),using' which you can save your files at the Apple Website, and your Mac sees your directory on the Web as another folder on its desktop. The SunRay (obviously, from Sun Microsystems) or a similar thin client could well Wake the second scenario come alive.The Sunray saves all files oh the server, and you can access them using your smart card. Pull out your smart card and your applications and data are SunRay on the network, and you can resume from wherever you left off.

What we're waiting for here really is economies of scale. And that could be one long wait.

ALWAYS ON

Typically, you pay for your internet connection on the bais of the bandwidth you use and the time you stay connected to the; service. Thus, you would have,to pay different amounts for 33.6 k dialup, 64 k ISDN, 128 k ISDN, and so on. In each of these cases, you pay for every hour you stay connected, irrespective of whether you do anything on your machine or not.

Now consider your cable TV service. Do you pay by the number of hours you Watch TV or by the number of channels you get at home? Obviously not. You pay a fixed amount every month. And sometimes, you may pay extra for some extra channels. More importantly, the cable service is always on (except for power cuts, if your service provider like mine doesn't invest in a generator), whether your TV is on or not. Very soon, your internet service would also become like that. That is, it would always be available at your end. You just have to switch on your computer,or set-top device or appliance to get going. You would pay for the bandwidth, you've opted for, along with either a fixed monthly fee or a fee based on actual data transmitted and not:for connect time.

This, too, is already happening. Many cable ISPs are. charging by the month. Even other ISPs, Dishnet for example, have begun offering packages where you pay a fixed amount and surf as long as you want. Look forward to this becoming more widespread.

APPS ON DEMAND

This one, in a way, extends the Web as your computer paradigm, but has already started happening. The concept is like this. What if the computer applications you need are treated as services and not as applications? Why should you pay a huge one-time cost for an application that you may not be using all 24 hours? Why not pay for actual usage instead? Something like pay-per-view movies. Why not use the Net to host such applications that users can connect to when they require?

Typical candidates for such a model are high-value products like ERP and billing software on one end and mass application packages like office suites on the other. As mentioned earlier, this one has already arrived, courtesy application service providers. The Indian-made ERP package—Makess—is already up. So is SAP with Mysap.com. Sun Microsystems is coming up with the Star portal for Star Office. The vendors are ready. What about the users?

Again, the critical, but missing ingredient is bandwidth. Lots of it.

WILL E-COM SURVIVE?

E-commerce is big business today. Enough and more has been written about it. Here we'll concentrate on just one thing. What is it that holds e-com up? Or as the business consultants say, what's the value proposition?

Unfortunately, the value proposition for moste-com sites seems to the novelty factor of shopping online, discounts and other freebies, and huge advertising spends. Hardly the stuff thai can hold a business up for long. No wonder then that most online business-to-customer setups are deep in the red.

So, unless e-com sites are able to deVebp value propositions for potential customers that'll simultaneously give them a healthy bottom line too, they'll find it difficult to survive. In other words, if the value they offer is going to be just the convenience of the Web (discounts and freebies must come to an end someday), then they may face a very tough challenge from established brick-and-mortar businesses that can go online and offer the same convenience.

In short, we may see the decline and fall of most clicks-only businesses, unless they go the clicks-and-mortar way. In fact, the first symptoms of this are already available in the West, Amazon.com is quietly making heavy investments in conventional distribution infrastrusture. CDNow, which at one time was heralded as th model for the future, is now facing very tough time. The others better watch out.

HTML IS DEAD

Way back, in the early days of the Net, all URLs used to end with either HTM or HTML, signifying that they were HTML pages. How many URLs do you see today that do the same? Today, you have ASP pages and PHP pages and God knows what else. So, is HTML dead?

Yes, HTML in its pure form is more or less dead, but not because of ASP or PHP.

HTML is a non-interactive layout language. It can lay out the text and graphics, color, bold fonts, blinking fonts, et al. And it slops pretty much there. The biggest limitation of pure HTML is that it can't interact with the user, accepting inputs from him and responding to that. Communication is all about interactivity, and if the Net is about communication, then HTML is just ground zero. One had to go beyond simple HTML to achieve interactivity.

On the Web, you can do this by using a mixed bag of tricks. The Web designer uses various scripting languages, evolved layout languages like XML (eXtended Markup Language), and add-ons like Flash to make the Web a live and happening medium. Today, HTML-only pages are more or less dead. Long live HTML.

Glossary

GLOSSARY OF JARGON AND ABBREVIATIONS

An alphabetic list of abbreviations follows this glossary of common computing terms. (See also main text of book, accessed through index.)

JARGON

Absolute Address	The actual location number of a word in computer store (see Relative address)
Access Time	Time to transfer information between backing store and main memory
Accumulator	A location (register) in the ALU where arithmetic operations are carried out
Acoustic Coupler	A device which connects a digital computer system to an analogue telephone via sounds rather than an electrical connection (see Modem)
Ada	High-level programming language for real-time applications. Developed for US Department of Defence and named after Countess Ada Lovelace
Address	The way a particular location in computer store is referenced (see Absolute, Relative and Symbolic addresses)
ALGOL	High-level programming language suitable for structured programming; used mainly for scientific applications. Inspired other languages like Ada and Pascal
Algorithm	A set of rules or defined process which performs a particular task; a mathematical formula or program procedure
Alphanumeric	A group of characters which includes a mix of numerals, alphabetic letters and (sometimes) punctuation marks and other symbols

Analogue A way of representing numerical values by a continuously changing physical quantity; for example the hands of a non-digital watch or sound-level display on a hi-fi set

AND A logic operator. Given statements *a* and *b*, the result of operation *a* AND *b* is true only if both *a* and *b* are true; if one or both of *a* and *b* are false, the result is false

APL A compact high-level programming language requiring little computing knowledge; used mainly for engineering, business planning and scientific applications

Application The user task performed by a computer (such as playing a game, making an airline reservation or processing a company's accounts). Applications software carries out the applications task (see also Systems software)

Application Language See End-user language

Architecture 1. The blueprint design which defines how the components within a computer system are interrelated. 2. The internal structure of a computer, such as the number of bits in the basic word length and the instruction set specification. 3. The design of computing elements and information flows in a network

Archival Store Files stored for historical reasons and infrequently accessed

Arithmetic and Logic Unit The part of a computer where arithmetic and logical operations take place using accumulators and special circuits. Sometimes referred to as the Arithmetic Unit

Array An ordered group of information elements, such as a list or table. Each element is identified by a subscript which specifies its relative position within the array. An array can have any number of dimensions

Array Processor See Parallel processing

Artificial Intelligence	The study of how computing can be applied to perform tasks that involve intellectual, communications and sensory activities akin to those in human beings
Assembler	1. Software to translate a low-level language program into machine-readable code. 2. An assembly language
Assembly Language	A low-level programming language, similar in structure to machine code but using mnemonic instructions and symbolic addressing
Asynchronous	Events unco-ordinated by regular time sequences. Asynchronous data transmission co-ordinates sending and receiving devices by Start and Stop codes in front of and after the transmitted data
Availability	The percentage of time a computer system is operational
Backend Processor	A system which acts as a processing support to the main general computer, typically a database processor
Backing Storage	Computer store (such as magnetic media) used to hold large amounts of information as a backing to main memory
Back-up	1. Doubling up on systems components to improve availability, with the stand-by moving into action if its twinned element fails. 2 Information held separately from current data which can be used to reconstitute the information base to a recent state, if the current data is corrupted or destroyed. 3. A computer installation which could be used to run work normally processed on another computer that is out of action for some reason
Bandwidth	Measurement of the information transmission capacity of a telecommunications link (see Narrowband, Wideband)
Bar Code	A code made up of lines of different widths which can be read by a special scanner; often attached to products to provide direct input to a computer system (see Light pen, Point of Sale, Wand)

Baseband	1. The 0 Hz band on which digital transmission signals are centred; digital transmission is sometimes called baseband. 2, A general term for the waveband occupied by unmodulated signals
BASIC	Easy-to-learn, high-level programming language, popular on microcomputers
Batch Processing	Form of data processing where input is gathered in batches in a computer installation, with the work processed sequentially from a batch queue in which some programs may be given special priorities.
Baud	Measurement of data transmission speed, equivalent to bits per second
Benchmark	A test to measure the performance of a system
Binary	A two-state system which can be represented by the digits 0 and 1. Digital computers perform information processing, store data and transmit information as binary digits
Binary Coded Decimal	A way of coding information in which each decimal digit or character is represented by a number of bits
Bipolar	A transistor with two n or p poles in the form of a pnp or npn sandwich (see n-type and p-type regions)
Bit	Abbreviation for Binary digiT. Takes the value of 0 or 1
Bit-slice	A technique of building up the word-length of a microprocessor architecture from chips containing thin slices of shorter word lengths (eg four 2-bit slices would make an 8-bit processor)
Bits Per Second	Measure of speed of digital transmission
Black Box	Colloquial expression for processor and memory inside the hardware packaging of a computer
Boolean	An algebra based on logical operators and true/false binary values; named after George Boole (1815-1864)
Bootstrap	Initialising routine which sets up the required program when a system is started up

Broadband See Wideband

Bubble Memory A compact form of solid state mass memory in which bit's are represented as magnetic domains in a thin film of material such as garnet

Bug An error; usually used in relation to program errors

Bureau An organisation which offers access to its own computer processing capabilities, software and applications expertise, usually on a commercial basis

Bus The means of exchanging information between the components of a computer and of providing connections to external input, output and storage. Includes specialised buses for data and other functions

Byte A group of 8 bits, generally the length of a coded character but some machines have different bit-lengths for characters

Cartridge A container for a magnetic disk or tape

Cassette Tape A self-contained magnetic tape device for storing computer data; the same as music cassettes (see Backing store. Mass storage and Serial access)

Cathode Ray Tube A tube which acts as an electronic gun focused onto a phosphor-coated screen to create a display; used in VDUs and TV sets

Central Processing Unit The main control unit in a von Neumann architecture; includes at least the ALU and CU and, in some systems, also main memory

Character A basic unit of coded computer data (see Byte)

Charge Coupled Device A solid state volatile mass memory in which the application of an external electrical field causes charges to be passed from one storage element to the next

Chip A piece of material (such as silicon) about a quarter-inch square containing integrated transistor circuits

Circuit 1. An interlinked set of electronic components and gates which creates a path through which electrons

	can flow to perform certain tasks; 2. The communications link between two or more points.
Circuit Switching	Linking devices in a network by directly connecting transmission circuits via switching centres or exchanges, as in the traditional public telephone network
Clock	A control linked to the processing unit which generates regular pulses to synchronise actions in the computer
COBOL	High-level language widely used for commercial applications
CODASYL	Body which defined COBOL and monitors its development; also has a task group on database management systems
COMAL	A high-level language which combines the easy-to-learn capability of BASIC and the structured programming features of languages like Pascal
Common Carrier	Organisation operating a telecommunications network available to the public and other organisations
Communications Processor	A computer system whose main task is to co-ordinate and route information in a communications network
Compatibility	1. The ability to run a program on machines with different architectures. 2. The ability for devices to communicate with each other in a communications network although they may have been initially developed to handle incompatible protocols.
Compiler	Software which translates a high-level language into machine code
Complementary MOS	Type of integrated circuit with low power consumption, often used in devices with limited energy supplies, such as a watch or calculator
Computer	Consists of (at least) a processor, memory and ports for input/output
Computer Aided Design	Application that assists in the design of new products and buildings and in the drafting of design drawings

Computer Aided Instruction	Application which provides a preprogrammed self-learning educational course
Computer Aided Learning	Same as CAI but generally with broader educational aims
Computer Aided Manufa-	Application which covers all stages of the production
cturing	process; can be linked directly to a CAD system
Computer Aided Training	Same as CAI but applied to the training of new skills rather than other types of educational objectives
Computer Axial (Aided)	Computer-controlled scanner which can present three
Tomography	dimensional X-ray images
Computer Managed Learning	A system which helps manage student records and monitor learning progress, as well as offering CAL capabilities
Computer NC	Computer control of NC machines
Computer Output Microfilm	Archival backing store produced on microfilm by a computer
Conditional Branching	A branch in a program where the point to which control is moved can vary according to different conditions
Configuration	The elements which comprise a computer system
Constant	Storage location in a program with a fixed value
Contents Addressable File	Technique of retrieving information by direct reference
Store	to its contents rather than indirectly via an index or by a location address
Contract Staff	Computer staff employed temporarily on a set contract
Control Unit	The part of a computer which controls the sequence of actions by the program and input/output operations; contains circuits (registers) which decode instructions and addresses (see Central Processing Unit)
Core	Main memory consisting of a magnetisable ferrite core; replaced valves as main memory in the 1950s

	and was superseded by transistors and ferrite core in the 1960s. Main memory is often called 'core store', even when it is made from another material
Crash	Colloquialism for a breakdown in the running of a computer
Cursor	Pointer on a VDU screen which indicates where the next typed character will be placed
Daisy Wheel	A print mechanism consisting of a hub and spokes (called petals). The character printheads are at the ends of the petals. The wheel rotates to position the printheads
Data	Synonymous with information but generally used for the representation and processing of information by a computer system
Data Description Language	A language used to specify data structures and relationships. Sometimes known as a Data Definition Language
Data Dictionary	An important component of a Database Management System which contains data definitions and other information to help control, monitor and protect the database
Data Flow Architecture	Computers controlled by data rather than program actions
Data Manipulation Language	A language used to store, retrieve and update items in a database; can be incorporated within a high level programming language
Data Preparation	Converting data usually collected manually on forms into a medium suitable for subsequent computer input
Data Processing	Could apply to any type of computerised information processing but generally used to describe administrative, accounting and commercial computing work
Data Processing Manager	Manager of department responsible for computing and data processing activities in an organisation
Databank	A large database

Database	Computerised information organised to make its storing, updating and retrieval efficient and reliable
Database Administrator	Job function responsible for establishing, developing and controlling the database
Database Management System	The design and software techniques used to organise the database structure and provide access to information in it
Database Processor	A computer system whose main task is to handle database-related operations
Database Task Group	Established by CODASYL to develop standard database management techniques
Debug	To search for and eliminate errors (see Bug)
Decision Support System	Software which provides information and modelling aids to help users make decisions
Declare	Describe explicitly the nature of data elements in a program
Denary	The ten-digit decimal number system
Desk-top System	A complete computer small enough to fit on an office desk
Digital	Representation of information by discrete numerical quantities
Diode	The simplest transistor of single p- and n-regions together as a pn junction
Direct Access	Access to information on computer storage by going directly to the required item, wherever it is held on the medium; disks are direct access devices
Direct Numerical Control	NC and other machine tools controlled by a central computer (see Flexible manufacturing)
Disc	Alternative spelling for disk (see Video disc)
Disk	See Magnetic disk
Diskette	See Floppy disk
Distributed Data Processing	See Distributed processing
Distributed Processing	A system or network where computing capabilities are in many locations rather than at a central point;

	also known as distributed computing or distributed data processing
Dot Matrix	See Matrix output
Dumb Terminal	A terminal which does not incorporate any of its own computing capability and can operate only when linked on-line to a computer
Dump	Regular copying of information to backing store which helps to provide a security safeguard in case data is corrupted or destroyed (see Back-up)
Duplex	A communications link which allows transmission in two directions simultaneously (see Half-duplex and
Dynamic Memory	Storage of information as an electric charge that can leak away over time, so must be refreshed frequently
Editor	Software which enables the user to edit information stored in a computer, such as updating and revising the draft of a document or amending a program to correct a bug
Electronic Funds Transfer	Carrying out a financial transaction through electronic
System	transmission of information rather than by a direct exchange of cash
Electronic Mail	The transmission of messages, documents and other information by electronic means, such as via the telephone and by linked communicating word processors
Electronic Mailbox	See Store and forward
Electronic Office	General term to encompass future office procedures and jobs where a variety of computer-based systems and electronic devices are used
Electrosensitive	A form of non-impact printer where specially-treated conductive paper is sensitised to produce the printed image
Emulation	Making a system behave like another system; used to predict the actions of a new computer service before it is implemented

End User — A term often used by computer professionals and manufacturers to refer to the person who uses the final service or product

End-user Language — Language which enables programs to be written by an end user without any programming expertise (see Nonprocedural language.)

Enquiry Language — See Query language

Erasable PROM — A PROM whose program can be erased, say by shining an ultra-violet light onto the ROM; the ROM can then be reprogrammed

Ergonomic — The study of people and equipment in the working environment to provide satisfying and safe, as well as efficient and effective, working conditions. Often used to mean the physical design of equipment

Error Messages — Output from a computer to warn the user that something has gone wrong and what, if anything, can be done about it

Ethernet — One form of Local Area Network

Exclusive OR — See XOR

Execute — To initiate and carry out an instruction or a complete routine or programme (see Run)

Expert System — A system programmed in a logic language to follow the 'human reasoning' used by an expert to deduce certain findings, reached through a judgement based on experience, which has been distilled into the program (see LISP, PROLOG)

Exponent — A mathematical notation to indicate the power to which a number is raised; for example, the square of 8 (64) is expressed as 8^2, where the 2 is the exponent

Facsimile — Electronic transmission of the image of a document from one point to another; a 'telecopier'

Fax — Abbreviation for facsimile

Fetch — The action of getting an instruction from memory and decoding it in the Control Unit

Fibre Optic Cable	Telecommunications cable composed of hair-thin glass fibres; data is transmitted as pulses of light down the fibres
Fiche	Microfilm in the form of a rectangular piece of film, like a card
Field	The basic structural element in a file; a number of fields go to form a record and records are grouped to form files
Field Effect Transistor	A type of transistor consisting of a single pn junction but acting like a bipolar junction; relatively compact, low cost and requiring low power consumptions (see Metal Oxide Silicon)
Fifth Generation	A range of computer architectures and capabilities designed for ease and naturalness of use as its prime objective; originated with a report in 1981 for the Japanese" government
File	Information organised into an interrelated set of records, such as a student file or product file
File Processing	A form of data management where information is structured into separate files; this is more inefficient and inflexible than database management systems where the same data item can form part of many different files and data structures
Firmware	Software stored in hardwired form, typically in ROM
Fixed Point	Computer calculations which assume that the decimal point is at a particular position within one or more words used to represent each number (see Floating point)
Flexible Manufacturing	Application where a number of machine tools and NC machines are controlled by a central computer; the production process can be changed by altering the control program rather than re-engineering machine tools
Flip Flop	A circuit which can be in one of two states; the state is changed by a pulse and remains fixed until another pulse is received. Used for static memories

Floating Point	Computer calculations performed by representing each number as a mantissa and exponent; the mantissa is multiplied by a base (say 10) raised to the power defined by the exponent; needs a special unit attached to the processor
Floppy Disk	Disk storage made of thin flexible material, similar in size to a 45 rpm record (see Magnetic disk)
Flowchart	A graphical representation of the structure of a system, software, file or database (see Structured design)
FORTRAN	A programming language used mainly for scientific applications
Front-end Processor	A system which removes some of the processing load from a central computer, typically handling communications co-ordination functions before the data is sent to the central system for processing
Gallium Arsenide	A semiconductor alternative to silicon chips
Garbage In/Garbage Out	A warning that incorrect input will produce incorrect output, however good the program processing it
Gate	An electronic device which has one or more input signals and one output; the output value is dependent on the logic-operations performed by the gate's circuit. Logic gates (for operations like AND and OR) can be built into the circuits of a computer processor
Gateway	A switching centre that interconnects two independent networks
Graceful Degradation	The ability of a computer to continue operating despite the failure of a component within it, probably at a reduced performance level
Graphics	Information in the form of drawings, graphs and pictorial images rather than alphanumeric text. There are special graphics terminals and input and output devices (see Light pen, Tablet)
Half-duplex	A communications link which allows data transmission in two directions, but not at the same time

Hard Copy	See Printout
Hard Disk	A rigid magnetic oxide-coated disk with higher capacity than a floppy disk and held in a cartridge container
Hardware	The physical equipment of a computer system
Hardwired	Fixed electronic circuit patterns (see Microcode)
Hertz	Unit of measurement of transmission signal frequency (cycles per second)
Heuristic	Method of solving problems through successive 'trial-and-error' attempts at a solution, rather than by a predetermined algorithm; used in AI systems
Hex	Abbreviation for hexadecimal
Hexadecimal	A number system with 16 digits used for data representation in a computer
High-level Language	A programming language designed to match the information processing needs of the application; uses commands and statement structures similar to a restricted form of a natural language (see low-level language)
Holographic Memory	A form of mass storage where information is held on a film and read using a laser.
Housekeeping Routines	Systems software which helps organise the use of available resources, particularly in the allocation and deployment of storage space
Human Factors Engineering	Generally synonymous with ergonomics, used mainly in the US
Impact Printer	Printer which creates an image by the physical contact of a printhead shaped as the required character
Inclusive OR	The OR logic operation
Index Sequential Filing	A form of file organisation where records are stored sequentially on a direct access medium and accessed directly via an index.
Informatics	Used synonymously with information technology; anglicised version of the French informatique, which

	is more the equivalent of data processing (see Telematique)
Information Management	The co-ordination of all information services in an organisation
Information Provider	An organisation or individual who provides information to be stored on a public viewdata system like Prestel
Information Retrieval	The use of a computer to search and extract information from a database
Information Technology	The devices and techniques used to store, process, manage, transmit and communicate information; encompasses various technologies such as computing, microelectronics and communications
Initial Programme Load	The routines needed to initialise a system before the software is loaded (see Bootstrap)
Ink Jet Printer	Non-impact printing technique which creates characters as a matrix of dots squirted at, high speed from ink jet nozzles
Input	Information entered into a computer system for processing; the act of entering data
Installation	The location of the main computer hardware
Instruction Set	The basic machine code operations provided by a particular computer architecture; each instruction initiates and performs a processing action once it has been decoded in the Control Unit (see Microcode)
Instructions Per Second	Measurement of the power of a processor
Integer	A whole number (1,2,3. . . , etc.)
Integrated Circuit	Circuits composed of many transistors which have been reduced in size and placed together in a single physical element, typically into a silicon chip
Intelligence	The capability provided by a computer processor, memory and software
Intelligent Terminal	A device which incorporates its own computing intelligence
Interactive	An application where the user is involved in a continuous dialogue with the system

Interactive Video	CAL techniques combined with video disc or tape
Interface	The junction between two devices, software modules or other elements involved in the operation of a computer
Interpreter	A program that translates a high-level language program into machine code statement by statement, rather then by analysing the complete program at once, as a compiler would do; typically used with an interactive language like BASIC
Interrupt	When the Control Unit stops processing to handle some external need, such as performing an I/O task
Inverter	See NOT
Iteration	Achieving a result by performing the same process repeatedly (see Repetition)
Job Control Language	The language used to tell the operating system how to organise and process the workload on a computer
Josephson Junction	Form of digital processing and storage which exploits the fact that some metals become superconductors at low temperatures; an alternative to silicon chips
Jump	See Branch
Junction	The place where n- and p-regions meet to form a transistor
Key	One or more characters within an information structure used to identify the whole structure, for example the name field in a student file
Keyboard	Means of typing input to a computer; input part of a VDU
Keypad	Compact keyboard with only few keys or buttons which could look like a TV remote control unit or a calculator's push-buttons
Key-to-disk/tape	A data preparation method which creates information on a disk or tape from keyboard input
Keyword	The most significant word or words which identify what the user is seeking in an information retrieval

	application; keywords can be combined by logic operators to aid information retrieval
Label	A number or word identifying a particular program statement, used in branching operations
Language	See Data Description, Data Management, End-user, Natural, Programming and Query languages
Large Scale Integration	A measure of the circuit density on a chip, typically in thousands of gates; between Medium and Very Large Scale Integration
Laser	An amplifier and generator of coherent light energy which can travel over vast distances without being dispersed; abbreviation for Light Amplification for Stimulated Emission of Radiation
Laser Printer	Non-impact method using lasers on light-sensitive material
Light Emitting Diode	A semiconductor display made of a substance, such as gallium arsenide, which glows when connected to an electron flow
Light Pen	A pen-like device which emits electric pulses; used for graphics input and to read bar codes
Line Printer	Impact printer which prints a line at a time
Linear Programming	A mathematical technique which calculates the optimum solution to a problem involving many variables which interact within a framework of known constraints
Liquid Crystal Display	A form of display composed of a liquid crystal substance sandwiched in a glass cell and activated by the application of a tiny voltage across the cell
LISP	A logic programming language
Local	Computing capability close to the user's location (see Remote)
Local Area Network	A means of interlinking, computers, terminals and other devices within a building
Logging on/off	The procedures needed to initiate and terminate a session at a terminal, including, for example, giving a secret password to identify the user

Logical Inferences per Second	Measure of speed of a logic program, like an expert system
Logic Operators	The basic actions and rules which determine the results used in Boolean algebra (see AND, NAND, NOR, NOT, OR, XOR)
Logic Programming	A development of formal logic principles similar to the way expert systems reach conclusions by following logical inferences; suited to AI, expert systems, parallel processing, educational and other applications
LOGO	An easy-to-learn language designed to enable students to learn by experience by controlling a movable object via LOGO
Loop	A section of code repeated a given number of times
Low-level Language	A programming language based on the format of the machine code of each architecture (see Assembly language)
Machine Code	The numeric codes which form a computer's instruction set (see Low-level language)
Magnetic Card	Cards coated with magnetic material for data storage; used with early word processors
Magnetic Disk	Disks coated with magnetic material, similar to music records, used to store computer data (see Direct access, Floppy disk. Hard disk and Winchester disk)
Magnetic Ink Character Recognition	Computer input by automatically reading characters printed with a special magnetised ink
Magnetic Media	Backing store which stores information as bits according to the magnetisation of tiny elements in the surface of the medium (see Magnetic cards, disks and tape)
Magnetic Tape	Tapes coated with magnetic material, similar to tapes for a domestic tape recorder, used to store computer data (see Cassette tape, Serial access)
Main Memory	Memory linked directly to the processor which holds programs and data required for immediate processing; sometimes regarded as part of the CPU

Mainframe	A computer with high capability, larger than other computers and generally provided with comprehensive applications and software support from the supplier
Management Information System	A range of computing services which provide management and administration staff with timely and accurate information and aids to assist carrying out their work (see Decision Support Systems)
Mantissa	Element in a floating point number
Man/Machine Communications	See User/system interaction
Mass Storage	Backing storage which contains large amounts of information
Matrix	A two-dimensional array consisting of a number of rows or columns
Matrix Output	Characters formed as a matrix of dots either as a dot matrix printer or on a display screen
Mean Time Between Failure	Average time between system breakdowns
Medium-Scale Integration	Between Small- and Large-Scale Integration as a measure of the circuit density on a chip; typically measured in hundreds of gates
Memory	Synonymous with computer storage but usually used in relation to main memory
Memory Map	A summary, often as a diagram, of the way main memory is allocated to different types of systems software and user programs
Menu	A form of user/system interaction where the user selects an action from a menu of options
Metal Oxide Semiconductor	A transistor made from layers of a metal, an oxide and a semiconductor
Microcode	Code used in a microprogram to turn a machine's instruction set into the appropriate signals to implement machine code; a microcoded instruction set can be altered whereas a hardwired implementation is fixed

Microcomputer A complete computer, the smallest and cheapest computers available commercially

Microfiche See Fiche

Microfilm Storage of reduced images of a document on film

Microprocessor A processing device on a chip

Microprogram See Microcode

Mill Colloquial term for the processor; mill time is time spent processing

Minicomputer A computer generally between a microcomputer and maxi/mainframe in price and performance, although demarcation between categories is fuzzy; often packaged as part of a small business system, word processor or intelligent terminal (see Original Equipment Manufacturer)

Modelling Software which simulates a system manipulating a number of variables which interact with each other; can answer "What if...?" questions to predict behaviour of the modelled system depending on how the variables are altered (see Decision Support Systems)

Modems Devices needed at the ends of an analogue transmission line to translate between the digital code of computers and the analogue wave form; an abbreviation for Modulator-DEModulator

Modulation Translating information into the required wave form for the link used for telecommunications

Module A self-contained hardware or software unit which links with other modules to form a complete system (see Structured design)

Mouse A device which moves the cursor on a screen in the same direction that the mouse is moved on a flat surface

Multifunction Workstation A workstation from which a variety of electronic office functions can be carried out

Multiprogramming The ability to run more than one program at a time in the same computer

N-type Region	A negatively charged area because it has an extra electron following the doping of a semiconductor with material which has an extra valence electron to the semiconductor
NAND	Logical operator which gives the opposite result to AND; abbreviation for Not AND
Nano-	A prefix signifying one thousand-millionth (often known as one billionth)
Narrowband	Telecommunications bandwidth that permits a limited volume of information to flow through it, less than a wideband link
Natural Language	A language used by people, like English
Network	The interlinking of many computers, terminals and other devices by telecommunications links according to a structured architecture and agreed protocols for communication
Nibble	A unit of four bits; half a byte
Node	1. A switching centre in a network. 2. A basic unit in a structured diagram
Non-impact Printer	Printing technique which creates an image on paper without physical contact between a printhead and paper (see Electrosensitive, Ink jet. Laser and Thermal printers)
Non-procedural Language	A programming language designed for end users which matches applications processes rather than the algorithmic procedures of other programming languages
Non-volatile Memory	Memory which retains information when its power supply is switched off
NOR	Logic operator which gives the opposite result to OR; abbreviation for NotOR
NOT	Logic operator which changes a true value to false and a false to true (or a 0 to 1 and 1 to 0); also called an inverter
Number Cruncher	Colloquialism for an application involving many complex calculations

Numerical Control Machine	A machine tool controlled by a program on a paper tape loop; a computer numerical control machine has more sophisticated control by computer software
Object Code	The binary machine code produced by a compiler, assembler or interpreter after translating the source program
Octal	A number system with 8 digits, used for data representation in a computer
Office of the Future	Another term for electronic office
Off-line	Activities related to computer tasks carried out when the user, local computer, terminal or peripheral is not in direct communication with a central computer (see also Spooling)
On-line	Activity in direct communications with a computer, say by a terminal linked to a remote system
Open Systems Interconnection	Standards set by ISO to offer a structure for open systems networks which provide compatibility across the network between various computing devices and systems
Operating System	Essential systems software which co-ordinates and controls the scheduling of work on the system and the use of the system's resources
Operator	Person who supervises and carries out the necessary physical tasks (like loading magnetic media) and is involved in processing work on a computer system; a word processing operator is a secretarial function which consists primarily of typing on a word processor
Optical Character Recognition	Input method which automatically recognises printed characters
Optical Fibre	See Fibre optic cable
Optical Mark Reading	Input method which recognises the absence or presence of a mark in a standard position on a form
OR	A logic operator. Given statements *a* and *b*, the result of operation *a* OR *b* is false if both *a* and *b* are false; if one or both of *a* and *b* are true, the result is true. Also known as inclusive OR

Original/Other Equipment Manufacturer — A company which produces a complete system or device which incorporates key components, or a whole computer, made by another supplier

Output — The results of computer processing which could, for example, be presented on a VDU display or on a printer

P-type Region — A positively-charged area which has one too few electrons following the doping of a semiconductor with material which has one less valence electron than the semiconductor

Package Software — Software which performs an applications task and which can be bought as a complete system

Packet Switching — A method of data transmission where information is sent in a 'packet' that includes an address at the front; this address is used to route the package to its destination via switching exchanges (see X25)

Paddle — Input device with a joystick control, particularly used with computer TV games

Paging — A form of virtual storage where programs are divided into a number of fixed-length storage units called pages

Paper Tape — Input, output or storage medium which uses holes punched in a reel of paper tape to represent coded data

Parallel Processing — A computer architecture, such as an array processor, which allows many processors to work on the same problem simultaneously

Parameter — A variable in a program or procedure which can be given a specific value for a given run or implementation of a program or to tailor packaged software to a specific user environment

Pascal — A high-level language used for a variety of applications; an evolution of ALGOL suited to structured programming. Named After French mathematician and philosopher Blaise Pascal

Password	A codeword used as part of the logging-in procedure to help check that data is accessed only by an authorised person
Peripheral	Input, output and backing store devices which form part of a computer system
Personal Computer	A microcomputer whose main application is for personal use rather than for corporate problem solving
Personal Computing	A capability provided on a terminal in a computer network which offers similar functions to a personal computer
Personal Identification Number	A personal number used as a security check with plastic cards in automatic transactions, such as obtaining money from a computer-controlled cash dispenser
Petal Printer	Another term for daisy wheel printer
PL/1	A high-level language which combines the capabilities of COBOL and FORTRAN
Plotter	Device used for graphics output
Plug compatible Manufacturer	A manufacturer which produces processors, peripherals or terminals that behave in exactly the same way as similar equipment from another manufacturer
Point of Sale	A computer-based or electronic system used at the point where a retail sale is made, such as at the checkout in a supermarket
Port	Connection where an external device can be linked to the internal bus of a computer or where communications channels are linked to a computer system
Portability	The ability to move a program from one computer to another; one objective of high level languages
Prestel	First public viewdata service, run by British Telecom
Private Automatic Branch Exchange	A computerised switching exchange used within an organisation and linked to PSTN or other external carrier

Private Branch Exchange Non-computerised PABX but sometimes synonymous with PABX

Printed Circuit Board A board, typically made of plastic, on which is printed, usually in copper, the interconnections between elements of an electronic circuit

Printer Output device which prints results on paper (see Daisy wheel, Dot matrix, Electrosensitive, Impact, Ink jet, Line, Laser and Non-impact printer)

Printout Output on a printer, also called hard copy

Procedure Part of a program which performs a specific task or calculation; an algorithm or subroutine

Process Control Application of a computer to monitor and automatically control a production process (see Real time)

Processor Hardware unit which performs arithmetic and logic operations, controls the sequence of processing and coordinates input, output and storage activities (see Central Processing Unit, Parallel processing)

Program A sequence of detailed instructions stored in a computer which automatically controls the actions of the hardware

Programmable ROM A Read Only Memory which is programmed by the user rather than the supplier but which cannot then be reprogrammed (see Erasable PROM)

Programming Language The vocabulary and rules (a formalised and restricted equivalent to grammatical and spelling conventions for natural languages) which can be used to write programs (see End-user, High-Level and Low-level languages)

Programmer A person whose prime occupation is developing software

PROLOG A logic programming language

Protocols A well-defined set of rules and conventions; agreed protocols must be used to provide compatibility across communications links (see X25)

PIT	National, usually government-owned, telecommunications authority
Public Switched Telephone Network	Telecommunications network available to the public
Pulse Code Modulation	A technique for transmitting information in digital code
Punched Card	Input, output or storage medium which uses holes punched in a card to represent coded data
Punched Tape	See paper tape
Query Language	An easy-to-learn language used to access information in a database
Query-by-example	A means of retrieving information by specifying the items being searched for in the appropriate position of a standard format displayed on a screen
QWERTY	The standard layout of a typewriter keyboard which has the letters QWERTY in the top alphabetic characters
Random Access	See Direct access
Random Access Memory	Main memory on a chip which allows the user to read from and write to it, so that programs and data in it can be changed; read/write memory is a more apt description
Raster Scan	Technique of generating images on a display by focusing an electron beam on a phosphor coated screen; used in VDUs and TV sets
Read Only Memory	Main memory on a chip with hardwired/firmware programs and data (see Erasable PROM and Programmable ROM)
Real Number	A non-integral number, ie a number with a fractional or decimal part
Real Time	The current moment; application, such as process control, where the computer must respond instantaneously to particular inputs
Record	A data structure which forms part of a file; usually composed of a number of fields

Register — Locations in the ALU and CU used for special functions, such us the accumulator and instruction decoder

Relational Database — A database management technique which relies on creating various relationships between basic data elements which are stored as tables with rows and columns

Relative Address — An address relative to the start of the program in which it is located, with the first word of each program having a relative number of 0 (see Absolute address)

Remote — Computing capability, such as a terminal, at a distance from the main computing capability

Remote Job Entry — Input and output facilities often with local processing and storage capabilities, located at distance from - and linked to — a main computer centre

Repetition — A basic programming function which enables a group of instructions to be repeated for a required number of times

Report Generator — Software which allows the formats of displayed or printed output to be changed by a user who is not a skilled programmer

Response Time — The time taken for the computer to respond to a user input

Rigid Disks — See hard disks

Ring — A form of Local Area Network

Robot — A computer-controlled machine which carries out some human-like physical movements; typically used on a production line, to carry out a repetitive action involving limited physical arm and hand manipulations

Run — The act of initiating and performing a program

Schema — A detailed 'map' which describes the structure and relationships between items in a CODASYL-like database management system

Scrolling — Using the VDU display frame as a 'window' moving vertically or horizontally to scan text; needed because the frame size may be smaller than a full page of text. A feature of word processing systems

Semantic The meaning of a language. A semantic program error is a fault in the program logic although the syntax may be correct

Semiconductor A substance, such as silicon, halfway between a conductor and insulator in allowing the flow of electronic current; suited to the construction of transistors

Serial Access Access to data by searching sequentially through a storage medium such as magnetic tape

Shared Logic See Shared resource

Shared Resource Word processing system where more than one workstation can share the same processing, storage and output capabilities

Silicon A semiconductor widely used to make computer chips

Simplex A communications link which permits data transmission in only one direction

Simulation To represent the behaviour of one system by another, often using mathematical and modelling techniques which can be implemented by software; emulation is a form of simulation in which one system actually behaves like another rather than predicting how it might behave

Small Scale Integration Lower than Medium Scale Integration as a measure of circuit density on a chip; typically measured in tens of gates

Smart Synonymous with intelligent, as in intelligent terminal

Software Generic term for computer programs which are stored in and control the operation of hardware (see Firmware)

Software Engineering Techniques and aids which make software development, testing, amendment and enhancement a systematic and predictable process; structured design is an example of a software engineering method

Software House A company dealing exclusively with the provision of software

Software Publishing The packaging, distribution and marketing of software products

Solid State Devices, such as memories, which have transistors and integrated circuits as their active elements, without valves or mechanical components

Sort Ordering elements according to certain rules; arranging records in a file according to a key, such as ascending sequence by part number

Source Code Software in the language written by the user before it has been translated into machine-coded object form

Specification A precise, detailed statement of software and/or hardware requirements

Spooling A technique to improve efficiency by writing printed output first to a magnetic media and then transferring it to a printer or other slower output device later, when the processor is engaged in other activities: also known as off-lining

Stand-alone A computer-based system or device which can operate independently from any other computing resource

Stand-by A duplicate computer or component to provide a back-up to ensure high availability of the system

Static Memory Storage which retains information without having to be continuously refreshed, as dynamic memory has to be

Store and Forward A service provided in a computer network where a message is held in computer storage until the recipient requests to see it, say on a word processor or VDU (see Electronic mail)

String A data structure consisting of a sequence of characters

Structured Design	A systematic and well-documented approach to design which emphasises the use of modules within a framework that clearly identifies the necessary applications processes; structured design charts differ from flowcharts, which relate more to program rather than applications processes
Structured Programming	Techniques of program design and implementation with similar objectives to structured design
Subschema	A grouping of data elements defined in a schema
Subroutine	Program code which performs a specific task and can be used by or incorporated in other programmes
Symbolic Address	Using a name rather than a number to identify a memory location
Synchronous	Events co-ordinated by a regular time sequence; synchronous transmission sends information as a stream of data bits with a control character at the start of the message and the receiving and transmitting devices co-ordinated by timing mechanisms
Syntax	The formal grammatical and spelling rules of a language (see Semantics)
System	All hardware and software which interact to carry out an applications task
System Control Language	Similar to a Job Control Language but usually more flexible and comprehensive
Systems Analyst	A skilled job function responsible for analysing an information management requirement and preparing a detailed specification from which programs can be developed
Systems house	Company which sells total hardware and software package, usually incorporating systems from other suppliers
Systems Software	Software, such as an operating system, concerned primarily with coordinating and controlling hardware and communications resources rather than applications tasks

Tablet	Flat board used in conjunction with a light pen as a graphics input device
Telecommunications	Transmission of information from one location to another by other than physical transportation, for example by electronic data links
Telematique	French term which covers computing and telecommunications activities
Teleprocessing	Computer processing using telecommunications links for data input and output
Teletex	An electronic mail service defined by international standards for text telecommunications which can link to traditional telex networks
Teletext	A form of videotex which disseminates information by broadcast transmission to receiving devices, such as TV sets or VDUs
Teletypewriter	A terminal which looks like a typewriter but can be linked to a computer; output from the computer is automatically printed on the teletype (the abbreviated name is derived from Teletype, the company which makes many such devices)
Terminal	A device used for input, output and communications with a computer over telecommunications links
Text Processing	Computer-based handling of information primarily in textual form, such as memos, reports and publications
Thermal Printing	A non-impact printing technique which uses heat sensitive paper
Time Sharing	A system which handles many on-line terminals simultaneously
Top-down Design	A design approach which starts with the most general concepts or objectives and subdivides them into greater levels of detail within a structured framework
Transaction Processing	Processing discrete user transactions (like airline reservations) made via on-line terminals

Transistor	A small electronic device which can act as a switch or amplifier and can be built into integrated circuits for use as computer processors and memories
Transistor-Transistor-Logic	Integrated circuit logic elements where an output signal is produced by a pair of transistors
Tuple	A record in a relational database
Turnkey System	A computer system delivered ready for the user to 'turn the key' to become operational
Unbundling	Charging for software separately from hardware
Unconditional Branch	A branch which transfers control automatically to the position in the program indicated by a label in the branch instruction
User	General term for the person, group or organisation operating the computer to perform an applications task
User Friendly	Appealing to a user with no previous computing expertise
User/system Interaction	Term used in this book for what is sometimes called man/machine communications or interface; the aspects of human factors engineering and ergonomics concerned with the techniques of communication between the user and the computer system
Utilities	General housekeeping systems software programs
Valence	The outermost layer of electrons surrounding the nucleus of an atom of a substance; the valence of a semiconductor is used in creating n- and p-regions, which are the basic building blocks of transistors
Validation	Using software to make automatic checks on the validity of input data
Value-added Network	A network which provides information services (like electronic mail and viewdata) in addition to basic telecommunications transmission and switching capabilities
Variable	An entity which can assume different values; used in program procedures and to specify data areas

	which can take new values for each program run or can change during a run
Very Large Scale Integration	Measure of the circuit density of a chip, greater than Large Scale Integration; could be measured in millions of gates per chip
Video Disc	The medium used for home video entertainment can also store and retrieve computer-coded information by laser recording and reading techniques
Videotex	Transmission and presentation of information which includes graphics and text data. Viewdata is interactive videotex and teletext is broadcast videotex
Viewdata	A form of videotex which allows the user to communicate with the system and other users, as well as retrieving information from a database
Virtual Machine	An operating system capability which makes each user in a multi-user system appear to have sole access to the required resources or which enables a computer to run a number of different operating system environments
Virtual Memory/Storage	An operating system capability which enables a program to run on a system which has less main memory available to it than the length of the program
Visible Record Computer	A small computer which uses a ledger card with magnetic media input and storage (on a magnetic strip) and printed output
Visual Display Terminal	See Visual Display Unit
Visual Display Unit	A device with a TV-like display screen and associated keyboard
Voice Recognition	Input by direct human speech which is automatically analysed by a computer
Voice Response	Computer output in the form of speech
Volatile Memory	A storage device which loses its memory when its power supply is switched off

Von Neumann Architecture An architecture built around the concept of a sequential central processing unit; named after computer pioneer John von Neumann

Wand A light pen attached to a Point of Sale unit used for automatically reading bar codes

Wide Area Network A network covering a wide geographical area

Wideband A telecommunications bandwidth which allows the flow of a large volume of information organised in many different channels; higher volume information throughput than narrow-band

Winchester Disk A compact, high capacity hard disk, typically of 8-inch diameter and held in a sealed cartridge

Word A set of bits handled as a basic storage unit; can be of different bit lengths on different architectures

Word Processing Application of computing to the typing process; can be carried out by a purpose-built word processor or a software package on a general purpose computer (see Text processing)

Word Processor A device purpose-built for word and text processing applications

Workstation A device (such as a VDU or word-processor) or desk incorporating a number of devices from which people carry out work using electronic information handling techniques

X25 CCITT standard covering transmission protocols to be used in packet-switched networks

XOR A logic operator, also known as exclusive OR. Given statements *a* and *b*, the result of the operation *a* XOR *b* is true if *a* and *b* are of different values; the result is false if *a* and *b* are of the same true/false values

ABBREVIATIONS

Definitions of the following abbreviations are provided in the glossary above and in the body of the book, as referenced through the index.

ACK	ACKnowledge character
AI	Artificial Intelligence
ALGOL	ALGOrithmic Language
ALU	Arithmetic and Logic Unit
AM	Amplitude Modulation
ANSI	American National Standards Institute
APL	A Programming Language
ASCII	American Standard Code for Information Interchange
ASK	Amplitude Shift Keying
AU	Arithmetic Unit
BASIC	Beginner's All-purpose Symbolic Instruction Code
BCD	Binary Coded Decimal
bps	bits per second
CAD	Computer Aided (Assisted) Design
CAD/CAM	Computer Aided Design/Computer Aided Manufacturing
CAFS	Contents Addressable File Store
CAI	Computer Aided (Assisted) Instruction
CAL	Computer Aided (Assisted) Learning
CAM	Computer Aided (Assisted) Manufacturing
CAT	1. Computer Aided (Assisted) Training 2. Computer Aided (Axial) Tomography
CCD	Charge Coupled Device
CCITT	Consultative Committee on International Telephones andTelegraph (an organisation with representatives from PTTs around the world)
CMOS	Complementary Metal Oxide Semiconductor
CML	Computer Managed Learning
CNC	Computer Numerical Control
COBOL	COmmon Business Oriented Language
CODASYL	COnference on DAta SYstem Languages

COM	Computer Output to Microfilm
COMAL	COMmon Algorithmic Language
cps	characters per second
CPU	Central Processing Unit
CRT	Cathode Ray Tube
DBMS	DataBase Management System
DBTG	DataBase Task Group (of CODASYL)
DDL	Data Description (or Definition) Language
DDP	Distributed Data Processing
DML	Data Manipulation Language
DMS	Data(base) Management System
DNC	Direct Numerical Control
DOS	Disk(-based) Operating System
DP	Data Processing
DPM	Data Processing Manager
DSS	Decision Support System
EBCDIC	Extended Binary Coded Decimal Interchange Code
ECMA	European Computer Manufacturers' Association
EDP	Electronic Data Processing (equivalent to DP)
EFTS	Electronic Funds Transfer System
EPROM	Erasable Programmable Read Only Memory
FEP	Front End Processor
FET	Field Effect Transistor
FM	Frequency Modulation
FORTRAN	FORmula TRANslation
FSK	Frequency Shift Keying
G	Giga-one thousand million (usually called 1 billion)
GIGO	Garbage In/Garbage Out
Hz	Hertz
IC	Integrated Circuit
IFIP	International Federation for Information Processing
I/O	Input/Output
ips	instructions per second
ISAM	Index(ed) Sequential Access Method

ISO	International Standards Organisation
JCL	Job Control Language
K	Kilo-1000 in decimal; 1024 (2^{10}) in binary system
LCD	Liquid Crystal Display
LED	Light Emitting Diode
lips	logical inferences per second
LISP	LISt Processing
LSI	Large Scale Integration
M	Mega-1 million in decimal; 1,048,576 (2^{20}) in binary system
MICR	Magnetic Ink Character Recognition
mips	millions of instructions per second
MIS	Management Information System (or Services)
MOS	Metal Oxide Semiconductor
MSI	Medium Scale Integration
MTBF	Mean Time Between Failures
NC (or N/C)	Numerical Control machine
NCC	National Computing Centre
NMOS	N-channel Metal Oxide Semiconductor
OCR	Optical Character Recognition (Reading)
OEM	Original/Other Equipment Manufacturer
OMR	Optical Mark Reading
OOF	Office Of the Future
ops	operations per second
OSI	Open Systems Interconnection
PABX	Private Automatic Branch eXchange
PBX	Private Branch eXchange
PCB	Printed Circuit Board
PCM	Plug Compatible Manufacturer
PIN	Personal Identification Number
PL/1	Programming Language/1
PoS	Point of Sales (also POS)
PROLOG	PROgramming in LOGic
PROM	Programmable Read Only Memory
PSS	Packet Switched Service

PSTN	Public Switched Telephone Network
PTT	Post Telephone and Telegraph (describes a national telecommunications authority)
QBE	Query-By-Example
RAM	Random Access Memory
RJE	Remote Job Entry
ROM	Read Only Memory
SCL	System Control Language
SOS	Silicon On Sapphire
SPC	Stored Program Control
SSI	Small Scale Integration
tips	thousands of instructions per seconds
T^2L	Transistor-Transistor-Logic
TP	Transaction Processing
TTL	Transistor-Transistor-Logic
VANS	Value Added Network Services
VDT	Visual Display Terminal
VDU	Visual Display Unit
VLSI	Very Large Scale Integration
VM	Virtual Machine or Virtual Memory
VRC	Visible Record Computer
VS	Virtual Storage
WAN	Wide Area Network
WP	Word Processing

Bibliography

Aarseth, E. (1991). *Texts of Change. Towards a Poetics of Nonlinearity.* Unpublished M.A. thesis. Bergen: Department of Comparative Literature, University of Bergen, Norway.

Agar, M., Hobbs, J. (1982). Interpreting discourse. In *Discourse Processes,* 5 pp. 1-32.

American Psychiatrict Association (1994). *Diagnostic and statistical manual of mental disorders* (4th ed.). Washington, DC: Author

Annenberg Public Policy Center (1999, Spring). Parent's fear internet's influence on children. *Media Report to Women: Vol. 27* (pp. 7-9). Washington, DC: Author

Asby, W. R. (1968). Principles of the Self-Organizing System. In *Modern Systems Research for the Behavioural Scientist,* ed. Buckley, W. Chicago.

Baudrillard, J. (1983a). *Simulations.* New York: Semiotext(e).

Baudrillard, J. (1983b). *In the Shadow of the Silent Majorities.* New York: Semiotext(e).

Bell, D. (1979). The Social Framework of the Information Society, in *The Computer Age: A Twenty-Year Perspective,* eds. Dertouzos, M. L. and Moses, J. Massachusetts: The MIT Press, Cambridge.

Brier, S. (1987). Naturvidenskab, humaniora og erkendelsesteori. In *Kritik* vol. 79/ 80. Copenhagen.

Bush, V. (1945). As We May Think. *Atlantic Monthly* 176, July 1945, pp.101-108.

Callinicos, A. (1989). *Against Postmodernism.* Cambridge: Polity Press.

Christensen, L. T. (1991). The Marketing Culture: The Communication of Organisational Identity in a Culture without Foundation. Paper submitted to the International Conference on "Organisational Culture", Copenhagen, June 26-28.

Comte, A. (1830-42) *Cours de philosophic positive.* Paris.

Comte, A. (1844). *Discours preliminaire sur l' esprit positif.* Paris.

Davis, R. (1999). Is internet addiction real? *Victoria Point Multimedia* [On-line]. Available: http//:www.victoriapoint.com/Addiction%20% 20not.htm

Delany, P., Landow, G. (1991). *Hypermedia and Literary Studies.* Cambridge, Mass.: The MIT Press.

Demarco, T. (1979). *Structured Analysis and System Specification.* Englewood Cliffs: Yourdon Press.

Dvorak, J. (1997). Net addiction. *PC/Computing. 10.* 85-87

Evensen, L. (1988). Lokal og global koherens i elevers skriving. In *TRANS — Trondheim Papers in Applied Linguistics,* IV.

Fainaru, S. (1998). Experts fear video games breed violence. *The Boston Globe. October 19* [On-line] . Available: http://wwwadn.com/stories/T98110984.html

Greenfield, D.N. (1999). *Virtual addiction.* Oakland, CA: New Harbinger Publications, Inc.

Grohol, R. (1998). Re: internet addiction (long). *Psychology of the Internet* [On-line]. Available: http://lists.cmhc.eom/research/l 998/041 6.html

Habermas, J. (1981). *Theorie des kommunitativen Handelns.* Frankfurt a. M.: Suhrkamp Verlag.

Habermas, J. (1987) *The Philosophical Discourse of Modernity. Twelve Lectures.* Massachusetts: The MIT Press, Cambridge.

Harpold, T. (1991). Threnody: Psychoanalytic Digressions on the Subject of Hypertext In *Hypermedia and Literary Studies,* eds. Delaney, Landow, pp.171-181. Cambridge, Mass.: The MIT Press.

Harvey, D. (1989). *The Condition of Postmodernity.* Oxford: Basil Blackwell.

Hassan, I. (1987). *The postmodern turn.* Ohio: Ohio State University Press.

Hiltz, S. R. (1984). *Online Communities. A Case Study of the Office of the Future.* Norwood, New Jersey: Ablex Publishing Corporation.

Huws, U., Korte, W.B., Robinson, S. (1990). *Telework Towards the Elusive Office.* Chichesten John Wiley.

Jablin, F. M., Putnam, L, L., Roberts, K. H., Porter, L. W. eds., *Handbook of Organisational Communication. An Interdisciplinary Perspective.* Newbury Park: Sage Publications.

Jameson, F. (1988). Cognitive Mapping. In *Marxism and the Interpretation of Culture,* eds. Nelson, G., Grossberg, L. Chicago: University of Illinois Press.

Jameson, F. (1991). *Postmodernism, or The Cultural Logic of Late Capitalism.* London: Verso.

Jensen, O. M. Storgaard. K. Information Technology and Ways of Life. In *Danish Experiments,* New Social Science Monographs, eds. Cronborg, T., Duelund, P., Jensen. O. M., Qvortrup, L. Copenhagen.

Krone, K. J., Jablin, F. M., Putnam, L. L. (1987). Communication Theory and Organisational Communication: Multiple Perspectives. In *Handbook of Organisational Communication. An Interdisciplinary Perspective,* eds. Jablin, F. M., Putnam, L. L., Roberts, K. H., Porter, L. W. Newbury Park: Sage Publications.

Laing, A. (1991). Changing Business: Post-Fordism and the Workplace. London: DEGW.

Landow, G. (1991). The Rhetoric of Hypermedia: Some Rules for Authors. In *Hypermedia and Literary Studies*, eds. Delaney, Landow, pp.81-103. Cambridge, Mass.: The MIT Press.

Luhmann, N. (1975). *Macht.* Stuttgart.

Luhmann, N. (1976). Generalised Media and the Problem of Contingency. In *Explorations in General Theory in Social Science 1-2, Essays in Honor of Talcott Parsons*, eds. Loubster, J. J. et al. New York.

Luhmann, N. (1984). *Soziale Systeme. Grundriss einer allgemeinen Theory.* Frankfurt a. M.: Suhrkamp Verlag.

Luhmann, N. (1990). *Essays on Self-Reference.* New York: Columbia University Press.

Lynch, K. (1960). *The Image of the City.* Cambridge, Mass.: The MIT Press.

Males, M. (1998). For Adults, Today's Youth' Are Always the Worst. L.A. Times [On-line]. Available: http://www.latimes.com/cgi-

Maturana, H., Varela, F. (1980). *Autopoiesis and Cognition, D.* Dordrecht: Reidel Publishing Company.

Mcknight, C., Dillon, A., Richardson, J. (1991). *Hypertext in Context.* Cambridge: Cambridge University Press.

Morgan, G. (1986). *Images of Organisation.* Beverly Hills: Sage Publications.

Moulthorp, S. (1991). Reading from the Map: Metonymy and Metaphor in the Fiction of Working Paths. In *Hypermedia and Literary Studies*, eds. Delaney, Landow, pp.119-132. Cambridge, Mass.: The MIT Press.

Nelson, T.H. (1965). A File Structure for the Complex, The Changing and the Indeterminate. In *Association for Computing Macinery Proceedings of the 20th National Conference*, pp.84-100.

Nelson, T.H. (1987a). *Computer Lib.* Redmond: Microsoft Press.

Nelson, T.H. (1987b) *Dream Machines.* Redmond: Microsoft Press.

Putnam, L. (1983). The Interpretive Perspective: An Alternative to Functionalism. In *Communication and Organisations: An Interpretive Approach*, eds. Putnam, L., Pacanowsky, M. Beverly Hills: Sage Publishing Company.

Putnam, L. L. (1985). Bargaining as Organisational Communication. In *Organisational Communication: Traditional Themes and New Directions*, eds. McPhee, R. D., Tompkins, P. K. Beverly Hills: Sage Publications.

Putnam, L. L., Scott Poole, M. (1987). Conflict and Negotiation. In *Handbook of Organisational Communication. An Interdisciplinary Perspective*, eds. Jablin, F. M., Putnam, L.L., Roberts, K. H., Porter, L. W. Newbury Park: Sage Publications.

Qvortrup, L. (1984). *The Social Significance of Telematics.* Amsterdam/Philadelphia: John Benjamins Publishing Company.

Qvortrup, L. (1988). *Det levende eller del dode samfund* (The Living or the Dead Society). Copenhagen: Blytmanns Forlag.

Qvortrup, L. (1992). Telematics and Organisational Communication: Trends in Organisational Communications Theories. In *Telematics and Work,* eds. Andriessen, J. H., Roe, R. A. London: Lawrence Erlbaum Associates.

Qvortrup. L. (in press). Telework: Visions, Definitions, Realities, Barriers. In *Handbook on Cities and New Technologies.* Paris: OECD and Urba 2000.

Redding, W. C. (1972). *Communication Within the Organisation: An Interpretative Review of Theory and Research.* New York: Industrial Communication Council.

Redding, W. C. (1985). Stumbling Toward Identity: The Emergence of Organisational Communication as a Field of Study. In *Organisational Communication: Theoretical Themes and New Directions,* eds. McPhee, R. D., Tompkins, P. K. Beverly Hills: Sage Publications.

Rousseau, J.J. (1968). *Du contrat social ou principe du droit politique.* (1762) here quoted from the English translation *The Social Contract.* London : Penguin Books.

Shannon, C. E. (1972). Information Theory. In *Encyclopedia Britannica. Volume 12.* Chicago et al.: William Benton, Publisher.

Shannon, C. E., Weaver, W. (1964). *The Mathematical Theory of Communication* (1948). Urbana: University of Illinois Press.

Simon, H. A. (1945). *Administrative Behavior.* New York: Free Press.

Simon, M. (1997). How internet has an effect on the social skills of children. *The Vocal Point* [On-line]. Available:

Steier, F. ed. (1991) *Research and Reflexivity.* London: Sage Publications.

Steier, F., Smith, K. K. (in press). The Cybernetics of Cybernetics and the Organisation of Organisation, in: *Organisation — Communication. Emerging Perspectives,* Volume III, ed. Thayer, L. Norwood, NJ: Ablex.

Suler, J. (1996). Review of the internet aggression by Norman Holland. The Psychology of Cyberspace [On-line]. Available: http ://www,rider.edu/users/suler/psycyber/holland rev.html

Suler, J. (1999a). Computer and cyberspace addiction. *The Psychology of Cyberspace* [On-line]. Available: http://www.rider.edu/users/suler/psycyber/cybaddict.html

Suler, J. (1999b). Internet demographics 1998. *The Psychology of Cyberspace* [Online]. Available: http://www.rider.edu/users/suler/psycyber/stats.html

Tapscott, D. (1999). The kids are alright: technology doesn't make them 'little criminals'. Victoria Point Multimedia [On-line]. Available: http://www.victoriapoint.com/child technology.htm

U.S. Census Bureau. (1997). Computer use in the United States. Washington. DC: Author [On-line]. Available: . http://www.census.gov/prod/99pubs/p20-522.pdf

Valenza, J. K. (1996). Lonely and bored children may use computer as escape. School Crossings [On-line]. Available: http://crossings.phillynews.com/archive/kl2/SKUL25.htm

Venturi, R., Brown, D. S., Izenour, S. (1972). *Learning from Las Vegas*. Cambridge, Mass.: The MIT Press.

Von Foerster, H. (1979). Cybernetics of Cybernetics. In *Communication and Control in Society*. Krippendorff, K. New York.

Wade, P. (1999). Practice agenda - technology 3rd question. *American College Personnel Association* [On-line]. Available: http://www.acpa.nche.edu/tech3.htm

Wallace, A. (1999). *The psychology of the internet*. New York: Cambridge University Press

Watzlawick, P. J., Beavin, J., Jackson, "D. (1967). *Pragmatics of Human Communication*. New York: Norton.

Weick, K. E. (1987). "Theorizing About Organisational Communication." In *Handbook of Organisational Communication, An Interdisciplinary Perspective*. eds. Jablin, F. M., Putnam, L. L., Roberts, K. H., Porter, L. W. Newbury Park: Sage Publications.

Weinstein, M. A. (1998). *Net game - an american dialogue*. [On-line]. Available: http://www.ctheory.com/gal.12-net_game.html

Wiener, N. (1950). *The Human Use of Human Beings'. Cybernetics and Society*. Boston: Houghton Mifflin Company.

Young, K. S. (1998). *Caught in the net*. New York: John Wiley & Sons, Inc.

Index